Public Relations Writing

The Essentials of Style and Format

EIGHTH EDITION

Thomas H. Bivins

University of Oregon

Mc Graw Hill

Connect Learn Succeed™

PUBLIC RELATIONS WRITING: THE ESSENTIALS OF STYLE AND FORMAT, EIGHTH EDITION

Published by McGraw-Hill, a business unit of The McGraw-Hill Companies, Inc., 1221 Avenue of the Americas, New York, NY, 10020. Copyright © 2014 by The McGraw-Hill Companies, Inc. All rights reserved. Printed in the United States of America. Previous editions © 2011, 2008, and 2004. No part of this publication may be reproduced or distributed in any form or by any means, or stored in a database or retrieval system, without the prior written consent of The McGraw-Hill Companies, Inc., including, but not limited to, in any network or other electronic storage or transmission, or broadcast for distance learning.

Some ancillaries, including electronic and print components, may not be available to customers outside the United States.

This book is printed on acid-free paper.

1 2 3 4 5 6 7 8 9 0 DOC/DOC1 0 9 8 7 6 5 4 3

ISBN 978-1-259-06037-3
MHID 1-259-06037-3

www.mhhe.com

This book is dedicated to my wife, Lonnie.
She has watched me work on it through eight editions for more than
twenty years, and has encouraged me every step of the way.

Contents

CHAPTER 5   Media Relations and Placement   67

CHAPTER 8   ## Controlled Publications   154

Preface

PREFACE

This is a handbook for those who, by intention or by accident, find themselves in the position of writing for public relations. In my years of experience, I have had as many questions concerning public relations writing from those not in public relations as from those in the field. Countless inquiries have come from those who, suddenly having been "appointed" publicity chair for a committee, find they don't know the first thing about publicity; or the office manager who has been assigned, ad hoc, the job of putting out a newsletter; or the small-company president who wants to create her own brochures on the new desktop publishing software, which she just acquired, but doesn't have the faintest idea how to proceed. That's why you'll find this book begins with the basics and pretty much sticks with them.

It is designed to aid both the beginner and the advanced public relations writer. In it you will find most of the forms of public relations writing, including news releases, backgrounders, broadcast scripts, magazine and newsletter articles, brochures, and Web and social media copy.

This latest edition has been updated to include more information on writing for digital environments and using social media to communicate. There is still a chapter on the basics of writing for the Web and for social media, including advice for blogging and micro-blogging (Twitter, etc.), and how to get the most out of online tools like Facebook, LinkedIn, and others. In addition, many of the chapters now include companion sections on how to produce digital versions of traditional forms. For example, Chapter 7 on news releases includes a section on digital releases, Search Engine Optimized (SEO) releases, and Social Media Releases (SMR). Likewise, Chapter 8 on controlled publications includes advice on how to write for and produce online and digital newsletters.

Other changes to this edition include a section on ethics in Chapter 2 for public relations writers working in digital forms including blogging and word-of-mouth marketing codes, and best practices. Chapter 4 includes a new section on buying the Internet. And, in Chapter 5 on media relations and placement, you will find information on creating online newsrooms and a new section on producing digital media kits.

Many of the recommendations contained in this book are based on years of experience as a writer, both in public relations and in general business practice. It is my belief that any public relations writer worthy of the name should become familiar with all forms of writing. After all, good writing is good writing, no matter what the form. The truly good writer can work in any medium, like the good artist.

This book is an attempt to put most of the reference material that you, as a public relations writer, would need to successfully complete the work which is so vital a part of your chosen profession—writing.

Acknowledgments

A number of people have helped make this new edition possible. John Mitchell, a longtime friend and faithful user of this book, was especially helpful with his many examples of fine work. Marilyn Milne, a professional and friend, provided examples of pitch letters and advisories. Seth Walker, formerly of Intel, provided me with numerous examples of that organization's fine work. My brother, Chris, also provided me with a number of examples from his vast design repertoire for a varied clientele. I am also indebted to the educators who reviewed the last edition of the book and made incredibly constructive suggestions for this latest edition: Sallyanne Holtz, University of Texas at San Antonio; Amiso M. George, Texas Christian University; Amber Erickson, University of Cincinnati; Robert M. Kucharavy, Syracuse University; Katrina Marie Olson, University of Illinois at Urbana-Champaign; and Mary Frances Casper, Boise State University. Every new item and nearly every change that appear here are based on their recommendations.

I am also grateful to Nicole Bridge, at McGraw-Hill for her suggestions, foresight, and diligence in keeping me on schedule. And, I can't forget my excellent project manager, Jessica Portz, she caught every detail. Finally, I am grateful to the many professionals around the country whose ideas and creativity inspired and contributed to much of this revision. They have been uniformly generous in their willingness to share their work with me. Nearly every time you see a footnote in this book, it is there to thank those generous individuals and organizations. This new edition is truly a result of their hard work as well as my own. My thanks go to them all. They share in whatever usefulness this book provides to you, the reader.

About the Author

Thomas H. Bivins is a professor and the John L. Hulteng Chair in Media Ethics in the School of Journalism and Communication at the University of Oregon. He received his PhD in 1982 in telecommunication from the University of Oregon and taught for 3 years at the University of Delaware before returning to the University of Oregon. Bivins received a BA in English and an MFA in creative writing from the

University of Alaska, Anchorage, and has over 30 years of professional media experience, including work in radio, television, advertising, public relations, graphic design, and editorial cartooning.

Additional Resources

An Online Learning Center for this text is available at www.mhhe.com/bivins8e. This Website contains a workbook for students and a password-protected manual for instructors. Please ask your McGraw-Hill representative for access information.

This text is available as an eTextbook at www.CourseSmart.com. At CourseSmart your students can take advantage of significant savings off the cost of a print textbook, reduce their impact on the environment, and gain access to powerful Web tools for learning. CourseSmart eTextbooks can be viewed online or downloaded to a computer. The eTextbooks allow students to do full text searches, add highlighting and notes, and share notes with classmates. CourseSmart has the largest selection of eTextbooks available anywhere. Visit www.CourseSmart.com to learn more and to try a sample chapter.

CHAPTER

1

Writing for Public Relations

In This Chapter, You Will Learn

- Why good writing is important to a public relations professional.

- The difference between uncontrolled and controlled information.

- The most often–used tools of public relations writing and how they differ.

- The process of public relations writing.

WHAT IS PUBLIC RELATIONS?

Before we begin to discuss writing for public relations, it's probably a good idea to get a grip on exactly what public relations is. That's not an easy question to answer. If you were to think that public relations is about putting a client's best foot forward, you'd be right. If you proposed that public relations is about dealing with the media (either keeping your client's name in the media or out of it), you'd be right as well. If you believe that public relations is helping clients and organizations get along with their constituencies, you'd be right again. In fact, public relations is all of these and more. Public relations is everything from planning entire communications campaigns to writing a letter to the editor. It involves any activity that enhances the reputation of your client, mediates disputes between various publics and your client, helps achieve mutual understanding among all parties involved in an issue, advocates on behalf of a client or cause, provides guidance and direction, and results in positive and mutual well-being. A quick query on Google nets the following definitions for public relations found on the Web:

- The business of generating goodwill toward an individual, cause, company, or product (www.motto.com/glossary.html)
- The acts of communicating what you are to the public. This is not to be confused with publicity, which is just one of the methods used in communicating the image (www.nejaycees.org/about/jargon.asp)
- Activity, communications, or press coverage that is designed to enhance the prestige or goodwill of a company (http://rdsweb2.rdsinc.com/help/bi_ct_expdef.html)
- Any activities or events that help promote a favorable relationship between a company and its customers and prospects; activities used to influence the press to print stories that promote a favorable image of a company and its products or services (www.garyeverhart.com/glossary_of_advertising_terms.htm)
- Communication with various sectors of the public to influence their attitudes and opinions in the interest of promoting a person, product, or idea (http://fourps.wharton.upenn.edu/advertising/dictionary/p.htm)
- An activity meant to improve the project organization's environment in order to improve project performance and reception (www.mccombs.utexas.edu/faculty/Linda.Bailey/glossary.htm)
- Professional services in promoting products by arranging opportunities for exposure in the media (http://freespace.virgin.net/brendan.richards/glossary/glossary.htm)
- A deliberate, planned, and sustained effort to institute and maintain mutual understanding between an organization and its publics (Institute of Public Relations definition) (http://wps.pearsoned.co.uk/wps/media/objects/1452/1487687/glossary/glossary.html)
- A promotion intended to create goodwill for a person or institution (http://wordnet.princeton.edu/perl/webwn)

- Public relations deals with influencing public opinion, through the presentation of a client's image, message, or product (http://en.wikipedia.org/wiki/Public_relations)

In fact, modern public relations is an eclectic package encompassing a great many job descriptions, titles, and functions. The federal government even forbids the use of the term *public relations* to refer to roles whose functions in the business world would be identical. The practice is rife with terms synonymous with yet subtly different from *public relations. Press agentry,* for instance, is usually taken to mean the role of providing media exposure, whereas *promotion* combines media exposure with persuasion. *Public affairs* most often refers to those who deal with community or government relations; and the federal government's decided-upon replacement term is *public information.*

Despite the myriad terms applied to the practice, there does appear to be a rather limited number of actual functions assigned to these roles. Nearly 30 years ago, James Grunig and Todd Hunt proposed a set of four models, and although these have undergone some changes over the years, they remain relatively accurate today.[1] The models are press agentry/publicity, public information, two-way asymmetric, and two-way symmetric. In the press agentry/publicity model, the practitioner acts as a one-sided propaganda specialist. The public information model presents the practitioner as journalist, carefully disseminating balanced information to the public. Practitioners in a two-way asymmetric model are seen as "scientific persuaders," using social science techniques to gather information on attitude and behavior characteristics of their publics and then adjusting their messages accordingly to influence those publics. Finally, the two-way symmetric model uses practitioners as mediators between organizations and their publics.

A broader categorization views the roles of public relations divided neatly into communications manager and communications technician. Managers analyze, plan, carry out, and evaluate public relations campaigns. Technicians provide the support for the programs in the form of writing, design, layout, production, and publication within all of the possible delivery systems. Thus, the role of the public relations writer is generally that of communications technician. However, that is not to say that there is always a clear divide between the two roles. No respectable communications manager would be incapable of writing a news release, and frequently communications technicians are involved in various stages of the planning process, as we will see. All public relations practitioners write at some time. Public relations is, after all, communication, and the basic form of communication is still the written word.

Regardless of the prevalence of television, radio, cable, satellite television, and the Internet, the written word is still powerful. Even the events we witness on television and hear on the radio were written down originally in the form of scripts. News anchors on television are not recounting the day's events from memory; they are reading from a teleprompter. Nearly every entertainment

---

[1]James E. Grunig and Todd Hunt, *Managing Public Relations* (New York: Holt, Rinehart and Winston, 1984), 21.

program is precisely scripted—from your favorite sitcom to the *MTV Video Music Awards.* And although it may not seem so, most of what you see on the Internet has been carefully thought out and written prior to its placement on the Web, or should be, especially if you're a professional working in public relations.

It is no wonder today's employers value employees who can communicate through the written word. Employers want people who can write and communicate ideas—who can pull complex or fragmented ideas together into coherent messages. This requires not only technical skill but also intelligence. It requires a love of writing as well. Be forewarned: The subjects of public relations writing can seem to many to be crashingly dull; however, for writers who love their craft, the duller the subject, the greater the challenge. Even the most mundane subject can shine with the right amount of polish.

So, the place of writers in public relations is assured. From the president or vice president of public relations to the support staff, writing will be a daily part of life. From enormously complex projects involving dozens of people and whole teams of writers to the one-person office cranking out daily news releases, editing weekly newsletters, or updating Web pages, writing will continue to be the number-one concern of public relations. Through it, your publics will come to know you and, for better or worse, develop a permanent image of who you are. It is in your best interest and that of the people for whom you work to ensure that this image is the one you want to portray.

What is needed before you begin to write, however, is knowledge. Being able to spell and string words together effectively does not make a good writer. First and foremost, a good writer must be able to think. To be a good writer you must be aware of the world around you and understand how your writing is going to affect that world.

It is essential that you think before you write; otherwise, your writing will be only empty words, disconnected from reality, or, worse, unintentionally misleading or false.

WHAT IS PUBLIC RELATIONS WRITING?

All public relations writing attempts to establish positive relations between an organization and its various publics, usually through image-building techniques. Most writing in the realm of public relations falls into two rather broad categories: uncontrolled information and controlled information.

Uncontrolled Information

Information that, once it leaves your hands, is at the mercy of the media is **uncontrolled information.** In other words, the outlet in which you want the information placed has total editorial control over the content, style, placement, and timing. Such items as news releases are totally uncontrolled. For example, you may write what you think is the most effective, well-thought-out news release ever presented to your local paper, but you never see it in print. Or maybe the paper does use it, but leaves out all of your skillfully crafted sentences about your employer. In these cases, the newspaper editors have exercised their prerogative to control your information. Once you put it in their hands, they get to decide what to do with it.

Then why, you're probably asking yourself about now, even use uncontrolled information? For at least two reasons. First, it's generally cheaper because you don't have to pay for production or placement costs. Second, your message gains credibility if you can pass it through the media on its way to your target publics. I've sometimes referred to this technique as "information laundering" (humorously, of course). The fact is that our messages are often viewed by our target publics as having a vested interest—which of course they do. However, when those same target publics see the same message served up by the media, it seems to gain credibility in their eyes. Obviously, this is also true for passing the information through any credible second party such as magazines, opinion leaders, or role models. Thus, the loss in control is usually more than balanced by the overall gain in credibility.

Controlled Information

Information over which you have total control as to editorial content, style, placement, and timing is **controlled information.** Examples of controlled information are institutional (image) and advocacy advertising, house publications, brochures, and broadcast material (if it is paid placement). Public service announcements (PSAs) are controlled as far as message content is concerned but uncontrolled as to placement and timing. To get the most out of any message, you should send out both controlled and uncontrolled information. That way, you can reach the broadest possible target audience, some of whom will react more favorably to one type or the other of your approaches.

TOOLS OF THE PUBLIC RELATIONS WRITER

As with any trade, public relations writing uses certain tools through which messages are communicated. The most common are listed here.

- *News releases* are the most widely used of all public relations formats. News releases—both print and broadcast—are used most often to disseminate information for publicity purposes and are sent to every possible medium, from newspapers to radio stations to Internet sites.
- *Backgrounders* are basic information pieces providing background as an aid to reporters, editors, executives, employees, and spokespersons. This information is used by other writers and reporters to "flesh out" their stories.
- *Public service announcements* are the broadcast outlet most available to nonprofit public relations. Although the PSA parameters are limited, additional leeway can be gained by paying for placement, which puts it in the category of advertising.
- *Articles and editorials* are usually for newsletters, house publications, trade publications, or consumer publications. In the case of nonhouse publications,

public relations articles are submitted in the same way as any other journalistic material. Editorials can be either paid for or submitted uncontrolled and vie for placement with comments from other parties.

- *Collateral publications* are usually autonomous publications, such as brochures, pamphlets, flyers, and other direct marketing pieces, that should be able to stand on their own merits but can be used as supporting information for other components in a package. They might, for instance, be part of a media kit.
- *Speeches and presentations* are the interpersonal method of imparting a position or an image. Good speeches can inform or persuade, and good presentations can win support where written methods may fail.
- *The Internet* has increasingly become one of the most important communications tools available in public relations. Writing for the Web is challenging and exciting and can garner results often quicker than any other format.

Although these are not the only means for message dissemination at the disposal of the public relations writer, they are the methods used most often. Knowing which tool to use requires a combination of experience, research, and intuition. It is also good to keep in mind that learning the basics of writing (even if the basics deal with "traditional" forms) will prepare you to write in any format, for any medium. If you can write a traditional news release, you can write a Search Engine Optimized release. If you can write a feature story, you can write an interesting blog post. Thus, unless you learn to write in the traditional forms, you won't have a grounding in the basics you need to write well in any form. The following chapters attempt to provide you with a framework, or template, from which you will be able to perform basic tasks as a public relations writer. The rest is a matter of experience, and no book can give you that.

THE PROCESS OF PUBLIC RELATIONS WRITING

All forms of writing for public relations have one thing in common: They should be written well. Beyond that, they are different in many ways. These differences are related primarily to purpose, strategy, medium, and style and format. As you will see, these elements are interrelated; you can't think about a single element without conceptualizing the others. For example, purpose and strategy are intimately related, and choice of medium is inextricably bound to style and format.

As to purpose, a public relations piece generally is produced for one of two reasons: to inform or to persuade. Strategy depends almost completely on the purpose of a given piece. For instance, a writer might choose a persuasive strategy such as argument to accomplish his or her purpose, which is to persuade a target audience to vote for a particular mayoral candidate.

The medium that you choose to deliver your message will also dictate its style and format. For example, corporate magazines typically use a standard feature style common to journalism. Newsletter writing, by contrast, is leaner and shorter and frequently uses a straight news reporting style. Folders (commonly referred to as brochures) are, by nature, short and to the point. Copy for posters and flyers is shorter still, whereas pamphlets and booklets vary in style and length according to purpose. Writing for the Internet may incorporate any or all of these styles in slightly to greatly abbreviated formats.

Beginning here and continuing throughout the book, we will deal with these elements of public relations writing: purpose, strategy, medium, and style and format.

KEY TERMS

uncontrolled information
controlled information

CHAPTER

2

Ethical and Legal Issues in Public Relations Writing

In This Chapter, You Will Learn

- Some of the ethical considerations of public relations writing, including unethical persuasive techniques and unethical language use.

- Guidelines for how to ghostwrite ethically.

- Guidelines for making ethical decisions.

- Public relations and the Internet

- The legal aspects of public relations writing, including defamation, invasion of privacy, and copyright and trademark considerations.

Public relations is fraught with ethical dilemmas. No one working in the field would deny this; however, for the writer these dilemmas take a slightly different form than the types of problems faced by others in the field. For instance, many of the ethical quandaries facing public relations people have to do with decisions on large issues—whether to handle a particular political candidate or ethically suspect client; how to deal with the media on a day-to-day basis without lying; what to keep confidential and what to disclose; and whether to do what the client says, no matter what.

It's not that such decisions are beyond the scope of the public relations writer. It's that a writer spends much more time dealing with the technical aspects of his or her job than with the bigger picture. This tight focus, however, comes with its own set of ethical considerations, among which are such quandaries as how to persuade without violating the basic tenets of ethics and good taste and how to write words that will later be claimed by someone else as his or her own.

ETHICAL CONSIDERATIONS OF PERSUASION

Some people consider persuasion unethical by nature. They believe in a very strict version of the "marketplace of ideas" theory that if you provide enough unbiased information for people, they will be able to make up their own minds about any issue. Of course, we all know that isn't true. Although our political system is based on this theory, to some extent it is also based on the notion of reasoned argument—that is, persuasion. People who believe fervently enough in a particular point of view aren't going to rely on any marketplace to decide their case. They're going to get out there and argue, persuasively, for their side.

Since the time of Aristotle, we've had access to a number of persuasive techniques. We also are aware of how easily many of these techniques can be turned to unethical purposes. In fact, the most frequent complaint against any form of communication is that it is trying to persuade unethically. This complaint may seem to be leveled most often at advertising, but public relations hasn't gotten off the hook entirely.

Discussed here are a number of techniques that, in varying degrees, can be used unethically. All of these techniques have been used in propaganda campaigns, but you will recognize many of them as still being used in both public relations and advertising.

Logic Fallacies

By far the most unethical of the techniques are those codified by the Roman orators over a thousand years ago. These are commonly referred to as **logic fallacies** because they are both illogical and deceptive by nature. Let's look first at these:

- *Cause and effect.* We see this in operation all the time. It means that because one thing follows another in time, the second was caused by the first. This tactic is most often used to infer that one thing is the result of the other. Politicians are particularly adept at using this argument. For example, an incumbent may suggest that the national drop in the crime rate is the result of his policies when, in fact, it is the continuation of a drop that began before his administration. Or a television ad for the plastics industry may imply that we are a healthier society because meat is no longer sold in open-air markets, exposed to the elements. Although this may be partially true, the overall longevity of any society is the result of multiple factors, not just one.

- *Personal attack.* This is a technique used to discredit the source of the message regardless of the message itself. Again, we see this time and again in politics, where policies are left unconsidered while personality assassination runs rampant. Anytime that you see an argument turn from issues to personality, this unethical strategy is being used.

- *Bandwagon.* This is an appeal to popularity. In other words, if everyone else is doing it, why aren't you? McDonald's has been using this strategy for years in its "xxx billion sold" byline. Because human beings are, by nature, group oriented, they already tend to want to go with what's popular. However, as Henry David Thoreau pointed out, the group isn't always right.

- *Inference by association.* This is an argument based entirely on false logic, most often thought of as "guilt by association" or, in some cases, credit by association. The argument usually takes the following form:

Chemical weapons are evil.
X company makes chemical weapons.
X company is evil.

Of course, the argument is logically inconsistent. Although chemical weapons may in themselves be evil, this does not automatically make the entire company evil. The same sort of argument can be made by associating a product or idea with another, already accepted idea. For example, "From the people who brought you. . . ." This statement assumes that because one product is successful or satisfying, all products from the same company will be. And, of course, this argument is used in all those celebrity endorsements: "Wheaties, the breakfast of champions!"

Other Tactics

Several other tactics closely related to inference by association are not necessarily unethical by nature but can be used unethically. Some of the most common tactics are as follows:

- *Plain folks.* This tactic appeals to our need to deal with people who are like us. The technique proposes that the speaker is just like the listener and so "wouldn't lie to you." Again, politicians are adept at this approach but so are corporate executives who sell their own products.

- *Testimonials.* This tactic is directly related to inference by association; however, the technique actually implies that the celebrity spokesperson uses the product or supports the cause. And, of course, this may or may not be true.

- *Transfer.* This technique involves the deliberate use of positive symbols to transfer meaning to another message, not necessarily related. The use of religious or patriotic symbols such as a "heavenly choir" or an American flag during a commercial not directly related to such symbols is an example of transfer. Most recently, the ubiquitous use of Beethoven's Ninth Symphony ("Ode to Joy") in everything from the Olympic Games to cable channel promos is a blatant attempt to bring a sense of high, nearly religious, meaning to the message being imparted.

Unethical Language Use

A final area of ethical consideration, as it relates to persuasion, has to do with the actual use of language. Often called **language fallacies,** these techniques are nearly always used intentionally. The most common are as follows:

- *Equivocation.* Words can be and often are ambiguous. Many words have more than one meaning. Equivocation refers to using one or both meanings of a word and then deliberately confusing the two in the audience's mind. For example, the word *free* is tossed about quite a bit by advertisers, but does it really mean without cost? When you purchase that big bottle of shampoo that claims you are getting "12 more ounces free!" are you really getting it free? When a press release states that a senior executive has "resigned," does it mean that she has quit or that she was fired? In fact, the word *resign* has become something of a euphemism in business and government for being asked to leave.

- *Amphiboly.* This approach uses ambiguous sentence structure or grammar to mislead. For example, "new and improved" products imply that a logical comparison is to be made. However, what are the newness and state of improvement being compared to? How about "X cereal: part of a nutritious breakfast"? What part? Is it nutritious without the other parts? What are the other parts? And if something only "helps" you obtain whiter teeth, what else plays a part?

- *Emotive language.* This technique uses emotionally charged words to shift response from the argument itself to the images invoked by these words. This is a bit like transfer except that it uses words instead of images. Think of the ads that use words such as *freedom, miracle, powerful,* or *younger looking.* Or the news release that refers to a product as revolutionary or a person as dynamic. When we use these words, we've strayed from fact to opinion.

Ultimately, whether or not what you have written is ethical will depend on your ability to be as objective as possible about your own motives. If you wish to deceive, you will. A technically good writer has access to all the tools needed to write unethically. The decision is yours. Remember, persuasion is ethical; manipulation is not.

Ethics and Ghostwriting

Ghostwriting refers to writing something for someone else that will be represented as that person's own point of view. Public relations writers ghostwrite speeches, letters to the editor, annual report letters from the president, and even quotes. Ghostwriting is ubiquitous, to say the least. Rhetoricians point out that no president since Abraham Lincoln has written his own speeches in their entirety. Recall that Lincoln wrote the Gettysburg Address on a train ride between Washington and Gettysburg—and, by most accounts, did a fairly nice job.

The days have long since vanished when the busy corporate executive or politician had the time (or the skill) to write his or her own speeches. In fact, we can no longer take it as a given that most of what passes for their words—either in print or spoken forms—are really *their* words. When Ronald Reagan's press secretary, Larry Speakes, indicated in his book that he had made up quotes (even "borrowed" quotes from others and attributed them to Reagan), many seemingly incredulous journalists cried foul. Surely they, as most of us, realized that the president simply doesn't have the luxury to write his own speeches anymore. Even John Kennedy, famous for his speeches, didn't write his own. Speakes himself dismissed the accusations as "taking a bit of liberty with my P.R. man's license" to "spruce up the President's image."[1]

However—and this is a big "however"—something still bothers all of us about a writer we don't even know putting words into the mouth of someone we do know or thought we knew. So, the question is, If ghostwriting is to be taken as having been produced by or at least prompted by the person under whose name it will appear, is it unethical? Well, yes and no. Some of the best guidelines that I know of have been set down by Richard Johannesen in his book *Ethics in Human Communication*,[2] in which he analyzes the ethics of ghostwriting by posing a series of important questions:

- *What is the communicator's intent, and what is the audience's degree of awareness?* In other words, does the communicator pretend to be the author of the words that he speaks or over which his signature appears? And how aware is the audience that ghostwriting is commonplace under certain circumstances? If we assume, as most do, that presidential speeches are ghostwritten, then the only unethical act would be for the president to claim to author his own speeches.

- *Does the communicator use ghostwriters to make herself appear to possess personal qualities that she does not have?* In other words, does the writer impart such qualities as eloquence, wit, coherence, and incisive ideas to a communicator who might not possess these qualities otherwise? The degree to which the writing distorts a communicator's character has a great deal to do with ethicality.

- *What are the surrounding circumstances of the communicator's job that make ghostwriting a necessity?* The pressures of a job often dictate that a ghostwriter be used. Busy executives, like busy politicians, may not have the time to write all the messages that they must deliver on a daily basis. However, we don't expect the average office manager or university professor to hire a ghostwriter. Part of

[1] Larry Speakes, with Robert Pack, *Speaking Out: The Reagan Presidency from Inside the White House* (New York: Harcourt, 1989), 169–170.

[2] Richard L. Johannesen, *Ethics in Human Communication*, 4th ed. (Prospect Heights: Waveland Press, 1996), 138–139.

the answer to this question lies in the pressures of the job itself, and the other part has to do with the need and frequency of communication.

- *To what extent does the communicator actively participate in the writing of his own messages?* Obviously, the more input that a communicator has in his own writing, the more ethical will be the resultant image. We really don't expect the president to write his own speeches, but we do expect that the sentiments expressed in them will be his own.

- *Does the communicator accept responsibility for the message that she presents?* Most communicators simply assume that whatever they say or whatever they sign their names to is theirs, whether written by someone else or not. This is obviously the most ethical position to take.

Remember, if you ghostwrite, you are as responsible for the ethicality of your work as the person for whom it is written. Be sure that you have asked yourself these questions before you give authorship of your work to someone else.

What the Public Relations Society of America Has to Say

The Public Relations Society of America's (PRSA) Member Code of Ethics isn't designed specifically for writers; however, it does provide the following relevant guidance:

- Be honest and accurate in all communications.
- Act promptly to correct erroneous communications for which the practitioner is responsible.
- Preserve intellectual property rights in the marketplace (this has much to do with plagiarism and copyright, covered below).
- Investigate the truthfulness and accuracy of information released on behalf of those represented.

An example of a possible code violation includes lying by omission, in which a practitioner for a corporation knowingly fails to release financial information, giving a misleading impression of the corporation's performance. Another breach of the code would involve a member discovering inaccurate information disseminated via a Website or media kit and not correcting the information.

In addition, educator and ethicist Kathy Fitzpatrick, a member of PRSA's Board of Ethics and Professional Standards, suggests the following approach to ethical decision making that provides a useful method of analyzing ethical behavior overall.

1. Define the specific ethical issue/conflict. Not everything you do involves an ethical issue; however, being "morally sensitive" is a good character trait to acquire. Paying attention to some of the pitfalls mentioned earlier in this chapter will help sensitize you to potential problems.

2. Identify internal/external factors (e.g., legal, political, social, economic) that may influence the decision. Many of these are outside factors and often beyond the control of a writer; nonetheless, awareness of the pressures that

may be leading toward an ethical infringement will give you a deeper understanding of what's happening and why—which will provide you with a stronger ethical platform from which to object.

3. Identify key values. These values are pretty obviously laid out in PRSA's code. They include the following:

   Advocacy—We serve the public interest by acting as responsible advocates for those we represent. We provide a voice in the marketplace of ideas, facts, and viewpoints to aid informed public debate.

   Honesty—We adhere to the highest standards of accuracy and truth in advancing the interests of those we represent and in communicating with the public.

   Expertise—We acquire and responsibly use specialized knowledge and experience. We advance the profession through continued professional development, research, and education. We build mutual understanding, credibility, and relationships among a wide array of institutions and audiences.

   Independence—We provide objective counsel to those we represent. We are accountable for our actions.

   Loyalty—We are faithful to those we represent, while honoring our obligation to serve the public interest.

   Fairness—We deal fairly with clients, employers, competitors, peers, vendors, the media, and the general public. We respect all opinions and support the right of free expression.

   Note, however, that not every value will come into play for every situation that arises. Recognizing the relevant value or values will increase as your skill level as an ethical decision maker grows.

4. Identify the parties who will be affected by the decision and define the public relations professional's obligation to each. Use the following set of common obligations to help you decide who you owe and why.

   Fidelity—Have you made a promise that you must keep? Will you be breaking any contract you have made, either explicit or implicit?

   Justice—Will anyone be treated unfairly by your actions?

   Harm—Will anyone be harmed by your actions? If so, how can you best eliminate or mitigate that harm?

5. Select ethical principles to guide the decision-making process. These could be based on the PRSA code itself, which is ultimately pretty good at laying out the relevant principles for public relations professionals. Of course, one should never ignore personal principles when it comes to making an ethical decision. If they conflict with professional principles for any reason, it's time to stop and ask why.

6. Make a decision and justify it. Imagine the person most harmed by your actions. What would you say to that person to assure them that you had carefully weighed the consequences of your action?

PUBLIC RELATIONS AND THE INTERNET

Recent changes in technology have allowed organizations to reach out to their constituencies in ways never before imaginable. The Internet has allowed us to reconfigure our communications and our modes of delivery. Additionally, technology has expanded the scope of both internal and external communications beyond that of traditional media. The role of everything from the news release to the corporate magazine has been broadened by the ability to make what was once a static delivery system now interactive. There are a number of relatively new methods for getting a public relations message out over the Internet, all of which have great potential for clarifying information and for persuading audiences. They also are burdened with predictable pitfalls. We are going to concentrate here on blogging and social media marketing, but they are indicative of the types of ethical problems associated with much of the *new* media.

Blogging

The key thing to remember about blogging in public relations is that public relations people don't represent themselves. They represent their clients and/or organizations. In addition, public relations messages have to be economical and to-the-point, and, above all, accurate. However, there are ethical problems that can arise in relation to this form of communication, perhaps the most troubling of which is the lure of anonymity.

To be anonymous is to present yourself or your opinion publicly without disclosing your true identity. Although the Supreme Court has held that anonymity can be "vital to democratic discourse," anonymity in public relations is always ethically questionable.[3] It can allow for abuses without accountability, but more importantly, it complicates the issue of credibility. It is vital in public relations blogging that our publics not only know who we are, but also *why* we're saying what we're saying. In other words, they need to know our motivation. Once they know that, they can put our messages in the proper context. That's why all public relations communication should be transparent. Being transparent in public relations means that your identity, the identity of those whom you represent, and your motivation are apparent.

A good example is ghost-blogging (the online version of ghostwriting). Recent research shows that although many readers of corporate blogs may understand they are most often being written by someone other than, say, the corporate CEO, they don't especially like the practice. And, if your readers *don't* know you're ghost-blogging, once they do find out, all your credibility vanishes. This will not help you or your client. The takeaway from this research is to *always* disclose who you are and whom you represent. Remember, public relations professionals have a moral obligation not to hide their identities.

Other considerations are included here in a compilation of several blogging codes.

- Never intentionally deceive others.
- Be accountable for what you post.
- Reveal your identity.

[3] *McIntyre v. Ohio Elections Commission*, 514 U.S. 334 (1995). Cited in the Electronic Frontier Foundation, http://www.eff.org/Privacy/Anonymity/

- Reveal your personal affiliations and conflicts of interest.
- Cite and link to all sources referenced in each post.
- Note questionable and biased sources.
- Publish as fact only that which you believe to be true.
- If material exists online, link to it when you reference it.
- Publicly correct any misinformation.
- Write each entry as if it could not be changed; add to, but do not rewrite or delete, any entry.
- Do not self-censor by removing posts or comments once they are published.
- Do not restrict access to your blog by specific individuals or groups.
- Allow and encourage comments on your blog.
- Build relationships by responding to e-mails and comments regularly.

Social Media Marketing

There are a wealth of terms currently in use to describe techniques used to create "buzz." They all refer roughly to the same technique—spreading the word about an organization, a client, or an idea by using your publics to help promote it for you. Although this used to be the domain of advertising, it is increasingly used by public relations professionals.

As with blogging, there are numerous pitfalls associated with this approach, all having to do with transparency. Public relations writers are often asked to use existing blogs and social networks to increase the level of awareness of their client or organization. The idea is to put out information in various forms on blog sites and other social venues (such as Twitter and Facebook) in order to spread the word throughout the Internet much faster than traditional approaches can—thus, the term *social media marketing*. The driving concept is that people will pass on or "share" information, especially if it is exciting or creative. The rise of YouTube to the status of a multi-million dollar business in just a few years is a testament to this approach. The ethical downside is that information disseminated this way can take on a false credibility because it doesn't seem to come directly from an organization (or their public relations firm) but rather from people just like you and me. The ethical problem is that the public relations aspect of the message is often hidden beneath layers of person-to-person communication—seeming more like a conversation between friends in which information is exchanged spontaneously.

The fact is, social media marketing works, and because it works, public relations will continue to use it. With that in mind, here is one of the better codes developed for this type of communication. The Word of Mouth Marketing Association (WOMMA), a leading organization representing marketers who practice this technique, has developed a code of ethics aimed specifically at such practices as social media marketing. It clearly calls for what it terms "honesty of identity," which includes:

- Clear disclosure of identity is vital to establishing trust and credibility. We do not blur identification in a manner that might confuse or mislead consumers as to the true identity of the individual with whom they are communicating, or instruct or imply that others should do so.

- Campaign organizers should monitor and enforce disclosure of identity. Manner of disclosure can be flexible, based on the context of the communication. Explicit disclosure is not required for an obviously fictional character, but would be required for an artificial identity or corporate representative that could be mistaken for an average consumer.

- We comply with FTC regulations regarding identity in endorsements that state: "Advertisements presenting endorsements by what are represented, directly or by implication, to be 'actual consumers" should utilize actual consumers, in both the audio and video or clearly and conspicuously disclose that the persons in such advertisements are not actual consumers of the advertised product."

- Campaign organizers will disclose their involvement in a campaign when asked by consumers or the media. We will provide contact information upon request.[4]

PRSA's Most Recent Take on the Subject

Although PRSA hasn't addressed the issue of blogging, social media marketing, and transparency directly in their code, they have issued a "Professional Standards Advisory" providing some guidance. Under the heading, "Deceptive Online Practices and Misrepresentation of Organizations and Visuals," they say:

> Misrepresentation by organizations and individuals using blogs, viral marketing, and anonymous Internet postings with undisclosed sponsorships and/or deceptive or misleading identities or descriptions of goals, causes, tactics, sponsors or participants. (Note: The term "Flog" has been coined to describe a "fake blog," where an organization or its representative creates an online forum that appears to be from a private citizen expressing personal opinion or experiences, when, in fact, it is being maintained for hire with an undisclosed agenda.)

The stated reason for needing this "advisory" is that

> A number of websites and deceptive social networking postings have surfaced on behalf of issues, candidates running for public office, and products blindly sponsored by individuals, industries and organizations. PRSA members are reminded that open communication is essential for informed decision-making in a democratic society.[5]

THE LEGAL ASPECTS OF PUBLIC RELATIONS WRITING

All those who deal in public communications are bound by certain laws. For the most part, these laws protect others. We are all familiar with the First Amendment rights allowed the press in this country. To a certain degree, some of those rights transfer to public relations. For example, corporations now enjoy a limited First Amendment protection under what is known as non-commercial speech. **Non-commercial speech,** as defined by the U.S. Supreme Court, allows

---

[4] The WOMMA Ethics Code, http://www.womma.com/ethics/code/read/

[5] http://www.prsa.org/aboutprsa/ethics/professionalstandardsadvisories/

a corporation to state publicly its position on controversial issues. The Court's interpretation of this concept also allows for political activity through lobbying and political action committees.

But, as with most rights, there are concomitant obligations—chief among them is the obligation not to harm others through your communication. The most important don'ts for public relations writers concern slander or libel (defamation), invasion of privacy, and infringement of copyrights or trademarks.

Defamation

Defamation is the area of infringement with which writers are most familiar. Although it is variously defined (each case seems to bring a new definition), **defamation** can be said to be any communication that holds a person up to contempt, hatred, ridicule, or scorn. One problem in defending against accusations of defamation is that different rules exist for different people. It is generally easier for private individuals to prove defamation than it is for those in the public eye.

Celebrities and politicians, for example, open themselves to a certain amount of publicity and therefore criticism; whereas, a private individual suing for libel must prove only negligence, a public figure must prove malice. For defamation to be actionable, five elements must be present:

1. There must be communication of a statement that harms a person's reputation in some way, even if it only lowers that person's esteem in another's eyes.

2. The communication must have been published or communicated to a third party. The difference here is that between slander and libel. Slander is oral defamation and might arise, for example, in a public speech. Libel is written defamation, though it also includes broadcast communication.

3. The person defamed must have been identified in the communication, either by name or by direct inference. This is the toughest to prove if the person's name hasn't been used directly.

4. The person defamed must be able to prove that the communication caused damage to his or her reputation.

5. Negligence must also be shown. In other words, the source of the communication must be proved to have been negligent during research or writing. Negligence can be the fault of poor information gathering. Public figures must prove malice—that is, the communication was made with knowing falsehood or reckless disregard for the truth.

There are defenses against defamation. The most obvious is that the communication is the *truth*, regardless of whether the information harmed someone's reputation.

The second defense is privilege. *Privilege* applies to statements made during public, official, or judicial proceedings. For example, if something normally libelous is reported accurately on the basis of a public meeting, the reporter cannot be held responsible. Privilege is a tricky concept, however; privileged information should be given only to those who have a right to it. Public meetings are public information. Only concerned individuals have a right to privileged information released at private meetings.

The third most common defense is *fair comment.* This concept applies primarily to the right to criticize, as in theater or book critiques, and must be restricted to the public interest aspects of that which is under discussion. However, it also can be construed to apply to such communications as comparative advertising.

Privacy

Most of us are familiar with the phrase "invasion of **privacy.**" For public relations writers, infringing on privacy is a serious concern. It can happen very easily. For example, your position as editor of the house magazine doesn't automatically give you the right to use any employee picture that you might have on file or to divulge personal information about an employee without his or her prior written permission. Invasion of privacy falls roughly into the following categories.

Appropriation is the commercial use of a person's name or picture without permission. For instance, you can't say that one of your employees supports the company's position on nuclear energy if that employee hasn't given you permission to do so, even if the employee supports that position and has said so to you.

Private facts about individuals are also protected. Information about a person's lifestyle, family situation, personal health, and the like is considered to be strictly private and may not be disclosed without permission.

Intrusion involves literally spying on another. Obtaining information by bugging, filming, or recording another's private affairs is cause for a lawsuit.

Copyright

Most of us understand that we can't quote freely from a book without giving credit, photocopy entire publications to avoid buying copies, or reprint a cartoon strip in our corporate magazine without permission. Increasingly, however, the temptation to cut and paste from Internet sources overrides our best intentions. Most forms of published communication, including what appears on the Internet, are protected by **copyright** laws.

The reasons for copyright protection are fairly clear. Those who create original work, such as novels, songs, articles, and advertisements, lose the very means to their livelihood each time that novel, song, or advertisement is used without payment. Writers need to be aware that copyrighted information is not theirs to use free of charge, without permission.

Always check for copyright ownership on anything that you plan to use in any way. You may want to rewrite information, or paraphrase it, and think that as long as you don't use the original wording you are exempt from copyright violation. Not so. There are prescribed guidelines for use of copyrighted information without permission. For example, you may use a portion of copyrighted information if

- It is not taken out of context.
- Credit is given to the source.
- Your usage doesn't affect the market for the material.
- You use the information for scholastic or research purposes.
- The material used doesn't exceed a certain percentage of the total work.

Copyright expert and legal scholar Thomas G. Field, Jr., provides some excellent background and guidelines for those trying to unravel copyright laws. Most of the following is from his pages on the Franklin Pierce Law School Website.[6] According to Field, copyright arises automatically once some aspect of a project has been fixed in a tangible medium (including digital media). Notice is not required. Registration is required only if legal action is warranted. However, notice and prompt registration provide important remedial advantages in the United States.

Copyright Ownership and Duration

Employees. Absent contrary agreement, employers own all rights in works created by their employees within the scope of their employment. These are called "works for hire." Copyright in such works (as well as those created anonymously or under pseudonyms) lasts for 120 years from creation or 95 years from publication.

Commissioned Works. Under limited circumstances, commissioned work may be "for hire." When freelance authors agree in advance and in writing, their work may be so regarded if, for example, it introduces or illustrates a larger work.

Freelance Works. Some commissioned work aside, freelance authors own copyright in their work unless they later transfer rights to others. Freelance newspaper work, for example, cannot be included in electronic databases such as Nexus without explicit permission. Many writers complain, but now that implicit permission does not exist, informed publishers are likely to insist.

Copyright in not-for-hire works extend 70 years beyond the lifetimes of identified (or identifiable) authors. Also, assigned rights may be recaptured after approximately 35 years. This provision will begin to have an effect in 2013. That may discourage publishers' use of freelance work with a possible shelf life beyond 35 years, but it shouldn't. Publishers may continue to use freelance work in ways that predate exercise of a termination interest.

Joint Works. Absent agreement, all coauthors are free to use joint work, but anyone who receives income must share it equally. For such works, the 70-year component of the copyright term does not begin to run until the death of the last surviving coauthor.

---

[6] I am extremely indebted to Professor Thomas G. Field, Jr., of the Franklin Pierce Law Center, Concord, New Hampshire, for his permission to use his excellent guidelines to copyright law and copyright on the Internet, at www.piercelaw.edu/tfield/copyWrite.htm and www.fplc.edu/tfield/copynet.htm.

When Should Freelance Authors Register?

As noted, the best possible remedies are available if registration predates infringement of unpublished work. It should, however, also be noted that the need to sue is lessened by carefully selecting people with whom to do business. The results are likely to be more satisfying than being tied up in copyright litigation.

Infringement and Limits to Copyright

Substantial Similarity. The legal test for copyright infringement is "substantial similarity." This translates (roughly) into whether ordinary observers would regard a work as copied in whole or in part from an earlier one. But more is involved.

Works in the Public Domain. When copyrights expire, anyone is free to use a work. Yet, duration is substantial and varies according to several factors. See, for example, Professor Laura Gasaway's chart, "When Copyrights Expire" (www.unc.edu/~unclng/public-d.htm).

Expressions, Not Facts or Ideas, Are Protected. Reporters (or their employers) have rights in stories describing events; they have no rights in underlying facts (even if they turn out to have been fabricated). This explains, in part, stories in which one news source credits another but goes on to restate the facts. Giving credit may not be legally required, but it can be useful if the original contains errors or omissions (not to mention fabrications). A short story using only the basic plot from an earlier story does not infringe.

Independent Creation Is Permitted. A short story, identical to an earlier one, for example, would not infringe if it were independently created. In such circumstance, infringement is certain if access can be proven—a given if the author is the same. When access is doubtful, the better known the original and the more similar the alleged copy, the more likely that infringement will be found.

Fair Use. Partial or limited reproduction of others' work is sometimes permitted if it fosters public interests such as criticism, education, or scholarship. Uses that, for example, cut into others' income or potential income, however, are unlikely to be fair.

Bottom Line. People often wonder whether some particular use of a preexisting work is legally acceptable, but that is the wrong question. The vastly more important question is whether their use of the work is likely to generate a suit. Anyone who appreciates the significance of that proposition will either get permission or be sure that none is needed—most likely because the material to be used is in the public domain!

Copyright and the Internet

The Internet has raised new questions regarding copyright—questions that are, in some ways, similar to the ones stated above, and in others, quite different. For example, as with traditional copyright law, fair use is still ambiguous ground.

However, Internet copyright issues also include such things as e-mail lists, blogs, the entire content of Web pages, and even links to other sites from your own.

Following is a discussion of some of the ins and outs of copyright on the Internet. It specifically addresses U.S. copyright issues of concern to those who post to or own e-mail lists or host Web pages. It also deals with situations where someone might want to forward or archive another's e-mail posting or to copy material from another's Web page.

Basic Limits to Copyright

Although e-mail messages and Web pages may enjoy copyright protection, rights are subject to several fundamental limits. For example, only expression is protected, not facts or ideas. Also, later works that merely happen to be very similar (or even identical) to earlier works do not infringe if they were, in fact, independently created. Sources of general information on those topics are listed below.

Fair Use. Fair use, as covered above, is also relevant to Internet copyright. It permits some use of others' works even without approval. Uses that generate income or interfere with a copyright owner's income are not favored. Fairness also means crediting original artists or authors. Commercial uses of others' work are also disfavored. For example, anyone who uses, without explicit permission, others' work to suggest that they endorse some commercial product is asking for trouble! Yet, not all commercial uses are forbidden. Most magazines and newspapers are operated for profit; that they are not automatically precluded from fair use has been made clear by the U.S. Supreme Court.

Licenses Implied in Fact. Fair use allows limited uses of others' work without approval, but other uses may be approved by implication. For example, when a message is posted to a public e-mail list, both forwarding and archiving seem to be impliedly allowed. It is reasonable to assume that such liberties are OK if not explicitly forbidden. It seems logical that few who post to public lists would object if their messages are forwarded to others apt to be interested. In the same vein, it seems that few authors would object to having messages archived. That serves the interests of list members who may want to revisit topics addressed earlier. Indeed, most would prefer archives to seeing old topics rehashed—which is why one often sees lists of frequently asked questions (FAQs), with answers. However, when forwarding, archiving, or using part of a prior message to respond to an earlier message, be careful not to change the original meaning.

Express Licenses. Many e-mail copyright problems could be avoided if list owners would broadcast, at least on initial subscription, a notice such as the following:

> Members who post to this list retain their copyright but give a nonexclusive license to others to forward any message they post. They also give the list owner the right to archive or approve the archiving of list messages. **All other uses of messages posted to this list require permission of their authors.**

Remember, however, that this is not a foolproof way to avoid copyright or other problems.

Private Lists. "Private" lists are possible. All who sign up might expressly agree, say, not to forward list messages. Also, list messages could be archived anonymously, if at all, or access could be limited by use of passwords. Private lists should have few "fair use" problems; permission to use others' posts should be limited mostly by what they agreed to when joining, not by copyright law.

Authors' Rights

Registration: Web Pages. The entire contents of a Website no more require multiple registrations than a book with many chapters and numerous illustrations—or a CD with text and music, still and animated graphics, and software. Copyright Office Circular 66 (http://lcweb.loc.gov/copyright/circs/circ66.pdf) contains a brief discussion. However, the following could mislead those unfamiliar with copyright:

> *"Revisions and Updates*
> Many works transmitted online are revised or updated frequently. For individual works, however, there is no blanket registration available to cover revisions published on multiple dates. A revised version for each daily revision may be registered separately. . . . A separate application and $45 filing fee would be required for each."

While *new* text isn't covered by prior registrations, it is difficult to see why a court would allow someone to get away with copying a page of mostly registered content merely because it contains a few new sentences or other changes.

Registration: E-Mail. If a list owner wants to register threaded list contents, that should be possible—particularly if copyright has been assigned by members. The main thing that seems unclear is how much time could be spanned by a single registration. Given that "prompt" registration means within three months of "publication," that period makes sense.

The situation for e-mail authors is much more ambiguous. First, group registration of several periodical contributions by a single author is possible, but combining e-mail posts would require liberal interpretation of the term *periodical.* Alternatively, e-mail authors might register their "unpublished" collections, but that presents a different problem: Are messages to "public" lists "published" for all purposes, or might they be regarded as "unpublished" for registration purposes? Perhaps because no one has tried to register, the Copyright Office has so far posted no information.

Notice: Web Pages. For several years, copyright notice has not been required in the United States. Until then, however, that was not true; notice may be needed to rebut lingering notions that works published without notice can be used by others without restriction. Again, Web pages are simpler. Although a formal notice is not required, it is best to provide a simple notice of copyright.

Notice: E-Mail. Notice on individual e-mail messages (if blanket notice is not provided, say, in a welcome message) may also be useful. Something as straightforward as "Please do not forward this message without permission" should be legally adequate as well as honored by most recipients. It is hard to see any advantage to traditional notices.

Finally, copyright is *not* the sole legal basis for objection. Anyone who makes derogatory references to others (or their sites, products, or services), however it is done, invites trouble.

Users' Risks—The Bottom Line

Those who copy others' text are ever more easily found on the Internet with search engines. Titles, markers, and the like may also enable owners to locate improper copies of sounds or images.

Copyright law precludes most uses of others' works without explicit or implied permission. Because *some* uses are OK, people often ask *which* uses are acceptable. Such questions often miss the point. The most important risk is not of *liability*, it is of *suit.*

Consider graphics, for example. Those who use a relatively small amount of another's work—if not copied in detail—may face small risk. Still, it is much better to work from scratch. Things represented to be in the public domain may not be. People looking for graphics have an alternative—commercial clip art sold for such uses. Unlike freeware picked up on the Web, it should also have warranties against infringement.

Litigation is expensive. People concerned about, say, the nuances of fair use must not become so entangled in legal details that they forget that anything generating income or interfering with another's potential income dramatically increases the chance of suit.

The most compelling questions are (1) is a proposed use of another's work likely to offend, and (2) are expected benefits worth the bother and possible cost to resolve a dispute?

Why not ask? Only if the owner says no does the second question need to be addressed.

Misunderstandings Concerning Copyright

Finally, copyright expert Brad Templeton summarizes the most common misunderstandings about copyright law this way:

- These days, almost all things are copyrighted the moment they are written, and no copyright notice is required.

- Copyright is still violated whether you charged money or not; only damages are affected by that.

- Postings to the Internet are not granted to the public domain and don't grant you any permission to do further copying except *perhaps* the sort of copying that the poster might have expected in the ordinary flow of the Net.

- Fair use is a complex doctrine meant to allow certain valuable social purposes. Ask yourself why you are republishing what you are posting and why you couldn't have just rewritten it in your own words.

- Copyright is not lost because you don't defend it; that's a concept from trademark law. The ownership of names is also from trademark law, so don't say somebody has a name copyrighted.

- Fan fiction and other work derived from copyrighted works is a copyright violation.

- Copyright law is mostly civil law in which the special rights of criminal defendants that you hear so much about don't apply. Watch out, however, because new laws are moving copyright violation into the criminal realm.

- Don't rationalize that you are helping the copyright holder; often it's not that hard to ask permission.

- Posting e-mail is technically a violation, but revealing facts from e-mail you received isn't, and for almost all typical e-mail, nobody could wring any damages from you for posting it. The law doesn't do much to protect works with no commercial value.[7]

Additional Resources

In addition to the wealth of information on the Franklin Pierce Law School site, "Copyright Issues: Multimedia and Internet Resources" from the University of Texas Website is an excellent resource, especially regarding digital multimedia (available at www.utsystem.edu/ogc/intellectualproperty/mmfruse.htm).

Trademarks

Trademarks are typically given for the protection of product names or, in certain instances, images, phrases, or slogans (see Exhibit 2.1). For example, several years ago Anheuser-Busch sued a florist for calling a flower shop This Bud's For You. The reason, of course, is that the slogan was commonly recognized as referring to Budweiser beer. The Disney studios have jealously guarded their trademarked cartoon characters since the early 1930s, and their trademark appears on thousands of items. Charles Schultz's *Peanuts* characters are also used for hundreds of purposes, all with permission. Even advertisements that mention other product names are careful to footnote trademark information.

One of the main reasons for trademark protection is to prevent someone not associated with the trademarked product, image, or slogan from using it for monetary gain without a portion of that gain (or at least recognition) going to the originator. Another important concern is that the trademarked product, image, or slogan be used correctly and under the direction of the originator. Certain trademarked names, such as Xerox, Kleenex, and Band-Aid, have for years been in danger of passing into common usage as synonyms for the generic product lines of which they are part. The companies that manufacture these brand names are zealous in their efforts to ensure that others don't refer, for example,

---

[7] Brad Templeton, "10 Big Myths about Copyright Explained," available at www.templetons.com/brad/copymyths.html.

> ## Exhibit 2.1
>
> ### Symbols for Protected Material
>
> © **Copyright** Used to protect copy of any length. Can be "noticed"—or marked—either without actual federal registration (which limits protection under the law) or with registration (which expands the degree of legal protection). "Noticing" is simply stating that something is copyrighted, for example, "Copyright Thomas H. Bivins, 2007." This can be done with or without an accompanying copyright symbol.
>
> ® **Registered trademark** Used to protect any word, name, symbol, or device used by a manufacturer or merchant to identify and distinguish his or her goods from those of others. This mark indicates that the user has registered the item with the federal government, allowing maximum legal protection.
>
> ™ **Trademark** Similarly used but as a common law notice. In other words, material marked this way is not necessarily registered with the government and thus has limited and not full legal protection.

to photocopying as Xeroxing or to facial tissue as Kleenex. In fact, one of the legal tests for determining whether a brand name has become a synonym for a generic product line is whether it is now included in dictionaries as a synonym for that product.

As harmless as it may seem, using the term *Xeroxing* in a written piece to refer to photocopying or the simple use of a cartoon character on a poster announcing a holiday party may be a trademark violation. The easiest thing to do is to check with the originator before using any trademarked element. Often, the only requirement will be either to use the true generic word (in the case of a brand name) or to mention that the image, slogan, or name is a trademarked element and give the source's name.

KEY TERMS

logic fallacy	non-commercial	privacy
language fallacy	speech	copyright
ghostwriting	defamation	trademark

CHAPTER
3

Planning and Research

In This Chapter, You Will Learn

- The four steps in the planning stage of writing.
- What an issue statement is and why and how it is developed.
- The basics of Internet research.
- Why it is important to know your target audience before you develop a public relations piece.
- The two types of formal research and their advantages and disadvantages.
- The three types of objectives used in public relations writing.

Almost all writing goes through, or should go through, several stages—the first, and some say the most important, is planning. Planning incorporates practically everything you need to know, about both your subject and your audience, to produce a successful written piece; that is, a piece that accomplishes what you need it to do. The planning process includes developing an issue statement (the purpose), selecting the proper strategies for accomplishing that purpose, choosing the most effective media to deliver the message, and adhering to the correct style and format as dictated by the media choices. Inherent in all of these steps is research—research into whom to communicate with, how best to communicate your message, and then research into how well you communicated. We'll talk about the planning stage of writing in this chapter and the next. The discussion includes all the elements just mentioned, with the exception of style and format. They are the focus of the remainder of the book.

DEVELOPING AN ISSUE STATEMENT

All communication in public relations has some purpose. It may be to encourage people to vote, to join your organization, or to not litter, or it may be simply to raise their level of knowledge about your issue. Thus, the first step in any plan whose purpose is to reach a specified audience with a specified purpose in mind is to define the issue or problem being addressed by the communication.[1] Working without a precise definition of the issue is analogous to writing a college term paper without a thesis statement—you have no clear direction to show where you are going, thus no way to determine whether you have gotten anywhere when you've finished.

The first step in defining the issue is to develop an issue statement. An **issue statement** is a precise definition of the situation including answers to the following questions:

1. What is the problem or opportunity to be addressed?

2. Who are the affected parties? At this point, it is necessary to list only the concerned parties. A precise definition of *publics* is the next step in the planning process.

3. What is the timing of this issue? Is it an issue of immediate concern (one needing to be addressed right now), impending concern (one that will need to be addressed very soon), or potential concern (one that may need to be addressed in the near future)?

4. What are your (or your organization's) strengths and weaknesses regarding this issue?

---

[1]The terms *issue* and *problem* are relatively interchangeable depending on how you view the situation. *Issue* is a more generic term and covers both problems and opportunities; however, many people in public relations persist in viewing most responses in terms of problems. For our purposes, we will use the term *issue* as being more inclusive.

In answering these questions, be as precise as you can. Succinctness is important to clarity, and clarity is of primary importance in the planning process. It is often wise to answer these questions in outline form and then, working from the outline, to develop an issue statement. Consider the following example. It is necessarily simplistic for demonstration purposes. Most issue analysis at this stage is far more complex; however, the approach is the same and the need for precision and succinctness is no less important.

1. *Issue.* Your company has recently developed a new line of educational software targeted to school-aged children from first grade through high school. Development was time consuming and expensive and was based on previous research showing a marked trend in education toward computers in the classroom. Marketing and advertising of the new software will be handled by your company's marketing department and its outside advertising agency. From a public relations perspective, however, you see an opportunity to capitalize on the growth in educational computing by raising the awareness of key publics as to the importance of this trend and by tying your company's name to that growth.

2. *Affected publics.* Your publics have already been determined in part by the markets who will be using your new line of software. They are educators, administrators, parents, and students.

3. *Timing.* Because this is an opportunity and not a problem, timing is essential. Most opportunities require that you act quickly to capitalize on them. Your software is already developed, as is a marketing program. You need to move in advance of or, at the very least, simultaneously with the marketing effort.

4. *Strengths and weaknesses.* Your strengths include the availability of existing marketing research that has already determined your target publics, advance knowledge of how the new software will enhance the educational process so that you can focus on those elements, and a wide-open opportunity to set the scene for your product through some public relations advance work.

   Weaknesses might include competition, potential perception of vested interest in any philanthropic effort you might suggest, and the necessity to move almost immediately because of the availability of the product.

An issue statement based on this information might look like the following:

The recent development of our new line of educational software and the coincidence of current trends in educational computing present an opportunity for our company to align itself as a leader in modern education. To do this, we will need to raise the attention level of key publics concerning the importance of computers in the classroom so that we become closely associated with the trend. We are in a unique position to alert educators, administrators, and parents to the multiple uses of classroom computers and the availability of educational software as an answer to many current classroom problems. A well-placed publicity effort outside of and separate from our marketing plan could help pave the way for eventual increased sales of our software. This publicity effort should not seem to be connected to our product; however, we should not appear to hide our interests in increased sales either. A joint effort with an educational nonprofit organization might be the best approach to take.

This issue statement covers all of the questions posed earlier. The only qualitative difference between the original answers provided to the questions and this statement is the narrative format of the statement. Stating the issue in this form helps others conceptualize what you already understand and sets the groundwork for further analysis of the issue. Exhibit 3.1 describes how to use a direction sheet to plan your written piece.

Exhibit 3.1

Preparing a Direction Sheet

The first step any public relations practitioner takes before beginning to write is research. Every practitioner needs to understand thoroughly the audience, message, and medium for each communication. Intuition will not suffice. It is therefore important to lay the groundwork for any written piece by beginning with a *direction sheet*. A direction sheet is a series of questions that you should answer when you begin an assignment. No public relations writer should begin an assignment without one.

A basic direction sheet might include the following information:

- *Subject of the piece.* Is it going to be a new product publicity piece, an announcement of employee promotions, or news about a special event such as a fund-raiser or a grand opening?

- *Format.* What form will the information take? Is it to be a news release, a magazine article, a television public service announcement (PSA), or a brochure?

- *Objective.* What do we hope to accomplish by producing this piece? Do we want to educate the general public concerning our hiring policies? Do we want to make engineers aware that we have developed a new product for their use? Do we want to promote the Olympics by associating ourselves with the event?

- *Intended audience.* Exactly who is the target public? Is it homemakers, businesspeople, children, staff members? The audience with whom you decide to communicate will determine the form of the message and probably the medium. News releases, for instance, can be from one page to five pages long. Article length is usually determined by the publication for which it is intended. Brochure length varies according to layout.

- *Angle.* The angle hooks the audience and establishes the context of the message. It is all important and one of the toughest components to establish. The angle must be new and interesting. In a print ad, it could be a bold headline. In a television PSA, it might be a peaceful, scenic shot juxtaposed with abrasive audio. In a radio PSA, it might be a humorous context.

- *Key ideas.* These are the salient points that you wish to make through your communication. Establishing key ideas is important because they serve as an outline for writing a successful message.

- *Length*. Length largely depends on format. The length should be agreed upon in advance by the party requesting the piece and the writer.
- *Deadline*. This element is usually the most inflexible. Unfortunately, in public relations writing, as in most writing, the finished product is usually needed "yesterday."

When you receive an assignment, try to get as much information as you can in one client meeting. This means, be prepared ahead of time with a complete list of questions. Once you have left your client, it is usually difficult to get back in touch.

RESEARCHING THE TOPIC

As is the case in all forms of writing, you must know your topic before you can write about it. Research techniques for this purpose can run the gamut from conducting formal research, such as surveys and questionnaires, to simply checking the library or online services. Increasingly, for instance, information on thousands of subjects can be found free of charge on the Internet.

Regardless of whether it is online or in a file cabinet, organizational research material is generally readily available to most public relations writers. You can check with various departments within your organization for information on your topic and obtain previously published material from in-house and other sources. After you have been at this type of work for a while, you will undoubtedly have a well-stocked "swipe file" in which you have collected everything you or anyone else has ever written about your subject area. In essence, you become a standard journalist gathering background information for a story. You should never start writing until you have sufficient background on your subject.

For many articles, human interest is important. This is where interviews come in. Firsthand information is always best when you can get it. Interview those intimately involved with your topic and use their information when you write. Interviewing is a special skill, and it takes a lot of practice. The people you interview will determine how informative or interesting your interview will be. Although you can't always control whom you interview, you can prepare so that you can make the most out of your meeting. Exhibit 3.2 gives some tips for a successful interview.

Exhibit 3.2

Tips for a Successful Interview

- *Do your homework*. Collect background information on the people you're going to interview as well as on the topics you're planning to discuss. Don't

(continued)

(continued)

be embarrassed by your own ignorance of the topics; however, the better you know the topics, the more time you can save by asking for specific details rather than for in-depth explanations.

- *Prepare your interviewees in advance of the interviews.* Contact them well in advance, set a time for the interview that is convenient for them, and make sure that they know exactly what you are going to cover and why. That way, they can also prepare for the interview by gathering pertinent information as well as their thoughts. Ask if you can "talk with them" rather than "interview them." A talk puts people at ease; an interview can make them tense and formal.

- *Write down a list of questions that you want answered, working from the general to the specific.* But be prepared to let the interview range according to the interviewees' responses. Often, an answer will open new areas of inquiry or suggest an angle you hadn't thought of before. Be ready to explore these new avenues as they come up. Ken Metzler, journalist, educator, and author of *Creative Interviewing: The Writer's Guide to Gathering Information by Asking Questions* (Allyn & Bacon, 1996), claims that the best interviewers should not only expect but also ask for surprises in their willingness to explore rather than follow a strict set of questions.

- *If you're going to use a recording device, make sure it's charged and tested beforehand.* And, even though you are recording, always take notes. This physical activity usually puts the interviewee at ease by showing that you are listening, and it serves as a good backup if your recorder stops functioning or your battery runs out.

- *Keep the space between you and your subject free of any object that may be a source of distraction.* Your recorder should not occupy the space between you and your subject. Move it a little to the side, but make sure the microphone isn't obstructed. You should also keep your notepad in your lap, if possible, or simply hold it.

- *Break the ice.* Open your interview with small talk. Try a comfortable topic, such as the weather, or, if you know something about your interviewee, a familiar, nonthreatening topic. For example, if you know your interviewee is an avid golfer, ask if he or she has had a chance to play much lately. Almost any topic will do. Most of the time, something will suggest itself naturally.

- *As your interview progresses, don't be afraid to range freely but be sure to return occasionally to your preset questions.* Although the information that you gather exploring other avenues may add greatly to your collection of relevant facts, remember to cover all the ground necessary for your article.

- *If you are ever unsure of a quote or think that you might have misunderstood it, ask your subject to repeat it.* Even if you are taping the interview, accuracy on paper and in your own mind is worth the slight pause.

- *Finally, be prepared to have to remember some key conversation after your interview is officially over.* Most of us are aware of the phenomenon that Ken Metzler calls the afterglow effect, when dinner guests, for example, stand at the door with their coats on ready to go and talk for another 30 minutes. The same thing usually happens in an interview. You've turned off your recorder and put away your pad, and on your way out the door you have another 10 minutes of conversation. In this relaxed atmosphere, important comments are often made. Remember them. As soon as you leave, take out your notepad and write down the comments or turn on your recorder and repeat the information into it. However, always make sure that your interviewee is aware that you are going to use this information as well. Don't violate any assumed off-the-record confidences.

Remember, get as much as you can the first time out. Most interviews range from 30 minutes to 2 hours. A follow-up interview, providing you can get one, will never be as fruitful or relaxed as the first one.

Evaluating Internet Resources

The Internet has become the most-used information source in the United States and perhaps even the world. However, the safeguards that more traditional information sources have developed over the years to ensure accuracy of information don't exist for the most part on the Internet. Following, then, are some guidelines for evaluating Internet resources.

Purpose

Audience
- Consider the intended audience of the page, based on its content, tone, and style.
- Does this mesh with your needs?

Consider the Source
- Web search engines often amass vast results, from memos to scholarly documents.
- Many of the resulting items will be peripheral or useless for your research.

Source
- Author/producer is identifiable.
- Author/producer has expertise on the subject as indicated on a credentials page. You may need to trace back in the URL to view a page in a higher directory with background information.

- Sponsor/location of the site is appropriate to the material as shown in the URL. Some examples are
  - .edu for educational or research material.
  - .gov for government resources.
  - .com for commercial products or commercially sponsored sites.
- ~NAME in a URL may mean a personal home page with no official sanction.
- *Mail-to* link is offered for submission of questions or comments.

Content

Accuracy

- Don't take the information presented at face value.
- Websites are rarely refereed or reviewed, as are scholarly journals and books.
- Look for points of view and evidence of bias.
- Source of the information should be clearly stated, whether original or borrowed from elsewhere.

Comprehensiveness

- Determine if the content covers a specific time period or an aspect of the topic or strives to be comprehensive.
- Use additional print and electronic sources to complement the information provided.

Currency

- Be sure the site has been updated recently, as reflected in the date on the page.
- Be sure the material contained on the page is current.

Links

- The links should be relevant and appropriate.
- Don't assume that the linked sites are the best available. Be sure to investigate additional sites on the topic.

Style and Functionality

- Site is laid out clearly and logically with well-organized subsections.
- Writing style is appropriate for the intended audience.
- Site is easy to navigate, including
  - Clearly labeled *Back, Home, Go to Top* icons/links.
  - Internal indexing links on lengthy pages.
- All links to remote sites work.
- Search capability is offered if the site is extensive.

ANALYZING THE TARGET AUDIENCE

Imagine holding a complex conversation with someone you don't know. If you are trying to persuade that person of your point of view, you will have a better chance if you know his or her predispositions in advance. The same holds true for written communication. To write for an audience, you have to know that audience intimately.

A **target audience** is typically defined as the end users of your information—the people you most want to be affected by your writing. What you need to know about your target audience depends to a great extent on your objectives. As discussed previously, public relations writing is typically used either to inform or to persuade. The type of information that you gather on your target audience depends on how you will use your piece. If you are writing a persuasive publication, for example, you need to know not only who your prospective readers are but also how much they know about your topic, how interested they are, and whether they can or want to do anything about it. With this information in hand, you can inform them, address their concerns, and, it is hoped, move them to action. By contrast, think of all those publications you've seen at government agencies or received through the mail, or downloaded from the Internet as a result of having requested information. Writers of these types of pieces need to know only that you desire their information.

Knowing the audience for whom you're writing is probably the most important factor in planning your message. The success of your writing will be determined to a great extent by how well you've aimed your message. The best way to write is for an imagined reader, an individual to whom you are speaking directly. To understand this individual, you need to know him or her personally. You will need to develop a profile of this typical reader, citing both demographic characteristics (for example, age, sex, and income) and psychographic information (for example, behavior patterns, likes and dislikes, and attitudes).

Another important factor to consider at this point is how your target audience feels about your subject. In most persuasive endeavors, there are three types of audiences: those already on your side, those opposed to your point of view, and the undecided. As most experienced persuaders know, convincing the hard-core opposition is not a reasonable objective. Persuading those already on your side is like preaching to the choir: Unless you want to stir them to some action, it is a waste of time. Thus, most persuasion is aimed at the undecided. Remember, however, that even the undecided have opinions. Those opinions may not be fully crystallized, which leaves this group particularly open to persuasion.

Conducting Target Audience Research

Methods for collecting information on your target audiences range from informal methods such as simply asking the client who the audience is, through secondary research gathered from such sources as the library, the Internet, or your own organization, to fairly expensive formal research. Many writers are put off by having to gather hard-core information about their readers. Unfortunately, many a message has missed its audience completely because it was not built around this information.

Although an in-depth discussion of formal research techniques is beyond the scope of this book, you need to understand the importance of such techniques and a bit about how they work. At the very least, you should know enough to ask the right questions of the people you hire to do the survey for you and enough to translate their findings into plain English. Briefly, then, here are some of the things to look for.

There are essentially two types of formal research: primary research and secondary research. **Primary research** is data collected for the first time and specifically for the project at hand. This type of research is generally more expensive than secondary research because you will have to do everything from scratch, including developing the questions, setting up the survey, collecting the data, and analyzing them. Whether you hire a research firm or do it yourself, it will be costly and take more time. The upside is that it is completely relevant to your current issue (ideally, at least).

Secondary research includes data previously collected, often by third parties, for other purposes and adapted to the current needs. Such data can include demographic information already gathered by another department in your organization or information gained from research done by other parties outside your company. Secondary research is generally less expensive and quicker to obtain, compared with primary research. However, it does have to be adapted to your uses and will not always answer your questions. Conducting a combination of primary and secondary research is usually the best approach.

Regardless of the type of research you use, it must fit your needs. The best way to ensure this is to set an objective for your research and then compare the results of your efforts with your original objective. This is most important if you decide to do primary research.

Secondary Research

A visit to the library or the Internet can yield volumes of secondary data. For example, government documents such as the *American Statistics Index (ASI)* can be invaluable sources. *ASI* is a compendium of statistical material including the U.S. census and hundreds of periodicals that can be obtained directly from the sponsoring agencies, from the library itself, or on the Internet. *ASI* also publishes an alphabetical index arranged by subject, name, category, and title.

Other sources of market information include the Simmons Market Research Bureau's annual *Study of Media and Markets.* This publication includes information on audiences for over 100 magazines, with readership delineated by demographic, psychographic, and behavioral characteristics. When using such secondary research, you will find much information that is not directly applicable to your target audience. You have to know not only where to look but also how to decipher what you read and apply it to your needs.

Primary Research

Once you've decided to use primary research, you'll need to decide how to collect it. The two most common methods of primary research are focus groups and surveys.

Focus Groups. Focus groups have become a fairly commonplace practice for those in advertising, marketing, and public relations. The technique requires that you assemble a small group (usually not more than 10 people or so) from your target audience, present them with questions or ideas, and ask for their reactions. Your approach can be relatively formal (a written questionnaire to be filled out following the presentation) or informal (open-ended questions asked in an open discussion among the participants).

The key to a successful focus group is to design your questions in advance and cover all the areas that you need to analyze. Be sure to explore whether your message's language is appropriate to your audience. Some of the questions to be considered are as follows:

- Is the message difficult to follow or does it have too much jargon or too many technical terms?
- Does your audience understand the message?
- Does the message speak to them, or do they feel it is meant for someone else?
- Is the medium appropriate?
- Would your readers take time to read the message if it came to them in the mail? As an insert in their paychecks? In the corporate magazine?

Answers to these questions should give you a fair idea of how your larger audience will react to your message.

The best way to set up a focus group is to hire a moderator who is experienced in asking these questions and interpreting the responses properly. Don't assume that, because you are the writer and the closest to the project, you can interpret audience feedback clearly. Indeed, in most cases you are not the one best suited to act as the focus group's moderator. Moderators are generally trained in marketing or sociology and are used to eliciting responses from people without biasing the answers. This is not a skill that is beyond most public relations people, but it does take a bit of training.

Surveys. An equally important primary research option is the survey. The three most common methods of survey data collection are the face-to-face interview, the telephone interview, and the online questionnaire. Each has advantages and disadvantages.

The *face-to-face interview* allows you to interpret body language, facial expressions, and other nonverbal clues that help flesh out the responses that you're getting verbally. A good interviewer will know how to gauge these nonverbal clues and evaluate them within the context of the verbal answers. The disadvantages of face-to-face interviewing include potential inconsistency in the abilities of interviewers and the general lack of willingness of most people to agree to any but the most perfunctory personal interview.

The *telephone interview,* by far the most common type of interview, also has its advantages and disadvantages. It must be brief (usually 5 minutes or so) or people won't agree to it. You can interview far more people this way, but you don't get much depth. Random dialing is most often used for telephone interviews;

however, not everyone has a phone and thus the sample is not truly random. Last, not everyone likes to be interviewed over the phone. If the information that you need can be gathered in only a few questions, though, the telephone may be your best bet.

The *online questionnaire* is usually the most effective way of gathering in-depth information from a great many people at the same time. Although it may lack the ability to clarify ambiguous questions in the way that face-to-face interviews can, it does provide for more questions and longer responses than telephone interviewing. It also has a built-in consistency, which the other methods don't have. Answers aren't biased by interviewer miscues (facial expressions or body language), and each question is asked in a uniform way. However, as with telephones, not everyone has access to a computer, thus, the survey isn't random in the truest sense.

Generally, two types of data are collected by survey. **Descriptive data** basically "paint a picture" of the public being studied by their distinctive demographic characteristics—descriptors such as age, income, sex, education, nationality, and so on. This is information you need for your reader profile.

Inferential data allow you to generalize about a larger group or population. This means that the people you choose for your survey must be entirely representative of the larger population that you want to reach. This allows you to sample a small segment of your target public and infer from their reactions the reactions of the larger audience. However, inferential research can work only if the sample is chosen completely at random from your larger population. This means that everyone in your target public has an equal chance of being chosen.

How do you ensure an equal chance? Easy. Computers have made this type of selection process much easier than it was in the past. All you need is a list of your target population (usually gathered from voter lists, motor vehicles records, and such). Numbers are assigned each person, and a computer randomly selects those to be surveyed. You should be aware of some variations in the selection process, however. These processes, or sampling methods, are listed in Exhibit 3.3.

Exhibit 3.3

Sampling Methods

Several different types of sampling methods are used in survey sampling. Each fits a specific need of those asking the questions.

- *Simple random sampling* is the easiest. It involves simply selecting the number you need from a master list, at random. This will usually be sufficient if you have a relatively homogeneous group with few or no differentiating characteristics.

- *Systematic sampling* adds a bit more complexity to the process by assigning (again by computer) an interval number. This means that the computer will select, at random, a starting number and then another number that will decide who is chosen next. For example, the computer chooses person number 2,067 as the first person to be mailed a survey. It then picks an interval number, say, 43. This number is added to 2,067, giving us 2,100—the next person to be sent a survey—and so on. The same interval number is used each time.

- *Cluster sampling* is useful if you need to interview only the head of each household, for instance, or 20 out of 56 houses in a subdivision, or people in 4 of the 10 counties of a state. Clusters are chosen using the same methods as above, only the population list is shorter because you're using larger initial units than individuals.

- *Stratified random sampling* implies that you will randomly select your sample based on further defining characteristics. For example, if your population is divided by income level (say, 20 percent over $50,000, 30 percent $20,000–$50,000, and 50 percent under $20,000), you'd need to select the same percentages in your sample.

- *Quota sampling,* by contrast, uses a set number from each mutually exclusive grouping within your population. This way, every voice is given attention. So, for example, within your population you may have a group (say, rape victims) who comprise a very small percentage of the overall target public. Using a stratified sample, you might not get the input you need from this group. Why? Because in the sample you may end up with only one or two people who fall into that category even though their opinions may be very important to you. If you draw an equal number of people from each of the subgroups whose opinions you need, you will have a better idea of the variance of opinion. Or you may not get a valid reading of opinions within that group if you limit yourself to a truly representative sampling size relevant to the population. In fact, many researchers will simply oversample a smaller subgroup to get a valid response from within that group and then weight the response in the overall final analysis.

The final question on any survey is one you must ask yourself: What does it all mean? If you've asked the right questions and if you've selected your samples according to your needs and totally at random, then you should be able to analyze the answers in a way that is meaningful to you and your employer. This implies that you've carefully planned out the survey in advance, including the questions to be asked and the method of gathering the data. It also assumes that you or whomever you hire to do the asking knows what he or she is doing.

Typical problems in survey design include the following: not enough people were sampled; the sample wasn't truly representative of your overall population; important questions were left out or questions were open to too much interpretation (see Exhibit 3.4 for types of survey questions); and your findings aren't related to your objective. Think about the possible shortcomings of any survey prior to spending your valuable time and money on something that might not prove to be worth it.

Exhibit 3.4

Types of Survey Questions

1. An open-ended question:

   Who would you like to see elected president?

2. A closed-ended question, with unordered answer categories:

   Who would you like to see elected president?

   a. Larry   c. Curly   e. Donald Duck

   b. Moe   d. Mickey Mouse

3. A closed-ended question with ordered answer categories:

   For each of these candidates, please indicate how much you would like that individual to be elected president.

	Strongly favor his election	Somewhat favor his election	Somewhat oppose his election	Strongly oppose his election
a. Larry	1	2	3	4
b. Mo	1	2	3	4
c. Curly	1	2	3	4
d. Mickey	1	2	3	4
e. Donald	1	2	3	4

4. A partially closed-ended question:

   Who would you like to see elected president?

   a. Larry   c. Curly   e. Donald

   b. Mo   d. Mickey   f. Other (specify)

5. Ladder scale question:

   On a scale from 0 to 10, where 0 means you rate the job the president is doing as extremely poor and 10 means you rate the job the president is doing as extremely good, how would you rate the job President Fillmore is doing now?

   Extremely poor   **Extremely good**

   0   1   2   3   4   5   6   7   8   9   10

6. Likert scale question:

   How likely do you think you will be to vote for President Fillmore in the upcoming election?

   1. Very likely

   2. Somewhat likely

3. Neither likely nor unlikely

4. Somewhat unlikely

5. Very unlikely

7. Semantic differential question:

Question   How would you characterize Millard Fillmore as president?

Good -Bad

Weak - Strong

Decisive -Indecisive

Immoral -Moral

Intelligent - Stupid

AUDIENCE DEFINITION WORKSHEET

One of the best ways to list your audiences is to answer a set of questions about them in the form of an Audience Definition Worksheet.[2] For example, once you have determined exactly who your audiences are, ask the following questions:

- Of the audiences listed, whose knowledge, attitudes, and behaviors must be changed to meet your goal? (These groups now become your primary audiences.)

- Who else is affected if you succeed in your goal? (Secondary audience)

- Are there others who can influence primary and secondary audiences? (Tertiary audiences/opinion leaders) (You may wish to design a communication initiative to reach some of these audiences as well. Or you may see a role for these folks as "allies and partners.")

Once you have determined primary audiences, you will need to further segment them to gain discreet knowledge about each one. Answer the following questions for each audience:

- Describe what you know about the audience members' knowledge, attitudes, and behaviors as they relate to your issue.

- What are the barriers to this audience fully supporting or participating in reaching your goal? What are the benefits if it does?

- What are the characteristics of this audience? How do members spend their time? What is their gender, ethnicity, and income level? How have they been educated? What are the language considerations? What or who are they influenced by? What makes new information credible for them? What or who could motivate change or action?

[2] This is part of a very good sample communications plan developed for nonprofits by the W. K. Kellogg Foundation, online at www.wkkf.org.

Anticipating Audience Expectations

Once you know who your audience is and how its members feel about your subject, one final question must be answered if you expect to be successful: Why are they going to be paying attention to what you've written? If you don't know why your audience is reading your message in the first place, you certainly can't know what members expect to get from it. Ask yourself these questions:

- *What does my audience already know about my topic?* Never assume that people know anything about your subject, but don't talk down to them either. How do you reach a compromise? Find out what they do know. Remember, people like to learn something from communication. It is best, however, to limit the amount of new information so as not to overwhelm your readers.

- *What is my audience's attitude toward me or my organization?* Remember the three basic audiences for any persuasive piece. You'll need to determine whether your audience is on your side, against you, or unconvinced. To the extent possible, try to determine your audience's image of you or your organization. Determining audience attitude is often an expensive proposition because it usually requires formal research. If time or money constraints permit you to make only an educated guess based on a small focus group or even on intuition, that's better than nothing. It is much easier to convince others when you know that you already have credibility with them.

- *Is my publication to be used in a larger context?* In other words, is your publication part of a media kit, for instance, or a direct-mail package, or one of many handouts at a trade show? This knowledge will determine your readers' level of attention and their receptiveness. Always consider the surroundings in which your piece will be used if you want it to have the maximum impact.

SETTING OBJECTIVES

Although the overall goal of a public relations campaign will generally be broad (such as "to improve employee moral"), **objectives** set the concrete steps that you will need to take to reach your goal. For public relations writing, these objectives must relate to the purpose of your message and should be realistic and measurable. For public relations writing, there are three types of objectives: informational, attitudinal, and behavioral.

Informational objectives are used most often to present balanced information on a topic of interest to your target audience. For instance, if you are simply attempting to let your employees know that your organization has developed a new health-care package, your objective might read something like this:

> To inform all employees of the newest options available in their health-care benefits package by the beginning of the October open enrollment period.

Notice that the objective begins with an infinitive phrase ("to inform"). Objectives should always be written this way. Notice, too, that the number of employees is addressed ("all"), and a specific time period for the completion of the objective also is included. In a complete communications plan, this objective would be followed by the proposed tactic for its realization and a method by which its success could be measured. For example,

> To inform all employees of the newest options available in their health-care benefits package by the beginning of the October open enrollment period by placing informational folders in each employee's paycheck over the next 2 months. Personnel will keep a record of all employees requesting information on the new health-care plan during the open enrollment period.

If your objective is *attitudinal* or *behavioral* rather than informational, your message is probably going to be persuasive. There are three ways you can attempt to influence attitude and behavior:

- *You can create an attitude or behavior where none exists.* This is the easiest method because your target audience usually has no predisposition.

- *You can reinforce an existing attitude or behavior.* This is also relatively easy to do because your target audience already believes or behaves in the way you desire.

- *You can attempt to change an attitude.* This is the most difficult to accomplish and, realistically, shouldn't be attempted unless you are willing to expend a lot of time and energy on, at best, a dubious outcome.

An example of an attitudinal objective is as follows:

> To create a favorable attitude among employees concerning the changeover from a monthly pay disbursement to a twice-monthly pay disbursement.

Methods for measuring this type of objective range from informal employee feedback to formal surveys of attitudes some time after the changeover has gone into effect.

An example of a behavioral objective is as follows:

> To increase the number of employees in attendance at the annual company picnic by 25 percent by mailing out weekly reminders to the homes of employees 4 weeks prior to the picnic.

Obviously, measuring the effectiveness of this objective is easier, but if you don't see an increase in attendance, you will have to do some serious research into the reasons why. However, these reasons might not involve your message or its presentation at all. You might simply have picked the Sunday of the big state fair to hold your picnic. Don't automatically conclude that your message is the problem without exploring all variables affecting its desired results.

EVALUATION

A quick word here about evaluation. Assessing your writing/message effectiveness is critical to its continued success. You will need to evaluate the impact of your writing, even if it is only for your own information. A good evaluation will help you determine if your writing was successful (has met its goals and objectives). Larger public relations campaigns in which your writing is used may have preset evaluative processes built in. Regardless of who does the evaluation, you can use the results to determine the level of success of your messages, adjust your approach if needed, or simply impress your clients and employers.

Evaluation can take many forms and should be tailored to your specific needs. For example, you may do a readership survey to determine the effectiveness of a newsletter or company publication (covered in Chapter 8). Or, you may opt for more formal research, such as surveys—mentioned earlier in this chapter. Remember, the time to build in evaluation procedures is when you write your objectives. If an objective can't be evaluated, it's not a good objective.

TIMELINE

To stay on track and to meet deadlines (especially if you are juggling multiple clients or projects), you will need to develop a timeline. This should include each component of the project you are working on, responsibilities for each component (if you have others working on the project with you), and deadlines for the completion of each component. A simple timeline can be easily constructed with just these three headings. If you wish to include budget information on your timeline, then just add another column; however, budgeting can be pretty complex and is covered in more detail later in this chapter. So, for example, your timeline might include the following information in a simple chart:

List all activities (down the left side of the chart).
Extend these items across the page, following each activity:

- Outline the steps, in order, that will lead to its completion.
- Assign a budget estimate to each step.
- Assign a staffing-needs estimate to each step.

  Working backward from the activity-completion point, assign a date for each step in the activity.

You might also want to develop a Gantt chart as a timeline. In a typical Gantt chart, the date/timeline runs horizontally across the page, and tasks are listed in chronological order down the left-hand side. A line extends across the page from each task, showing the date work begins and ends on that task or subtask. This generally excludes budget. (See Exhibit 8.13 in Chapter 8 for an example of a Gantt chart.)

BUDGETING

So much depends on money. If you don't have the money, you can't do the job. Whether you're an independent writer or working in-house for a single employer, budgeting for your work is of paramount importance. There are potentially hundreds of factors that can make up a budget. Fortunately for most of us, it doesn't take that much effort to put together a budget for a single project—even if that project has multiple components. As already noted, budgets are often constructed along with timelines; however, they can also be stand-alone efforts. As long as it reflects the projected costs of a project accurately, your budget will be a success.

Constructing a Basic Budget

Before you begin to construct a budget, you must determine whether to bill by the hour or by the project. Some writers work very fast, so billing by the hour isn't rewarding for them. Charging by project is a good way to go if you're a fast worker. If you are working for the same client on a regular basis, you might want to develop a yearly budget (with some built-in discounts if the client agrees to keep you on contractually). You might also consider a retainer—a monthly fee just for the client to keep you as a "shop" even if you don't do anything in a given month. But whether you bill by the hour, by the project, or by the year, there are some common factors that you can apply to your budgeting process. In fact, constructing a budget "by the numbers" will allow you to charge a project fee that is reasonable, even if you are a fast worker.

1. Begin with a list of the project components. This could be a series of individual activities in an overall campaign such as media relations, writing, and analyst relations. For our purposes, the list will probably include only the components of a complete writing assignment. For example, news releases, case studies, white papers, media kits, and speeches for a multicomponent campaign. Or it could contain just one project (a newsletter, for example) and all of the elements that go into that type of project.

2. Next, determine how many hours would normally be devoted to each component and your cost-per-hour. This would include your hours and the hours of anyone else working on that component of the project. This is especially important if you are paying from a total billing that you are collecting. If you are part of an in-house department and only part of your time is devoted to this project, you will have to determine how much of your time it takes up. You will need to perform this calculation for each person involved in any part of the project for whom you or another department is paying. This calculation should include salaries and benefits.

3. Include all out-of-pocket expenses you incur while working on the project:
   - Photocopying.
   - Long-distance calls.
   - Travel expenses, including mileage, fuel, food, lodging, air travel, and the like.
   - Supplies, including all on-site supplies exclusive of printing supplies—such as computer/copier paper and toner cartridges—and all miscellaneous supplies no matter how small, such as pencils, pens, writing pads, and paper clips.

- Payments to other vendors whom you subcontract (for example, layout artists, designers, and printers).
- Office space if you lease an office. You must calculate the cost of rent or space allocation, including utilities, telephones, fax, and other office equipment such as photocopiers.
- Production costs including the costs of on-site equipment such as computers. Printing should be calculated based on design needs, frequency, and quantity.
- Distribution, including the cost of mailing or other methods of distribution—such as hand delivery—and mailing lists.

Do You Need a Contract?

Contracts include scope of work, timeline, and protection language (for both the client and you). These should cover clear information on fees and expenses, confidentiality, and so on. It is perfectly fine for you to draft the contract, but allow your client to edit it if that helps you reach a mutual agreement. On the other hand, it doesn't hurt to hire a lawyer to draft a basic contract for you that you can then adapt to the needs of specific projects. Remember, it's never a bad idea to get it in writing.

KEY TERMS

issue statement	secondary research	inferential data
target audience	descriptive data	objectives
primary research		

CHAPTER

4

Choosing the Right Message and Medium

In This Chapter, You Will Learn

- What a message strategy is and why it is important to develop one before you develop a public relations piece.

- The purpose of informative and persuasive public relations pieces.

- What message strategies work best for conveying information and for persuading, and how each of these strategies works.

- How to choose the appropriate medium (or media) for conveying the message.

- How to buy media time and space, including the Internet.

Message strategy has to do with developing a message, or messages, that will reach and have the desired effect on your target audience. Your message strategies should logically follow your objectives and contribute either directly or indirectly to them. You will need to develop individual message strategies for each of your target publics, based on what you have learned about them through your research. Remember, the strategy or strategies that you use will be determined largely by your audience's makeup, predispositions, and perceived needs.

Most public relations writing is either informative or persuasive by intent, and a number of strategies can be used to accomplish both of these outcomes. Information, for example, may be imparted in a straightforward, expository manner, indicating by style that the message is unbiased. Information may also be imparted using **entertainment,** as anyone who has ever watched *Sesame Street* knows. In fact, if you are trying to reach an ambivalent audience with information, getting attention through entertainment may help ensure your success. Persuaders may use entertainment as well as reason or emotion to convey their message.

Although persuasion may seem to be separate from "pure" information, it most certainly is not. Most public relations people know, for example, that whether or to what extent target publics change their minds is due to three variables: (1) whether they are even aware of the issue you are talking about, (2) whether they believe it is important to them personally, and (3) whether they believe they can do anything about it. The extent to which each of these variables is in play with any given target public will dictate the strategy that you use in your writing. For example, if the target public is largely unaware of the issue you are dealing with, you will need to inform the public first before anything else can be attempted. If the audience is aware of the issue but doesn't see its relevance to members' personal agendas, then you will have to do some persuading. If the public is aware of both the issue and its importance to members but feels constrained (for whatever reason) from acting, then your job becomes a combination of information and persuasion.

What you have found out about your publics from your prior research will then dictate what strategies to take in your information and persuasion approaches. For example, although entertainment may work well with children, something approaching logic (argument) might have a better effect on businesspeople. Both strategies could be said to be persuasive; their styles are dictated by the target public.

An informative piece should be balanced and complete. Its purpose is to let readers in on something that they may not know or about which they may have an incomplete picture. The intent may be to publicize a new product or service, to set the record straight on a vital issue affecting your organization, or simply to let your readers know what's happening in your organization. Whatever the intent, the informational publication has to stick to just that—information. If your point of view is so strong as to evoke opposition, you probably should be writing a piece to persuade.

Persuasive pieces usually are heavy on the positive attributes of your service, product, or point of view. They need to be written in terms that the audience can relate to, and they frequently benefit from the use of words with emotional impact. Informative pieces can get away with far fewer emotionally packed words and are frequently longer. After all, their aim is to inform what is assumed to be an audience that is already convinced of or at least interested in the subject.

Again, think of how hugely popular and effective *Sesame Street* has been, or how successful the show *Biography* has been for the cable network A&E. I address entertainment strategies further when I discuss persuasion, below. For a short prewriting checklist for information pieces, see Exhibit 4.1.

THE PROCESS OF PERSUASION

To write persuasively you must understand the process of persuasion, what it is and how it either works or doesn't work. **Persuasion**—moving someone to believe or act a certain way—is difficult in most cases. That's why so many public relations campaigns strive for understanding, not persuasion. The problem, as it turns out, is that human beings have an interesting and frustrating ability to not listen to what is being said to them. This is particularly annoying for public relations people, who are constantly trying to communicate with publics who are simply not paying attention. Once we understand why they aren't listening, we have a much better chance of getting them to pay attention. Ready for a little theory?

Exhibit 4.1

A Prewriting Checklist for Information Pieces

When writing an information piece, ask yourself the following questions:

- Why would my target audience want to know about this topic?
- What would it want to know about it?
- Is the topic tied to a particular strategy? If so, what strategy? If it is part of an overall persuasive campaign, why am I using an informative approach?
- How much material should be considered "further information" to which interested readers can be referred elsewhere?
- Am I expecting any results from this approach? Make your objectives clear enough to be measurable so that you can later evaluate the results of information dissemination effectively.

Remember, the most valid objective of information is to raise your target audience's level of knowledge or understanding. The reason behind public relations writing may ultimately be to persuade, but in information pieces, bias should be kept to a minimum.

Dissonance theory, formulated in the 1950s, says that people tend to seek only messages that are consonant with their attitudes; they do not seek out dissonant messages. In other words, people don't go looking for messages they don't agree with already (who needs more conflict in their lives, right?). This theory also says that about the only way you are going to get people to listen to something they don't agree with is to juxtapose their attitude with a dissonant attitude—an attitude that is logically inconsistent with the first. What this means (theoretically) is that if you confront people with a concept that radically shakes up their belief structure, you might get them to pay attention. For example, this is the technique used by some antiabortion activists when they force us to look at graphic images of aborted fetuses. Although the experience may be truly uncomfortable, it reminds even the most ardent abortion rights supporters among us of the costs of the procedure. The attempt is to shock unbelievers into questioning their loyalties.

Later research revealed that people use a fairly sophisticated psychological defense mechanism to filter out unwanted information. This mechanism consists of four so-called rings of defense:

1. *Selective exposure.* People tend to seek out only the information that agrees with their existing attitudes or beliefs. This accounts for our not subscribing to *The New Republic* if we are staunchly liberal Democrats.

2. *Selective attention.* People tune out communication that goes against their attitudes or beliefs, or they pay attention only to parts that reinforce their positions, forgetting the dissonant parts. This is why two people with differing points of view can come to different conclusions about the same message. Each is tuning out the parts with which he or she disagrees.

3. *Selective perception.* People seek to interpret information so that it agrees with their attitudes and beliefs. This accounts for a lot of misinterpretation of messages. Some people don't block out dissonant information; they simply reinterpret it so that it matches their preconceptions. For example, whereas one person may view rising interest rates as an obstacle to his or her personal economic situation, another may view the same rise as an asset. The first person may be trying to buy a new home; the second may be a financial investor. Both are interpreting the same issue based on their differing viewpoints.

4. *Selective retention.* People tend to let psychological factors influence their recall of information. In other words, we forget the unpleasant or block out the unwanted. This also means that people tend to be more receptive to messages presented in pleasant environments—a lesson anyone who has ever put on a news conference understands.

What does all this mean? For those of us in the business of persuasion, it means we have a tough job ahead of us. However, the outlook isn't all that bleak. Since the time of the ancient Greeks (and probably before), we have known that people can be persuaded. Once you know how resistant they can be, half the job is done. The rest is knowing how to break down those defenses (or, at least, how to get around them).

ELABORATION LIKELIHOOD MODEL

Some people seem easy to persuade and tend to believe almost anything, whereas others seem resistant to persuasion, have their own opinions, and often argue with those trying to persuade them. The fact is that audiences, or publics, exist in multiple forms and use multiple methods of reasoning out decisions, two of which have caught the attention of researchers over the past 30 years or so.

In 1986 Richard E. Petty and John T. Cacioppo developed what they called the **elaboration likelihood model** of persuasion in which they sought to explain these differences.[1] They suggested that persuasive messages were transmitted and received through two different routes: the central route and the peripheral route. The **central route** is used by people who think about messages extensively before becoming persuaded. In other words, they "elaborate" on a message and will be persuaded only if the message is cognitively convincing. The **peripheral route** is used by those who are unable or unwilling to spend time thinking about a message. Instead, recipients using peripheral processing rely on a variety of *cues* to make quick decisions, most of which don't bear directly on the subject matter of the message. These cues include such tactics as using well-known celebrities or authority figures, creating a sense of gratitude in the receiver of the message, and using peer pressure or a person's need to belong to a particular group.

Petty and Cacioppo stress that the central and peripheral routes are poles on a cognitive-processing continuum that shows the degree of mental effort a person exerts when evaluating a message. They are not mutually exclusive approaches. The more listeners work to evaluate a message, the less they will be influenced by cues not relevant to the message itself. The greater the effect of cues not relevant to the message, the less impact the message carries.

For central processing receivers, the cognitive strength of the argument being presented is extremely important. For these receivers, thoughtful consideration of strong arguments will produce the most positive shifts in attitude. In addition, the change will tend to be persistent over time, resist counterpersuasion, and predict future behavior. However, thoughtful consideration of weak arguments can lead to negative boomerang effects (the weak arguments are shown to be exactly what they are, and the idea loses the respect and attention of the receiver).

According to Petty and Cacioppo, however, most messages are processed through the peripheral route, bringing attitude changes without actually thinking about the issue. Peripheral route change can be either positive or negative, but it won't have the impact of message elaboration and the change can be short lived.

Things to Note about the Elaboration Likelihood Model

- Personally relevant issues are more likely to be processed on the central route; issues with little relevance take the peripheral route (cues take on greater importance).

[1] R. Petty and J. Cacioppo, *Communication and Persuasion: The Central and Peripheral Routes to Attitude Change* (New York: Springer-Verlag, 1986).

- Certain individuals have a need for cognitive clarity, regardless of the issue; these people will work through many of the ideas and arguments they hear and will generally use the central route.
- Distraction disrupts elaboration.
- Repetition may increase the possibility of elaboration.

Practical Advice for the Persuader

- If listeners are motivated and able to elaborate a message, rely on factual arguments—that is, favor the central route.
- When using the central route, however, remember that weak arguments can backfire.
- If listeners are unable or unwilling to elaborate a message, rely on packaging rather than content—that is, favor the peripheral route.
- When using the peripheral route, however, remember that the effects will probably be fragile.

PERSUASIVE STRATEGIES

Writing a message that persuades is not easy. First, you have to have a crystal-clear understanding of how you want your readers to respond. This means you have to be able to convey your message in the clearest possible terms and must also be responsive to opposing points of view.

The persuasive message is normally audience centered; that is, persuasive strategy is based on who your audience is and how members feel about your topic. The approach that you use probably will be based on audience analysis. For example, your knowledge of your target audience should indicate how receptive participants are to either an emotional or a rational appeal. Historically, audiences react best to a combination of both. There are times, however, when a purely emotional or purely rational appeal will be most effective.

In general, audience-centered persuasion will be more successful if you adhere to the following simple principles:

- *Identification.* People will relate to an idea, opinion, or point of view only if they can see some direct effect on their own hopes, fears, desires, or aspirations. This is why local news is more interesting to most people and why global issues remain so distant from most of our daily lives.
- *Suggestion of action.* People will endorse ideas only if they are accompanied by a proposed action from the sponsor of the idea or if the recipients themselves propose it, especially if it is a convenient action. For example, every time you see a tear-off coupon dispenser at a grocery store, the product manufacturer is following this principle.
- *Familiarity and trust.* People are unwilling to accept ideas from sources they don't trust. We will trust even celebrities if they are familiar to us and have

good reputations. We certainly trust them to recommend commercial products (such as athletic shoes); however, it is much harder to find spokespeople for image-related issues. That's why we often see occupations rather than specific people used in these pitches. An ecoscientist is a far better spokesperson for a company wanting to go "green" than is any celebrity.

- *Clarity.* The meaning of an idea has to be clear, whether it is an event, a situation, or a message. One of the most important jobs of public relations is to explain complex issues in simple terms. In today's "sound-bite" environment, this has become increasingly difficult. No one is more aware of this difficulty than political campaign advisors. When was the last time you saw a political ad that said anything substantive in 30 seconds? Even so, research shows that some of the best of these ads actually do work.

Remember, a hostile audience usually won't be convinced, a sympathetic audience doesn't need to be convinced, and an undecided audience is as likely to be convinced by your opposition as by you. Different strategies will be used for each of these audiences. For instance, if you are writing for a friendly audience, an emotional appeal may work well. For an undecided audience, a rational appeal supported by solid evidence may work best. If your audience is neutral or disinterested, you'll have to stress attention-getting devices. If it is uninformed, you'll have to provide information. And if it is simply undecided, you'll have to convince the audience.

As already mentioned, certain strategies are more appropriate to persuasion than to information dissemination. For example, emotional appeals are most often associated with persuasion, not information. That's why, for instance, straight news stories are generally free of such appeals. They are supposed to be as objective (informative) as possible. The most common strategies for persuasion are compliance strategies and argument strategies.

Compliance Strategies

Compliance strategies are persuasive strategies designed to gain agreement through techniques of persuasion based not on reasoned argument (although they may appear to be) but on some other method of enticement. For example, offering a reward for the return of stolen merchandise doesn't exactly appeal to altruism, yet it's considered an acceptable method for regaining what is yours. So, although some compliance strategies may appear at first blush to be unethical, a quick review of the following three compliance strategies will reassure you that they need not be.

Sanction Strategies

Sanction strategies use rewards and punishments controlled by either audience members themselves or as a result of the situation. For example, if I'm trying to persuade you that supporting the state lottery is a good thing because the proceeds go to fund education, I can offer you the potential reward of big winnings. Of course, you control whether you are eligible. If you buy a ticket, you are; if you don't, you're not. However, I made you aware and offered you the choice.

Appeal Strategies

Appeal strategies call upon the audience to help or come to the aid of the communicator or some third party represented by the communicator. For instance, I might urge you to "save the whales." I am counting on your sense of altruism to act, mostly because it is so difficult to tie the fate of whales to any personal interest beyond altruism. Of course, this strategy works only on publics prone to act sympathetically.

Command Strategies

Command strategies come in three forms:

- *They may use direct requests with no rationale or motivation for the requests.* The famous "I want you" poster for the U.S. Army is still a great example of this strategy. A more current example is "Got milk?"—the campaign of the American Dairy Council.

- *They may provide explanation accompanied with reasons for complying.* The army "Be all you can be" campaign is a good example of this one. One of the newer versions of that message plays heavily on the college tuition benefit, for example.

- *They may provide hints in which circumstances are suggested from which the audience draws the desired conclusions and acts in the desired way.* This technique implies that your audience shares certain connotative meanings. For example, the famous (or infamous) Virginia Slims ads suggested that smoking promotes thinness. Another example is the now-famous Godfatherly appeal, "I made him an offer he couldn't refuse." The implicit suggestion is understood between communicator and audience. Nothing explicit need be said.

Argument Strategies

Democratic debate is at the heart of our system of government. It is no surprise then that **argument strategies** are among the oldest types of persuasion at your disposal. Argument strategies, which are persuasive strategies designed to oppose another point of view and to persuade, come in two types: reasoned argument and emotional appeal. Both types attempt to persuade by arguing one point of view against another.

Reasoned Argument

Reasoned argument (also known as logical argument) uses the techniques of rhetoric as handed down from the ancient Greeks. For persuasive messages, it is important to understand the psychological state of your audience and build your message around it. This audience-centered approach includes three basic techniques of reasoned argument: the motivated sequence, the imagined question-and-answer (Q & A) session, and messages aimed at attitude change.

Motivated Sequence. A common tactic used by persuaders is the motivated sequence, which involves the following five steps:

1. *Attention.* You must first get the attention of your audience. This means that you have to open with a bang.
2. *Need.* Establish why the topic is of importance to the audience. Set up the problem statement—a brief description of the issue you are dealing with.
3. *Satisfaction.* Present the solution. It has to be a legitimate solution to the problem.
4. *Support.* Support fully your solution and point out the pitfalls of any alternatives. Otherwise, your audience may not be able to comprehend completely the advantages of your solution over others.
5. *Action.* Call for action. Ask your audience to respond to your message and make it as easy as possible to take action.

Imagined Q & A. In the imagined Q & A, the message is structured into a series of questions that the audience might have, followed by your answer to each. Ask yourself the questions your audience might be asking you, such as

- *Why even talk about this subject?* Tell audience members the importance of your topic to them. Tie your topic to their concerns.
- *For example?* Don't just leave them with your point of view. Give them examples. Support your proposal.
- *So what?* Let them know what all of this means to them and tell them what you want them to do.

Messages Aimed at Attitude Change. If you are going to try to change attitude, be aware of the most common techniques. Following are some guidelines for constructing persuasive messages designed for attitude or opinion change. The strategy used here is argument.

- *If your audience opposes your position, present arguments on both sides of the issue.* Remember, audience members already know you have a vested interest in giving your side of the story. By presenting both sides, you portray an image of fairness and willingness to compare arguments. The process appears to be more democratic that way. In most cases, it is advisable to address counterarguments only after you have presented your own side. Here's how it works:
  - *State the opposing view fairly.* Make your audience believe that you are fairminded enough to recognize that there is another side and that you're intelligent enough to understand it.
  - *State your position on the opposing view.* Now that you've shown you understand the other side, state why you don't think it's right—or better yet, not totally right. This indicates that you find at least some merit in what others have to say—even the opposition.
  - *Support your position.* Give the details of your side of the argument. Use logic, not emotion. Show that you are above such tricks; however, don't

avoid emotion altogether. Try to strike a balance while leaning toward logic and emotional control.

■ *Compare the two positions and show why yours is the most viable.* If you've done your work well up to this point, then your audience will already see the clear differences between the two sides. Strengthen members' understanding by reiterating the differences and finishing with a strong statement in support of your arguments.

● *If an audience already agrees with your position, present arguments consistent with its favorable viewpoint.* This will tend to reinforce audience members' opinions. Not much can be gained by presenting opposing arguments because they already agree with you. In fact, it might work against you.

● *If your audience is well educated, include both sides of the argument.* Intelligent people will judge your argument by how well you can refute counterarguments.

● *If you do use messages containing both sides of the argument, don't leave out relevant opposition arguments.* Audiences that notice the omission (especially well-educated ones) will probably suspect that you can't refute these arguments.

● *If your audience is likely to be exposed later to persuasive messages countering your position, present both sides of the argument to build audience resistance to the later messages.* This is known as the inoculation effect, which basically states that once you have heard me present both my side and the opposing side of an argument and heard me soundly refute the other side, you are far less likely to listen to the other side at a later time. You have, after all, already heard their side—from me.

Because emotion is common to all human beings, it should come as no surprise that the use of **emotional appeal** as a persuasive strategy is widespread. Most advertising uses emotional appeal to sell products. Parity products, especially, benefit from this technique. A *parity product* is one that is virtually indistinguishable from other similar products. Bath soaps, soft drinks, and perfumes are examples of parity products. Think about the types of ads you have seen that deal with these products: They are almost always based on an image created by emotional appeal. And not to let public relations off the hook, think of all those politicians who seem to be pretty much alike. How are they differentiated in our minds?

Emotional appeal can be fostered in several ways, the most important of which are the use of symbols, the use of emotive language, and the use of entertainment strategies. I discuss the use of symbols and emotive language in the section on ethics in Chapter 2. Here, I concentrate on entertainment as a way of creating emotional appeal.

Like the techniques of argument, the techniques of entertainment have been handed down to us from the ancient Greeks. The masks of comedy and tragedy are part of our cultural symbolism in the West. Entertainment, by nature, appeals to the senses. As a culture, we often refer to a person's sense of humor or someone's sense of the dramatic. As anyone who has kept track of the evolution in beer commercials knows, humor has become the primary focus of many beer manufacturers' ad campaigns. Think of the Budweiser campaign using frogs (and then lizards) to imprint name recognition or the "Bud Bowl," now a staple of Super Bowl mythology. Like many other products, beer is a parity item, and parity products are best differentiated by image, which is often the result of entertainment strategies.

It's easy to spot the uses of drama and humor in advertising, but public relations campaigns frequently use the same approaches to persuade. Humor, for example, is especially useful if what you have to "sell" either is opposed by your audience or appears to be distant from their experience. Politicians needing image revamps often turn to humor. The then vice president Al Gore could be seen some years ago cracking jokes about his own stiffness on *Late Night with David Letterman.* This was not an accident but rather a carefully planned public relations move to soften his image.

Emotional appeal, like compliance strategies, may seem to be unethical; however, using emotion to draw attention is not inherently so. It may be manipulative (in the sense that its sole intent is to hook the audience), but it is unethical only if it hides the true objective of the message: to persuade.

CHOOSING THE APPROPRIATE MEDIUM OR MEDIA

The final step in the planning process is choosing the appropriate medium or media for your message. Any assumptions that you make at this juncture could be disastrous. Selecting the right medium or media is a decision that should be based on sound knowledge of a number of factors. Public relations educators Doug Newsom, Judy VanSlyke Turk, and Dean Kruckeberg have suggested a series of important considerations to be used in choosing the right medium for your message:[2]

1. What audience are you trying to reach, and what do you know about its media-usage patterns and the credibility ratings for each medium? Many target audiences simply do not watch television or listen to the radio. Others don't read newspapers regularly or subscribe to magazines. You need to know, first, whether your intended audience will even see your message if it is presented in a medium they don't regularly use. Research tells us, for example, that businesspeople read newspapers more than do some other groups and that they rely on newspapers for basic news and information. Other groups may rely on television almost exclusively for their news and information. For each of these groups, the credibility of the medium in question is vital. For example, businesspeople cite newspapers as a more credible source for news and information than television; however, for many people, television is far more credible.

2. When do you need to reach this audience for your message to be effective? If time is of the essence, you'd best not leave your message for the next issue of the corporate magazine.

3. How much do you need to spend to reach your intended audience, and how much can you afford? It may be that the only way to achieve the result that you're looking for is to go to some extra expense such as a folder with more glitz or a full-color newsletter. Although every job has budget constraints, it's best to know from the start exactly what it will take to accomplish your objectives.

[2] Doug Newsom, Judy VanSlyke Turk, and Dean Kruckeberg, *This Is PR: The Realities of Public Relations,* 8th ed. (Belmont, CA: Wadsworth, 2003).

After you have answered these tough questions, you will need to ask four others:

1. Which medium (of those you've listed in response to your first three questions) reaches the broadest segment of your target audience at the lowest cost? The answer to this question will give you a bottom-line choice of sorts because cost is the controlling factor in answering it. Maybe you can reach all of an employee audience with an expensive corporate magazine but two-thirds of it with a less expensive newsletter.

2. Which medium has the highest credibility, and what does it cost? Here, the correct answer will give you the additional factor of credibility that is key if your audience is discriminating at all. There are always those for whom the least credible of sources is still credible (otherwise, gossip tabloids would go out of business). But, for the honest communicator, credibility is important to the success of any future messages.

3. Which medium will deliver your message within the time constraints necessary for it to be effective? Again, a critical letter distributed via the company intranet may be timelier than a well-written article in next month's corporate magazine.

4. Should a single medium be used or a combination of complementary media (media mix)? Remember, each element in an overall communications program may require a specialized medium for that portion of the message to be most effective.

The more that you know about your audience, the better you will be at selecting just the right medium for your message. However, you must also understand that media criteria often dictate message and message format. For instance, brochures demand brevity, as do flyers and posters; corporate magazines allow for fuller development of messages; newsletters offer more space than folders but less than magazines; pamphlets offer space for message expansion and place fewer demands on style; annual reports require strict adherence to Securities and Exchange Commission guidelines; and Web pages allow for detailed information on numerous topics. You must also consider cost and lead time for writing, editing, printing, and distribution.

In short, selecting the most appropriate medium for your message is a complex endeavor. Be forewarned that no assumptions should be made about the acceptability of any particular medium. Until you have considered, at the least, the questions posed earlier, you will probably only be guessing on your choice of an ideal medium.

Advantages and Disadvantages of Media Selections

Following is a list of potential media through which to send your message. Each has its advantages and disadvantages. These have to be balanced against the considerations already listed for media selection. Remember, it's the rare public relations writer who will restrict her or his output to a single medium.

Newspapers
Advantages

- Newspapers allow you to reach a huge number of people in a given geographic area.
- Newspapers have short deadlines.
- If you're placing advertising, you have flexibility in deciding the ad size and placement within the newspaper (your ad can be as large as necessary to communicate as much of a story as you care to tell).
- Exposure to your message is not limited; readers can go back to your message again and again if so desired.
- Newspapers provide immediacy of message.

Disadvantages

- Ad space can be expensive.
- Newspapers have short message life (most papers are read and then tossed).
- Your message has to compete against the clutter of advertisers and all the other editorial copy for attention.
- Poor photo reproduction limits creativity (although this is improving).
- There will invariably be some waste circulation (some people, perhaps many, won't be in your target public).
- The Internet is quickly overtaking newspapers in the editorial copy area.

Magazines
Advantages

- Magazines allow for better targeting of audience because you can choose magazine publications that cater to your specific audience or whose editorial content specializes in topics of interest to your audience.
- High reader involvement means that more attention will be paid to your message.
- Better quality paper permits better color reproduction (especially important if you're purchasing ad space).
- Magazines have a longer shelf life (most people keep magazines longer and pass them on to others).
- With the latest digital tablet technology, magazines can now be more portable than ever, and the image quality is fast becoming equal to the print versions.

Disadvantages

- Long lead times mean that you have to make plans weeks or months in advance.
- The slower lead time heightens the risk of your message getting overtaken by events.
- There is limited flexibility in terms of ad placement and format.
- Space and ad layout costs are higher.

Radio

Advantages

- Radio is a universal medium enjoyed by people at one time or another during the day, at home, at work, and even in the car.
- Radios provide good selectivity of geographic markets.
- The vast array of radio program formats efficiently target your advertising dollars to narrowly defined segments of consumers most likely to respond to your offer.
- During the past 10 years, radio rates have seen less inflation than those for other media.

Disadvantages

- Because radio listeners are spread over many stations, you may have to get out your message simultaneously on several stations to reach your target audience.
- Listeners cannot go back to your message to go over important points.
- Messages are restricted by time segments.
- Radio is a background medium. Most listeners are doing something else while listening, which means that your message has to work hard to get their attention.

Television

Advantages

- Television permits you to reach large numbers of people on a national or regional level in a short period of time.
- Independent stations and cable offer new opportunities to pinpoint local audiences.
- Television, being an image-building and visual medium, offers the ability to convey your message with sight, sound, and motion.
- Television has the perception of being more immediate.
- Television provides high message impact.

Disadvantages

- A message is temporary and may require multiple exposure to rise above the clutter.
- Preferred ad times are often sold out far in advance.
- Television has limited length of exposure because most ads are only 30 seconds long or less, which limits the amount of information that you can communicate.
- Television is relatively expensive in terms of creative, production, and airtime costs.

Direct Mail
Advantages

- Your message is targeted specifically to your target public.
- Marketing message can be personalized, thus helping increase positive response.
- Your message can be as long as is necessary to fully tell your story.
- Direct mail provides easy means for consumer action.
- Effectiveness of response to the campaign can be easily measured.
- You have total control over the presentation of your message.

Disadvantages

- Direct mail has a poor image ("junk mail") and is often discarded out of hand.
- Resources need to be allocated in the maintenance of lists because the success of this kind of campaign depends on the quality of your mailing list.
- Long lead times are required for creative printing and mailing.
- Producing direct-mail materials entails the expense of using various professionals—copywriter, artists, photographers, printers, and so on.
- Direct mail can be expensive, depending on your target market, quality of your list, and size of the campaign.

Outdoor (Billboards) and Transit (Posters)
Advantages

- Outdoor advertising is difficult to ignore.
- It has good geographic selectivity.
- It reaches large numbers of people at a reasonable cost.

Disadvantages

- Only a brief message is possible.
- Outdoor advertising has long lead time and considerable preparation.
- It needs to be in place a fairly long time to be effective.

The Internet
Advantages

- The Internet is relatively cost effective.
- The Internet provides good targeting of specific publics.
- It allows for immediacy of messages.
- It can be interactive.
- The Internet makes it easy to track responses for surveys, reader/viewer involvement, and the like.
- It can reach global audiences.

Disadvantages

- Set-up time can be extensive.
- Production and maintenance of a Website can be costly and time consuming.
- The Internet is crowded, and search engines are not always reliable.

NEGOTIATING MEDIA BUYS[3]

Once you know what media types you think you want to use, negotiations begin with media sales representatives (reps). First, you'll need to contact all the local sales reps for each vehicle that you think you may use. This step takes a lot of back-and-forth effort, so give yourself plenty of time for negotiations. Do this as far in advance as possible for the most favorable rates. You should have a rough budget in mind before you start as well as a good idea of the timing of your messages for best effect. Ask each sales rep whom you negotiate with for his or her best deal. Sometimes this may mean committing to a "package" in which the number of times your message appears can get you a reduced rate. Finally, negotiate the best deal that you can. This doesn't always mean getting the lowest price. Sometimes added value is more important than getting rock-bottom prices. Know what your objective is and go for the best deal to reach your goals. Negotiating involves the following:

1. *Negotiate rates.* There are almost endless rate discounts that can be negotiated. Even if your goal does not include rock-bottom pricing, the first proposal that you receive will rarely be the best rate you can negotiate. Consider the following discounts:
   - Frequency discounts
   - Corporate rates
   - Different rates for different seasons/months
   - Direct response rates

2. *Negotiate positioning.* Never place your message without knowing exactly where it will run. Ask for what you want; the worst that can happen is that you are told "that's not possible." Sample positioning requests include the following:
   - Specific sections and pages within the newspaper, along with a specific place on the page.
   - Specific dayparts or within a certain show on the radio. Ask for specific slots within the hour. Make sure that you don't run in the same break with competing messages (for example, opposing arguments or competing points of view).
   - Specific programs on television. Ask for specific slots within the commercial "pod" (break). Make sure that you have adequate competitive separation.
   - Specific out-of-home locations, facing a certain direction.

3. *Negotiate additional opportunities.* Most of the time, these are at no additional cost to you. These opportunities should flow naturally from your goals. Sample opportunities to ask for include the following:

---

[3] This information is a slightly edited version of the American Marketing Association's guidelines for buying local media, found at www.marketingpower.com. It also provides a software tool to plan buys that can be used online.

- Sponsoring local events
- Sponsoring special sections or programs
- Remote broadcasts at your establishment

4. *Negotiate added value.* This can take the form of "free" space or time and should be at no additional cost. Sample added value to ask for include the following:

- Free space in the newspaper in conjunction with your ad buy
- Bonus commercials to go along with your radio or television buy

Evaluating Your Media Buys

Your media buy is complete, and the plan has finished running. It has been great to see and hear your messages. But did you get what you paid for? Was your plan effective? Here are some tools to help you evaluate your buy so that you can plan and buy smarter the next time around.

Did You Get What You Paid For?

Every sales rep whom you worked with should provide a postanalysis of your buy. This postbuy analysis differs depending on the media type.

- *Radio and television.* This postbuy analysis will show what you purchased compared to what actually ran. It includes number of commercials, dayparts, and rating points (in television).
- *Newspaper.* You should receive the actual newspaper page that your ad ran on, torn from the paper (called a tear sheet). This will show you the reproduction quality, how cluttered the page was, and what section and actual page position you received. If you ran a local magazine ad, you should receive a copy of the publication to see where your ad fell in the magazine.
- *Outdoor.* You should receive pictures of each board you purchased. Is it facing the way you thought it should? Make sure that the entire board is visible from a couple of different distances. If you bought an illuminated board, make sure that you receive a picture taken at night. Ask to see the traffic figures for that location to ensure that you received as much exposure as you paid for.

If your postbuy analysis shows that you did not get what you purchased, negotiate a make-good or credit. A make-good is a free repeat of your ad at a mutually agreeable time/place. If your ad schedule is over, you should receive a credit against your buy.

Was Your Plan Effective?

What was your objective? Did you have a goal to receive a certain number of phone calls or to increase awareness by a certain percentage? It is important to measure your results so that your media plan can be tweaked or revised next time around. If you did not reach your goals, were you using the wrong media type or the wrong media vehicle? Did you reach your target? If you did reach your goals, good for you! What did you do right that can be re-created for the next plan? Can you test a new media type or new program the next time?

BUYING THE INTERNET

Public relations professionals have realized that any media buying mix these days has to include the Internet. Not that long ago, a successful media campaign was measured by how well it was covered in the traditional media—things like air-time on TV and radio or column inches in newspapers and magazines. Today, success may well be measured by mouse clicks. Adding this new medium to the mix has some definite positives. It's fast—really fast. You don't need to wait to find out who's paying attention, and you can make changes instantly when you need to. You can link to multiple elements of your campaign without cluttering someone's mailbox or annoying the local media with a flurry of news releases flowing across their desks. And, you can reach publics you never imagined without having to worry about geographical boundaries—especially if you're interested in national and international audiences. Recent findings from a joint study by the Transworld Advertising Agency Network and Worldcom Public Relations Group revealed that in 2010, 28 percent of PR agencies sampled reported that 15 to 33 percent of revenues came from social media. And, in 2011, that number jumped to 44 percent.[4] So, the writing is on the wall. Public relations is adopting the Internet, especially social media, as part of their overall media mix. The only problem is that not everyone understands exactly what to buy and whether it will actually work within their overall campaign. Following, then, is some advice based on what the experts are saying.

Begin with assessing your needs and the methods you will use. Ask yourself the following questions:

Whom Will You Be Talking To?

This isn't very different from the question you would ask any traditional medium. You'd want to know who *their* target audience is. Ask them for an audience profile. If they sell online opportunities for advertising and public relations, they'll have one. This applies to Websites, social media sites, and blogs (but only if they deal directly with your client's product or issue). Remember, you rarely need to reach everybody, so use a targeted approach, and select only those resources that will help you connect directly to your publics.

What Media Will Help Accomplish Your Objectives?

You have to be explicit about your objectives. For example, is your client announcing a new product release? Among other options, you will want to generate leads to your client's site. *Leads* are referrals routed to a specific web location (often called a "landing page" or "lead capture page") via a link from another site. Landing pages are often linked from social media sites like Facebook or LinkedIn, or they can be generated via banner ads on these sites or others.

Most clients assume that Twitter and Facebook are the default choices. However, these two are very different animals, so let's look at the differences. Twitter is a micro-blogging tool, not a social media "site" per se. Social media sites tend to be personal—Twitter is a bit more perfunctory. What Twitter is good for is keeping up with what's happening around your client and your client's products and

[4] http://www.emarketer.com/Article.aspx?R=1008290, March 21, 2011

issues. It's also great for initiating conversations and building subsequent "friend-ships." This includes identifying "influencers," those who specialize in an area that has some bearing on what you're trying to accomplish for your client, and to whom others look for thought leadership. For example, through Twitter, you can search for blogs that are known to have influence in the area you're concentrat-ing on. You can then subscribe to the blogs and follow their authors on Twitter.

Once you've made contact, you can often follow up by connecting with your new "friends" on a social media site. Sites such as LinkedIn and Facebook are excellent tools for establishing and maintaining relationships with targeted publics, including news media. Facebook and LinkedIn allow you the space to focus on details, rein-forcing messages, and linking to other sites with even more detail (lead capture).

Blogs can also be useful for creating a sense of community and sharing con-tent with your publics free of advertising (and the "pitch" that invariably comes with it). They can be less formal than LinkedIn and Facebook (yes, Facebook is often formal), and put your publics more at ease. Remember, this type of blog is generated by you. It is not the same as using other blog sites to generate leads, although you should certainly provide that opportunity from your own site.

Tool-Specific Options

In addition to the broad-based platforms available, some common tool-specific options are pay-per-click and banner advertising.

- *Pay-per-click*

If you're serious about driving targeted traffic to your Website, *Pay-per-click* (PPC) is a good option. PPC is one of the many ways Websites sell advertising. For example, search engine providers like Google and Yahoo will sell you listings (literally ads) that augment the usual returns someone gets when they search for a keyword. When a person clicks on your listing, they go straight to your Website (much like a lead). These "listings" are sold in an auction. The bidders pay for the cost of each click on their listing/ad based on a keyword. The more you pay, the more likely it is that your PPC listing will rank higher than some others, or be placed on the page where you want it. Keep in mind that others may be bidding on the same keyword, which could get out of hand if you're not careful.

Research your keywords carefully to get the most out of your investment. Then, balance your projected search volume against how much you're willing to pay, or can afford, based on your overall budget. The same questions asked above concerning how to determine the proper media mix apply here as well.

- *Banner Advertising*

Banner ads are similar to what you might see in traditional print publica-tions, except that they're clickable—and that's the payoff. And, depending on how much you're willing to spend, they can be pretty fancy, including changing images, animation, and sound. Banner ads are usually purchased directly from the Website, or through an ad network, especially if you're planning a broad-based campaign where you will be dealing with dozens of site purchases. As with lead referrals and PPC, banner ads can serve as a *click-through* point, bringing traffic directly to your site. And, like a traditional print ad, even if they don't click on it, it may still have some memory value. The more they see it, the more likely they will be to eventually click on it.

Here are some common terms associated with pricing these types of tools:

- **Clicks/Click-throughs:** The number of visitors who click on the banner ad linking to your Website. Sites often sell banner ad space on a cost-per-click (CPC) basis.

- **Page views:** The number of times a particular Web page has been requested from the server. Page views indicate the number of visitors who *could* have seen the banner ad—referred to in traditional media as *exposure*. And, as with traditional media, exposure doesn't measure effectiveness. Online banner ads are usually sold in cost-per-thousand impressions, or CPM—a fixed price per one-thousand visitors to the site housing your ad—not on the number of people who actually click on it. If that's an additional measurement you want, try *click-through-rate*.

- **Click-through rate (CTR):** The ratio of page views to clicks, expressed as the percentage of total visitors to a particular page who actually clicked on the banner ad.

Although you might focus on the measure most important to you and your client, you should at least consider as many measures as you can when judging the effectiveness of a banner ad.

Finally, because the Internet is a dynamic, changing environment, it's best to constantly monitor your placements for results and possible adjustments to message or location. You can add or subtract placements, change locations of those placements, and, above all, improve your copy to get the most out of your writing.

LEARNING TO ADAPT

One of the hallmarks of a good writer is the ability to adapt to the needs of the audience, the message, and the medium. Public relations writing, unlike many other forms of writing, requires this flexibility. In the following chapters, you will find a variety of writing styles used in different formats. The key to writing for public relations is to learn these formats and adapt your style to each as needed. The road to becoming a good public relations writer has many sidetracks, and it is quite easy to let yourself become specialized. But the trick to becoming the best kind of writer is not to let that happen. The greater the variety of writing styles that you can learn to use well, the better your chances will be of becoming an excellent writer.

KEY TERMS

message strategy	central route	argument strategy
entertainment	peripheral route	reasoned argument
persuasion	compliance strategy	emotional appeal
dissonance theory	sanction strategy	
elaboration likelihood	appeal strategy	
model	command strategy	

CHAPTER

5

Media Relations and Placement

In This Chapter, You Will Learn

- How journalists judge news value.
- The difference between hard news and soft news.
- How to work with the media, including getting to know journalists and their jobs.
- How to successfully get your public relations message placed in the media.

- How to create a media kit, including a digital version.
- How to create an online newsroom.
- How to reach journalists via social media.

Public relations practitioners are professionals. So are journalists. Professionals, in the ideal sense, work together for the public welfare. Why, then, do public relations people see members of the media as adversaries, going out of their way to dig up the dirt? And why do reporters often see public relations people as "flaks," paid to run interference for their clients?

Actually, there is a little truth in both points of view, and both sides have a number of legitimate complaints. Public relations people often are charged with covering up or stonewalling, whereas reporters often do seek only the negative in an issue. Obviously, this is far from a perfect relationship between professionals.

Part of the problem stems from a lack of real understanding in both camps of how the other operates. There is little you can do to make journalists find out more about public relations, but you can do much to improve your own knowledge of how the media operate, what media people want from you, and what they are capable and not capable of providing.

WHAT IS NEWS?

The most common stumbling block to a good working relationship between public relations and media professionals is a mutually agreed-upon definition of the concept of news. Research has shown that most journalists judge news value based on at least some of the following characteristics:

- **Consequence.** Does the information have any importance to the prospective reading, listening, or viewing public? Is it something that the audience would pay to know? Remember, news value is frequently judged by what the audience (and the advertisers who support the media) are willing to pay for.

- **Interest.** Is the information unusual or entertaining? Does it have any human interest? People like to transcend the everyday world. Excitement—even vicarious excitement—often makes good news.

- **Timeliness.** Is the material current? If it isn't, is it a whole new angle on an old story? Remember, the word *news* means "new." This is one rule frequently broken by public relations practitioners. Nothing is more boring than yesterday's news.

- **Proximity.** For most public relations people seeking to connect with the media, a local angle is often the only way to do it. If it hits close to home, it stands a better chance of being reported.

- **Prominence.** Events and people of prominence frequently make the news. The problem, of course, is that your company president may not be as prominent to the media as he or she is to you.

If your story contains at least some of the above elements, it stands a chance of being viewed as news by media professionals.

Journalists often make a distinction between hard news and soft news. Although there are no fixed definitions of these terms, some pretty self-evident differences exist between the two. **Hard news** is information that has immediate impact on the people receiving it. By journalists' definition, it is very often news that people need rather than news that they want. **Soft news** is just the opposite: It is news that people want rather than news that they necessarily need. A story about a local teachers' strike is hard news. One about a new swimming program at the YMCA is soft news. A story about a corporate takeover is hard news. One about the hiring of a new celebrity spokesperson is not.

The problem is that many public relations people believe that journalists view everything they send them as soft news. Of course, this isn't so, and many public relations writers have discovered that both hard and soft news often will be used by media outlets looking to fill time or space. In addition, much of what passes for soft news often is viewed as public interest information by the various media.

The other thing to understand about hard and soft news is that hard news frequently is perishable whereas soft news is not. In other words, a story on an important stockholders' meeting in which a buyout is announced is not only perishable but also timely. By contrast, a new development in a product line or a promotion within your organization probably is not perishable—it will still be news a week from now.

WORKING WITH THE MEDIA

The media are a powerful force, and they can do a lot for you—or a lot against you. The determining factor may well be how much you know about media professionals and appreciate their jobs, and how well you get to know them as people.

Get to Know Journalists' Jobs

Learn all you can about the media outlets and the individuals with whom you will be dealing on a regular basis. Journalists have a tough life. I know—so do you. Having some journalism experience goes a long way toward understanding the frustrations of the job. Many public relations practitioners have had prior journalistic experience or education. Most journalists, however, haven't experienced public relations work firsthand. Thus, it is often up to you to make the relationship work.

Talk to journalists. Ask them for their guidelines on gathering news. Get to know how they write and what they choose to write about. Most news outlets will gladly provide you with guidelines for submitting everything from feature stories to publicity. Follow them. Know their deadlines and stick to them as if they were your own—in a way, they are. At the same time, try to let media people know what you do. Show them your style. Ask them for hints on how to make it more acceptable to their needs. Everybody likes to be asked his or her professional opinion.

Get to Know Journalists as People

To begin working with media people, you have to meet them first. If you're new to your job, the first step is to get out and introduce yourself. Now, no self-respecting reporter is going to be in his or her office when you drop in. They're busy people, and they're probably out covering stories. If they have an 11:00 p.m. deadline, they may not be back in the office to write their stories until after 6:00 p.m. And with the advent of laptop computers, smart phones, and online transmission capabilities, many reporters now file directly from the field. So how do you meet them?

Call or e-mail first. Tell them who you are and how what you're doing relates to their work. Keep it brief, just a quick "Hello, I'm new in town. You'll be hearing from me soon; anything I should know?" If you get a chance to meet in person, do so. Again, be brief, keep it professional, and don't get away without asking them what you can do to make *their* jobs easier.

Remember, this is a two-way relationship. Journalists need your information as much as you need their medium for your messages. Be available at all times and make sure they know how to get in touch with you at a moment's notice. Always give them your cellphone number. News happens after five o'clock, too. If you cooperate, they'll cooperate.

Establishing a rapport with the media is your first concern; however, a word needs to be said here about courting the press. Most journalists who deal in hard news don't react well to being courted. That is, they aren't likely to change anything they think or write because you invited them out to lunch. Although we've all heard stories about unethical journalists, I prefer to assume that every reporter has professional scruples. You should too. They may well go out to lunch with you, especially if you have a story that may interest them, but they are very likely to pick up their own checks. The sole exception might be the trade press. Trade journalists are used to receiving samples of products that they are writing about. Everything from small parts to expensive equipment is loaned out to the various trade publications for these purposes. For most media, though, the golden rule of media relations is, *Let them know you by your work, not by your checkbook.*

Guidelines for Dealing with the Media

So now you're ready to meet the media in a working situation. What do you do? Although there are no guidelines that can cover every possible situation, following are a few that will help keep your encounters professional and as pleasant as possible:

- *Always be honest.* It takes a lot of hard work to build credibility, and nothing builds credibility like honesty. It takes only one mistake to ruin months of credibility building. If you are honest with the media, they will be fair to you. But remember, fair to them means balanced and objective. They will tell all sides of a story, even the negative. You should be willing to do the same.

- *Establish ground rules early on in your relationship.* Among the most important of these rules is that everything is on the record. If you don't want to see it or hear it the next day in the newspaper or on television—or in 20 minutes on their blog—you'd best not say it to a journalist today. Although I usually advise public relations practitioners (and others) to always stay on the record, there are some accepted circumstances under which journalists are *supposed* (and that's a big *supposed*) to honor your off-the-record comments.

- *Not-for-attribution.* This is the home of the "sources close to the White House" quote. Honest public relations practitioners generally stay away from this one. It smacks of leaks and fear of attribution. This is one of the key ways that the media often are manipulated into running with information on which they would normally require confirmation. Let's face it, without attribution, how does anyone know the opinion is even valid?

- *Background.* In my estimation, this is the only useful justification for going off the record. Going off the record to fill in background, without which a reporter might misconstrue your statements or misunderstand your position, is a legitimate procedure. Keep in mind, however, that it is open to the same potential abuse as any other off-the-record comment.

• *Always answer a reporter's phone calls.* Never avoid returning a call, either because you're afraid of what the reporter will ask (in which case, you're in the wrong business) or because you haven't done your homework. If the reporter doesn't get it from you, the ideal source, he or she will have to get it from less reliable sources, and you don't want that to happen.

• *Give media people what they want, not what you want.* Ideally, they can be the same thing. The key, of course, is to make your information newsworthy, following the criteria listed earlier.

• *Along the same lines, don't bombard journalists with a daily barrage of media releases or advisories.* Nothing that happens that often is newsworthy. The reporters and editors who receive your releases know this and are very likely to stop reading your information.

• *Don't assume that reporters are out to get you.* If you've established a good working relationship with them, they are probably going to seek out your help, not try to assassinate you.

• *Don't try to intimidate reporters.* They'll resent it. Don't let your boss talk you into this one. You are the liaison, the media relations person. It's your job to get along, and nobody wants a friend who tries to intimidate him or her into doing something.

• *Don't plead your case or follow up on stories.* The nature of publicity is to let the media handle it once you have released it. If you want more control than that, take out an ad.

Guidelines for Interviews

Just the act of being interviewed by reporters or setting up interviews between your clients and reporters can help you conceptualize the proper relationship between reporter and public relations practitioner. With that in mind, following are some guidelines for interview situations. Some are similar to the guidelines already covered; others are specific to a reporter interviewing *you.*

• *Keep everything on the record.* As with everything else in which a reporter is involved, keep any comments strictly on the record. If you don't want your words printed on the front page of tomorrow's paper, don't say them out loud to a reporter.

- *Provide background.* Give interviewers all the background they need to bring them up to speed on the topic at hand *before* you begin the official interview. They may not have read your media backgrounder or done any homework on your client prior to the interview (although they have if they're good reporters). As with everything else you say, keep the background information free of anything that you don't want to see in the news.

- *Know the topic.* If you don't know the topic, why are you being interviewed? The same applies to any spokesperson you may have chosen for the interview. Always choose the person who knows the most about the issue being discussed, not just the company president or yourself. Nothing is more embarrassing than to have to constantly beg ignorance.

- *Anticipate touchy questions.* If something hot is happening with your client, the interviewer is there to ask about it. Assume this always to be true. If the interviewer doesn't ask the tough questions, consider yourself lucky; however, be prepared to answer them with *your* spin.

- *Answer questions that are already a matter of public record.* For example, if you have just filed a quarterly return with the Securities and Exchange Commission and it contains information about your organization's economic status that is less than flattering, guess what? It's public information by law, and you might as well be prepared to address it if it comes up.

- *Be completely honest.* Truth is the major responsibility of all communicators. If you ever lie to a journalist, he or she will never trust you again. Remember, credibility is difficult to obtain, but it takes only one lie to lose it forever. The following three guidelines are related to this one.

- *Answer questions directly.* Don't rush, guess, dodge, or stonewall when answering questions. Reporters become frustrated quickly when you try to avoid answering a question. Ultimately, it's best to get to the point if you want to maintain your credibility.

- *If you don't know the answer, say so.* Offer to get back to the interviewer with the answer as soon as you can. You can also offer to put him or her in touch with someone who does know the answer, but then you lose control of the spin factor.

- *Keep it cordial, no matter what happens.* Never lose your cool. This puts you at a disadvantage because you automatically become defensive in such situations. If this happens, you lose control of the interview, and you hurt your own image as a public relations professional.

- *Look professional.* This may seem self-evident, but you're a professional. If you look like one, you will enhance your credibility, and this will enhance the importance of your message.

- *Offer help later if needed, and give it.* If you've promised to follow up, do it. Make yourself available for any follow-up questions that the interviewer may have and assure him or her that it is no trouble. However, don't call or e-mail the interviewer just to check on the progress of the story.

Guidelines for Correcting Errors

Finally, what do you do if you discover an error in the subsequent story a reporter produces? If the error is minor, ignore it—no sense badgering a reporter or editor over minor details. If the error is important, however (regardless of whether the error was caused by you or by the reporter), it needs to be corrected. Here are some guidelines for doing so:

- *Always be as diplomatic as possible.*
- *Contact the reporter immediately.* If it's your fault, say so and ask if it's too late to get the error corrected before publication. Don't take a great deal of time pointing out the error. Just mention it and ask if it can be fixed.
- *Remain calm and courteous.* If you seem agitated, the reporter will get suspicious. If it's the reporter's fault, he or she may even get angry.
- *If the story has already been run, ask for a correction.*
- *If the reporter is unwilling or unable to redress the error, don't automatically go over his or her head*—unless correcting the error is worth more than your relationship with the reporter.
- *If all else fails, call or e-mail the editor correcting the error.* Keep it short and to the point. And, above all, keep it rational. Don't pout and don't point fingers.
- *Finally, ask the reporter if there is anything that you can do in the future to prevent this sort of thing from happening again.*

MEDIA PLACEMENT

Knowing journalists will enhance your chances of placing valuable information with them. But you can't rely on personal contact for everything. Placing public relations materials with the media requires up-to-date information on all of the possible outlets for your materials, as well as the ability to physically get your message to the media.

Deciding Where to Place Your Message

Naturally, the number and type of media outlets will depend on your business. If you are in the automotive industry, trade journals will be a vital link between you and your publics. If you work for an organization that is strictly local, then your media contacts will be limited to the local media. Local interest news will be important, too, within the communities in which your plants or offices are located. If you work for a regional or even a national operation, then your contacts will expand accordingly. Whatever media you deal with, it is important to keep updated directories and lists that meet your particular needs with the least amount of wasted information.

Media Directories and Databases

A good directory is an indispensable tool for the media relations specialist. **Media directories** come in all sizes and address almost every industry.

Publishers of directories offer formats ranging from global checkers that include a variety of sources in every medium to specialized directories dealing with a single medium.

A number of excellent directories for media placement are available. Here are some of the major ones:

- **Bacon's Media Directories** (now part of Cision). Bacon's has been around since the early 1930s and provides a wealth of directories (collected into online databases) including extensive lists of media contacts and outlets around the country and around the world. They also provide directories specific to new media, including social media contacts and influencers lists. http://us.cision.com/

- **BurrellesLuce** provides a host of services ranging from media contacts to monitoring the results. As with other such providers, they now include social media monitoring. http://www.burrellesluce.com/

- **Standard Rate and Data Service** (SRDS), used primarily for marketing, is an extensive set of databases covering a wide range of media: business publications, consumer magazines, and traditional as well as digital media of all sorts. Access to their databases is through subscription. http://next.srds.com/home

- *Editor & Publisher* provides a database encyclopedia with listings and contacts for all dailies worldwide and all community and special interest U.S. and Canadian weeklies. Information includes ad trends, circulation size, rankings by circulation, and more. http://www.editorandpublisher.com/Subscribe/Yearbook/

One of the most important points to remember about media selection is to try to place your messages in a medium you're personally familiar with, or that you can easily evaluate personally before you approach them. What may sound like an excellent vehicle for your message when viewed through a directory or database may turn out to be second rate for your purposes. After some time in your particular field, you will become familiar with its leading media forms. Until then, review them all. Your image is tied to their image.

Media Lists

Directories are essential, but they are not the only tools you will need to keep up-to-date with media relations. **Media lists,** just as vital to your job, are a more personal tool than directories because they contain details about local contacts and all the information that you need to conduct business in your community. Media lists may include regional and even nationwide contacts, depending on the scope of your operation. Once compiled, the list should be updated at least once a month. It takes only a 30-second phone call to each of the media outlets on your list to verify names and addresses. In the long run, the routine of updating will pay off. Using a computer is a great way to compile and maintain a media list. Computer software designed specifically for media lists is available from a number of distributors.

In compiling a media list, you will need to include most of the following items:

1. Name of the publication, radio or television station, particular show (for talk shows), and so on.

2. Names of editors, reporters, news directors, and others.

3. Addresses, including mailing and street addresses if they are different. You may need to hand deliver something on occasion, and this can be difficult if all you have is a post office box number.

4. E-mail addresses, telephone and fax numbers for the media outlets as well as for each of the people on your list. Most media outlets accept computer-generated media releases, satellite-transmitted video, or audio actualities (prerecorded video or audio). Include such details in your media list.

5. Any important editorial information such as style guidelines, deadlines, times of editions (morning and evening), dates of publication for magazines, times of broadcasts, use of actualities, photo requirements, and use of fax or electronic transmission (and applicable phone numbers).

Getting Your Message to the Media

Once you have decided where to place your information, you have to get it there. Again, you have a number of choices, depending on what you are sending and to whom.

- *Transmit it electronically via computer.* This can be accomplished in several ways. You can use standard e-mail, e-mail attachments, Website message dumps, or direct dumps to the medium itself. Many media have direct lines for such purposes. One of the benefits of using a computer is that images can also be transmitted, often with excellent results.

- *Mail it.* This takes more time, but if your information is not perishable, it may work just fine. Thousands of information pieces are still mailed every day and sent via overnight delivery through companies like FedEx and UPS.

- *Hand deliver it.* Reserve this one for important or timely information. Hand delivery used to be the norm; now it's a lot of trouble. However, it can pay off in that it still receives a bit more attention than other forms of delivery.

- *Fax it.* Nearly everyone still has a fax machine. The biggest problem with this delivery method is quality. If all you're sending is text, then it's fine. But if pictures are an important consideration, this may not be your first choice.

In lieu of delivering the message yourself, you may choose to use a placement agency. **Placement agencies** are outfits that will take your information, such as a press release, and send it out to a great many media outlets using their regularly updated media lists and computerized mailing services. Many of these firms send out hundreds of releases for you—at a tidy cost.

Organizations such as *PR Newswire* (www.prnewswire.com) send out your release electronically, over a newswire—just like the Associated Press. Media outlets can subscribe (free of charge) to the service and will receive your release—along with hundreds of others—sorted by subject and other descriptors. They can scan by subject, look at the lead only, or pull up the whole release. This method substantially reduces the amount of paper they have to plow through and at least guarantees subjects of interest to them. Your advantage is that you can target locally, regionally, or nationally. Of course, the price of placing the release increases with its coverage.

Fitting Your Information to Your Outlet

You need to know as much as possible about the media outlet to which you are sending your information. Never submit information blindly to publications that you've never read or to stations that you've never watched or listened to. Picking a trade publication out of *SRDS* just because it has a large circulation doesn't ensure that it is the type of publication in which you want to see your story.

The key, of course, is to read the publication, watch the television station, or listen to the radio station first. By doing so, you also will learn about the outlet's style and will be able to tailor your release accordingly.

If you are writing for a trade journal, don't automatically assume that the one you have chosen is similar in style to others in the industry. Remember that publications often are differentiated by their styles when they deal with similar subject matter.

Understanding Radio and Television Placement

Despite the increasing popularity of the Internet, radio and television remain a good option for getting your word out. Radio is relatively cheap and can fit easily within most budgets, and television is still immediate and connects personally with viewers. Most people remember local commercials on TV, even if they find them occasionally annoying. Following are the basics of radio and television placement. Details are usually handled in face-to-face negotiations with the station advertising representatives, or through an agency that specializes in radio/ TV placement.

Before placing information on the radio, you will need to understand the concept of **format.** Whereas placement of your message on television requires familiarity with the various program offerings of the stations that you are dealing with, placement on radio is usually determined by the format of the station—usually designed around the type of music that it plays or information that it provides. For example, some stations play only top-40 hits. These stations usually cater to a teenage audience. Other stations play only classic rock or jazz, or provide news. Their listeners vary according to their format. A radio format, programming format, or programming genre refers to the overall content broadcast over a radio station. Some stations broadcast multiple genres on a set schedule. Over the years, formats have evolved, and new ones have been introduced. In today's age of radio, many radio formats are designed to reach a specifically defined segment, or niche, of the listening population based on such demographic criteria as age, ethnicity, background, and the like.

Determining what radio station you place your message on depends on what your target audience listens to, and that is determined through audience research. Any radio sales manager will be able (and quite willing) to provide you with detailed analyses of the station's listening audience. All you have to do is match your target audience profile with the station's listener profile. If, for instance, your target audience regularly listens to jazz, then you would be best served to place your message on a station using a jazz format.

Examine the formats and styles of all publications or broadcast shows that you would like to accept your information and then prepare your material in a style as close to theirs as you can. For example, if you are prerecording public service announcements for use on various stations, you might want to put a different music track on each spot, depending on the format of the station with which it will be placed. Nothing is quite as jarring to listeners of a classical music station as to have their entertainment interrupted with a message surrounded by a rock music background. Although a rock music station might carry a spot with a classical music background, the opposite is probably not true.

Television is much easier to figure out. It is a medium that still reaches a very broad segment of the population. Rather than depending on formatting to attract a single audience, television depends on different programs and times of day to attract different audiences. Program types include drama and adventure, news, talk, reality shows, and sports, among others. Each program type draws a particular target audience. Time of day is also a factor in determining when to air a television commercial. Standard television time blocks (known as day-parts) are listed in Exhibit 5.1, as are radio day-parts.

Just as in radio, a television sales manager will be able to give you detailed statistics on viewing audiences by program and time of day. You will need to consider the following questions before you place your message with either a radio or television station:

- If radio, what format does the station use? If television, what programs are appropriate to my message?

- Will the station take audio actualities (for interviews or reactions)? If so, what format? Although most stations now prefer digital formats, it's still a good idea to ask. If it is video for television, what format will they want?

- What length spot will the station use? 10-, 20-, 30-, or 60-second spots? Who will write the copy? Will I write and submit it, or will I simply give the station the information? Will the station use scripts I have written for its announcers to read?

- Will the station provide production services, or will I have to have my message prerecorded?

- How much lead time does the station need? For production? For placement?

Finally, be prepared to negotiate both cost and placement. Radio and TV sales managers can offer you a variety of options—some more expensive but more focused, and some less expensive but not in attractive time slots. For example, radio run-of-station (ROS) spots are cheaper because the station decides when to

Exhibit 5.1

Radio and Television Day-Parts

Day-parts. How the day is broken down for buying purposes:

Radio Day-Parts

- Morning drive 5 a.m.–10 a.m.
- Day 10 a.m.–3 p.m.
- Afternoon drive 3 p.m.–7 p.m.
- Evening 7 p.m.–12 p.m.
- Overnight 12 p.m.–5 a.m.

Television Day-Parts

- Early morning (EM) 5a.m.– 9 a.m.
- Day 9 a.m.–4 p.m.
- Early fringe (EF)/early news (EN) 4 p.m.–6 p.m.
- Prime access (PA) 6 p.m.–7 p.m.
- Prime 7 p.m.–10 p.m.
- Late news (LN) 10 p.m.–10:35 p.m.
- Late fringe (LF) 10:35 p.m.–1 a.m.
- Overnight 1 a.m.–5 a.m.

run them. That limits your effectiveness in reaching your target public. If you're willing and can afford to pay more, then morning and afternoon drive times are your best bet. You'll reach the largest audiences of the day.

Also, don't assume that buying standard commercial slots is your only option. Radio stations often allow for business sponsorships (not just limited to public broadcasting stations). For example, you might be able to sponsor a segment of the local news—say, the weather, or sports. And don't forget the stations' online audiences. Most radio and TV stations have Websites, and often stream their programming online. In fact, increasing numbers of people are accessing their "radio" and "television" exactly that way. It could actually cost less for you to buy some space or time online, and could reinforce your on-air messages.

MEDIA KITS

One of the most common methods of distributing information to the media is via the **media kit.** Media kits are produced and used for a variety of public relations purposes. They are handed out at product promotion presentations and press conferences; they are used as promotional packages by regional or local distributors or agencies; and they are part of the never-ending stream of information provided by organizations to get their messages out. When a media kit (also known as a media packet) is used properly, it can aid message dissemination by adding the right amount of unduplicated information to the media mix.

Not all industries still use the traditional, printed media kit. For example, in much of the high-tech industry, the media kit may be "going the way of the dodo bird."[1] Tech or business reporters tend to like technology and don't mind linking to Websites for more information or to download photos. Sometimes, an online media kit rather than a print version will be developed.

Intel, for example, delivers two major resources for tech and business reporters during major news and product launches (in addition to a news release over the Business Wire news portal, typical interviews, automated phone responses, and so on). First, it always updates its online newsroom. http://newsroom.intel.com/community/intel_newsroom. Journalists used to working with Intel know to go there first. Second, for big launches, Intel creates a "virtual media kit," which can also be viewed and downloaded at its online newsroom. In addition, Intel has at times held an online news conference during which media call into a phone bridge while following along with an online presentation from their desks.

Note, however, that traditional media kits are very much alive with mainstream media like *Ms.* and *Marie Claire* magazines. Many of the editors simply want to pull art from the kits and hand it to their art directors. They also don't like to search around on the Internet and jump from link to link. Media kits are also popular in many countries overseas where Internet access is limited or art budgets are severely constrained. In addition, countries such as Japan have well-known and well-established public relations practices that require public relations professionals to place printed material in certain venues for reporters. This, of course, doesn't stop the media from going online for traditional media kit material, but it certainly limits the practice.

A media kit usually is composed of a number of information pieces designed specifically for use by the media (see Exhibit 5.2). Enclosed within a folder with a cover indicating who is providing the kit and its purpose, a media kit usually includes something like the following:

- A table of contents
- A news release
- A backgrounder or a fact sheet
- One or two other information pieces such as
  - Preprinted brochures
  - Company magazines or newsletters
  - An annual report

[1] E-mail correspondence with Seth Walker, Intel Public Relations. Much of this discussion on the changing uses of media kits is from that correspondence.

Exhibit 5.2

Media Kit

Label on cover designates which medium and reporter receives this particular kit

Agenda, Welcoming Letter, List of Participants, Brochures

News Release & Backgrounder

Photograph

Business Card

Press Kit Folder (Inside pockets hold information)

- A feature story or sidebar, if appropriate to the subject matter
- A biography (or biographies) and accompanying photos

Anything fewer than these items is generally a waste of folder space. If you have only a few items to disseminate and wish to avoid the cost of producing folders, use plain, manuscript-sized envelopes. These are cheaper than folders, you might already have them in stock with your address printed on them, and they are ready for mailing.

The contents of a media kit can vary greatly, depending on the intent of the kit. For example, a media kit for a corporate product introduction briefing might include these items:

- News release on the new product
- Color photo and cutline (caption)
- News release on the product content (the material used to manufacture the product)
- Black-and-white photo and cutline of other products made from the manufactured material
- News release describing another application of the material
- Black-and-white and color photos of that application
- Backgrounder on the material
- In-house magazine article tear sheet on the material
- Color brochure on the material and its uses
- News release on new materials being developed
- Hard copy of the product presentation speeches

Media kits can serve many purposes and should include enough information to meet the needs of their audiences. The key to assembling a useful kit is to keep in mind the needs of those receiving the information.

If you are providing a media kit to the media for a press conference, it should include some, but not necessarily all, of the following items:

- A cover letter explaining the kit and a table of contents listing each item in the kit, with each item listed as appearing on the right or left side of the folder.
- A basic fact sheet outlining the participants at the press conference, the relevant dates, and any facts or figures that might be unclear.
- A backgrounder explaining the relevance of the current topic in a historical context.
- News releases of about one and one-half pages for both print and broadcast media. Give both releases to each reporter.
- Any feature stories or sidebar-type information that might be of interest to reporters. Be sure it is relevant.

- Any photos or other visual materials that might add to the stories. Include cutlines.
- Biographies on any individuals playing an important part in the event the press conference covers. Include photos as well, if available.
- Any preprinted information pieces that might be of interest to the media, such as brochures, in-house publications, and the like.

Once you have assembled a media kit, make sure that all members of the media get a copy, even those reporters who do not attend the event your media kit is designed to cover. Media kits are most effective when used with a good, up-to-date media list. By labeling your media kits with the names of the various media outlets prior to your event, you will know immediately after the event who showed up and who didn't. You can then mail the remaining kits to the prodigal media.

DIGITAL MEDIA KITS

Digital media kits (DMKS), also called **electronic media kits** (EPKs), are fast becoming the primary way to put out information formerly relegated to print media kits. They contain many of the same ingredients as a print kit, but have way more flexibility because they are digital. They're easy to update, and cost less to produce. In addition, they can be interactive: linking to other information, other locations, and presenting information and examples in demonstration format (including video).

What you include and in what format are key to a successful DMK. If your kit is exclusively online, you may not need to make every item printable; however, components such as news releases and white papers should always include a link to a downloadable version, usually in *portable document format* (PDF). If your DMK will be distributed via flash drive or e-mail, the bulk of the material will probably be in PDF.

Following are some guidelines for building your DMK. Naturally, you should tailor your kit to your needs. Product promotion kits will include a lot more specifics than a general company introduction. A single digital media kit won't cover everything. You will find that you'll probably need a basic "who we are" kit for the uninitiated and individually focused kits for specific products, services, and newsworthy topics. In the more focused DMKs, you can basically follow the list provided for print media kits.

Guidelines for Building a Digital Media Kit

- If your DMK is online, make it easy to find. A simple but clear link will suffice, usually from your home page, or a landing page that has been linked to from another location—perhaps a social media site.
- Digital media kits should have a unified look, just like their print counterparts (see Exhibit 5.2). Use a digital version of your letterhead and logo on each "page" of your DMK.

- Provide contact information clearly stating where you can be reached, including your phone numbers, e-mails, mailing address, and link to your Website. Also include links to your social media presence such as your Twitter stream, Facebook page, and LinkedIn profile. If you utilize a "contact button," make sure it's clear and easy to spot. It should also connect with a live person's name, phone, and e-mail. Avoid at all costs links to recorded messages or involved menus that require a lot of button pushing. If your DMK is targeted to news/trade media, the contacts should be the public/media relations person handling the subject.

- Make sure all your links are active and lead to the correct location.

- Include high-quality visuals wherever possible. Digital media demand high-resolution images, especially if you intend for them to be used by the news or trade media or by bloggers who may want to repost them.

- Provide multimedia when appropriate, including videos and audio clips. That will make it easy for others to incorporate elements of your information into their blog posts. You can also link to external resources, such as Flickr photos and YouTube videos. Video components are important to DMKs, although they do take up a lot of memory space if embedded directly. A general rule of thumb is to keep it short. Not many people perusing a DMK are going to watch a four-minute video interview with the company CEO. A minute should be the maximum time for any video you decide to embed directly into your DMK. If you're posting to YouTube, it can be longer.

- If your DMK is generic, create separate pages for a company overview explaining what you do and why anyone (especially the media) should care. Also, since people like to put faces to otherwise faceless organizations. Include bios of executives and key employees along with photos.

- A FAQ sheet (frequently asked questions) is always a good idea, but be sure to target the public you are trying to reach with your DMK. If it's the news media, anticipate the questions a reporter might ask. If it's consumers, it might be about your product or service as something they would be using personally.

- Whether you're providing information for customers or news media, previous media coverage can demonstrate the current "buzz" about your company or product/service. Link to relevant coverage, and keep it up to date. You may also provide recent media releases tooting your own horn, customer testimonials, and other information that puts you in a positive light.

- Organize everything into a folder and save a copy to your computer or file server. Nothing is quite as annoying as having to recreate the whole thing from scratch if it disappears into a black hole in the Internet.

- Finally, distribute your digital media kit. DMKs are distributed in several ways. Probably the most convenient is by uploading it to your online media room. Another common approach is to use flash drives (USB or "thumb drives"). They range in size, so you can probably find one that will hold your kit easily. This method is particularly useful for conferences and trade shows.

Another method is to send it out via e-mail. This requires some adjustment as many e-mail programs limit the size of attachments. Compressing the components into a "zipped" file is one way to do this. Most computers have a built-in compression program. And, be sure your recipients know that your DMK is coming. Reporters tend to ignore or label as "junk" information they haven't requested or been notified is coming.

Here are a couple of good examples of digital media kits—one from *The Wall Street Journal* and one from Healthcare Solutions.

http://www.wsjmediakit.com/digital/
http://www.healthcaresolutionsmediakit.com/

CREATING AN ONLINE NEWSROOM

Perhaps the single most important change in connecting with the media over the past 20 years has been advances in technology, especially the Internet. No chapter on media relations would be complete these days without some mention of online newsrooms.

The **online newsroom** has quickly become a fixture for clients and companies seeking publicity. Journalist and public relations practitioner Sherri Deatherage Green calls it "the media's front door to the company,"[2] and marketing consultant Robin Stavisky says that "online media rooms sit right on the nexus of the transition between old and new ways of communication, and they provide a stunning example of the power of the Internet to transform a humble servant into an information hub."[3]

Online newsrooms can distribute news through a broad range of communications methods. These can include streaming video and audio presentations, interviews, features, webcasts (Web broadcasts), **webinars** (Web seminars), and blogs (Web logs), along with more traditional printable materials such as media releases, white papers, backgrounders, articles, annual reports, and magazine articles. And, because this is all online, you can include additional links and suggested reading (such as trade articles)—all of which will enhance the user's experience and knowledge base.[4]

In many ways, the online newsroom may be replacing the media kit, which has been the standard publicity interface between public relations and news media for nearly the past 100 years (they were regularly used by movie studios at the turn of the 20th century). However, the "traditional media kit isn't dead," according to long-time publicist Bill Stoller.[5] There will always be a need for some physical manifestation of publicity. Its sheer novelty alone may capture

---

[2] Sherri Deatherage Green, "Online Pressrooms: All the News That's Fit to Download," *PRWeek*, April 26, 2004.

[3] Robin Stavisky, "Tale of the Lowly Pressroom: The Transformation of Communications," at www.marketingprofs.com/5/stavisky1.asp, April 19, 2005.

[4] Ibid.

[5] Bill Stoller, "Creating Your Online Newsroom." Also see Stoller's site at www.PublicityInsider. com, which has a wealth of information on obtaining publicity.

the attention of some journalists, and a physical handout is still your best bet at trade shows, pressrooms, and special events.

Putting an online newsroom together isn't complex, but you should follow some commonsense guidelines. Remember, you are serving the media here. Don't make it difficult for them—online or off.

What to Include in Your Online Newsroom

The basics include press release archives, executive bios, color headshots, and company backgrounders, but there are plenty of options including such things as searchable databases of on-staff experts and feature stories. Standard content might include:

- *Personal contact information.* The name, address, e-mail, phone number, fax number, and cell phone number of your primary media contacts should be easy to locate. If you have an instant messaging ID, put it in there, too.

- *Media releases.* Place media releases in chronological order (most recent at the top). Keep traditional press release formatting and use easy-to-read fonts.

- *Executive photos, product photos, charts, graphs, and other appropriate artwork.* Provide multiple versions—lower-resolution 72 dots per inch (dpi) for online publications and Websites and higher-resolution 300 dpi for offline publications. Put instructions such as "To download, right-click and choose 'Save'" next to the graphics. Make sure that your pitch letters and media releases provide links to the appropriate artwork on your site.

- *Backgrounders, executive bios, white papers, investor relations information* (if applicable), *fact sheets, speeches, awards, streaming media of press conferences, product demonstrations, president's speeches,* and so on.

- *Search tool.* Make it easy for journalists to find just what they want, by making all your materials fully searchable. This usually means making PDF files from the original documents, which will then be automatically searchable. Don't scan them. Scans are not searchable.

- *Video content.* Videos are making inroads in online newsrooms, but video files are usually quite large and can hinder downloading of anything approaching broadcast-quality images. This would seem to make it a bit pointless; however, video compression ratios are getting better literally every day, which should make including video on your site easier. And, even if TV reporters can't use your online video, it can pique their interest enough so that they might request a broadcast-quality version or a satellite feed. As with most public relations output, it helps to make the video available in "sound bytes," suited to broadcast time restrictions.

Some Do's and Don'ts

- Do keep it simple.
- Do post high-resolution color photos (editors can always convert them to black and white).
- Do link your online pressroom to your company's home page.

- Do make it clear at the top of your main page of your online newsroom what it is and whom it's for.

- Do provide a link to your consumer FAQs (frequently asked questions) page and an e-mail link for customer service to give nonjournalists a place to get their questions answered. This will save you a great deal of time responding to messages from nonjournalists asking, "Why am I looking at a press release?" or "How do I download a new driver?" or some such thing.

- Do offer the opportunity for journalists to enter their e-mail address if they wish to be kept abreast of the latest news from your company, but don't link it in any way to the ability to access any portion of the site.

- Don't force journalists to register or sign in for access. They're busy folks and may very well decide not to bother. Make life as easy as you can for them.

- Don't wait for information technology (IT) workers to post media releases. Find a way to do it yourself.

- Don't forget to include media contact phone numbers and the company headquarters' address in easy-to-find places.

- Don't incorporate software or animation that might not be compatible with reporters' computer systems or browsers. Don't use flash, heavy Java scripts, and other "bells and whistles." The face that you put forth to the media must be highly professional, and the ease of navigation and logical flow of the newsroom is vital.

- Don't try to lay out the online newsroom if you're not a talented Web designer. Hire a professional designer who has a portfolio that includes simple, easy-to-navigate, clean-looking sites.

On this last note, remember that your job as a writer is to write. Although you may enjoy dabbling in Website building, an online newsroom is a big undertaking and requires expert skill at both developing and maintaining the site. It's pretty much a full-time job. If you don't have in-house IT help, many outside vendors offer Website tools and templates that require little training or technical expertise.

For example, Red Door Interactive, an "Internet Presence Management" firm based in San Diego, offers a product called Interactive Press Center. Red Door cites a recent Middleburg/Ross study of more than 500 reporters indicating that 99 percent of reporters go online at least once daily, 92 percent use the Internet for research purposes, and on average, reporters spend 15 hours per week on e-mail and the Web. According to its own press release, this was the impetus for the development of its Press Center software.[6]

Specialty firms, public relations agencies, and news distribution services offer online pressroom development with a variety of features. TEKmedia's software package, for example, lets you know which journalists are accessing your media

---

[6] Red Door Interactive Website at www.reddoor.biz/aboutus/news/pressreleases/archive/2002/1582.

releases so that you can better target your message and track your efforts; ipress-room software includes podcasting services and an "online buss builder" package; and Vocus offers a range of public relations and government relations software packages including an online newsroom.

Whatever tool you choose to develop your online newsroom, experts generally apply the simpler-is-better rule when designing. It needs to be functional first. Skip the fancy stuff that slows download of information. Remember that many reporters will be writing from the road and may have only dial-up access.

Online Newsrooms to Study

In addition to the Intel site mentioned earlier, following are three of the online newsrooms that stand out in their usefulness (and, in some cases, uniqueness):

- http://www.microsoft.com/en-us/news/
- www.google.com/press/index.html
- www.crayola.com/mediacenter

As noted at the beginning of this chapter, the landscape is changing, mostly for the better. Access to publics is in many ways easier than ever before. The public relations writer can now reach directly to end users of information and begin a conversation that will certainly become more of a true dialogue than the old-fashioned one-way monologue. What won't change is the requirement to write well. The new generation of Internet entrepreneurs continue to champion good writing as the primary tool of public relations, now and in the future. Only the technology changes. Good writing will always be recognized as good writing.

THE SOCIAL MEDIA APPROACH

Increasingly, journalists are using social media to research and write stories. A joint 2010 study conducted by Cision and George Washington University's School of Political Management found that 89 percent of journalists use blogs for sourcing stories, 65 percent use social networking sites, and 52 percent use micro-blogging sites like Twitter. However, 84 percent said social media sources were "slightly less" or "much less" reliable than traditional media, with 49 percent saying social media suffers from "lack of fact checking, verification and reporting standards."[7] A more recent, 2011 survey from Oriella (an alliance of 16, worldwide communication agencies) reveals the following:[8]

- 47 percent of journalists use Twitter to source stories
- 35 percent use Facebook
- 72 percent look at blogs

---

[7] The full survey can be downloaded from http://insight.cision.com/content/GWU-request.

[8] Downloadable at http://orielladigitaljournalism.com/view-report.html#/6/.

In addition to sourcing via social media, many journalists are placing those stories back within social media venues. A *PRWeek*/PR Newswire 2010 survey showed:

- 62 percent of journalists are now required to write specifically for online news sections
- 39 percent of journalists are now required to blog
- 37 percent of journalists are now required to have a Twitter account

What this indicates is that social media are fast becoming one of the best methods for getting your information out to the news media. Journalists are now seeking information sources online, and that means you must have an online presence and you must develop professional relationships with journalists and editors. The most obvious choices are:

LinkedIn. A good LinkedIn network is a must for reasons other than connecting within your industry. It's a good way to connect with journalists. LinkedIn now provides a *LinkedIn for Journalists* group allowing journalists to find story ideas, scoops, and sources. LinkedIn advises the use of *LinkedIn Skills* to uncover trends about a particular beat a journalist might be covering. As LinkedIn notes, "For instance, if you write articles geared toward the working mom, you might want to see what skills are on the rise or on the decline for *childcare*. If you cover the mobile space, checking out the growth of *Android* as a skill might be of interest to you." Journalists can also follow companies through *LinkedIn Company Pages*, and search by keywords.

This means that journalists are looking for your information, and LinkedIn is focusing on acquiring content for their site that can be shared with journalists. You can use your presence on LinkedIn to connect with journalists you already know. This will put you on their radar and make you a source they are familiar with. A recently added tool is LinkedIn's sharing button. It's just like the ubiquitous Facebook sharing button you see on every site you visit. If enough people "share" information from your site using the LinkedIn button, that information is automatically featured in the *LinkedIn News*. Finally, be sure to link to your Twitter and Facebook accounts from your LinkedIn account. Spread the word as widely as you can.

Facebook. According to a 2011 report on CNN.com, Facebook is lagging behind other social media tools such as Twitter in adoption by reporters.[9] Even though Facebook has since launched a new page called *Journalists on Facebook*, they are still struggling to convince the news media to get on board—and, not all public relations professionals are sure it's the best social media platform for reaching reporters and editors. According to inVocus (an online media news center), many journalists find Twitter and LinkedIn more useful for new leads.[10] Some PR professionals find it too personal, blurring the professional lines in the

---

[9] http://www.cnn.com/2011/TECH/social.media/04/14/facebook.journalists/

[10] inVocus media blog, http://www.vocus.com/invocus/media-blog/reporters-and-pr-pros-divided-on-journalists-on-facebook-initiative/. InVocus main Web-site can be accessed at http://www.vocus.

relationship between public relations the news media. Others, however, find that Facebook allows them to be informal in their approach, alerting "friended" journalists to information that previously would have been the domain of traditional media releases.

Despite the pros and cons, recent research shows that journalists often do use Facebook to source stories, and, like LinkedIn, Facebook is a good way to maintain relationships with media—providing you already know them. Facebook is more personal than LinkedIn, and assumes "friends" are easier to talk to. The basic rule for dealing with reporters and editors is don't "friend" them unless you already "know" them. It's a little like begging for attention. Make initial contact through face-to-face meetings, email exchanges, or even Twitter feeds. Once you know each other, then it's okay to connect with them on Facebook. Even then, keep it professional.

Some tips:

- Treat your Facebook pages like a Website. Report your stories there, complete with links to what others are saying about you. Facebook isn't a Website, but you can strengthen the professional relationship you want to take with journalists by taking a professional approach on your Facebook page, at least as it relates to media contacts.

- Consider putting up a custom newsroom as part of your Facebook page. It broadens your reach to have it in more than one location, especially since reporters are tending to use social media and may spend less time visiting your corporate Website.

Twitter. Twitter is a micro-blogging platform, useful for short updates, comments, and, especially, media alerts. You should also post news that appears on your other social media sites to Twitter for quick results (which means they must be up-to-date). In addition, many journalists make themselves available on Twitter. You need to be aware of who they are and where they can be found. By following their Tweets, you learn more about what they are covering. Sometimes, journalists even post a call-out when they're looking for subjects or sources. All you have to do is find them. Once you get on a reporter's radar, he or she will be more likely to remember you and your client when looking for a source. Some suggestions are:

- JustTweetIt reporters listing
- Muckrack.com
- MediaOnTwitter.com
- Journalists directory on Twellow
- Journalists on WeFollow
- Journalists on Listorious

A word of caution, however. Twitter is a great tool, but there is still a protocol involved with pitching the news media. As with Facebook, it's probably best to have already established a relationship with reporters before pitching them, or, at least, having notified them in advance that you are sending them something (and they've agreed to look at it).

Finally, one of the best resources for meshing your needs with that of reporters is the Website, *Help A Reporter Out* (HARO). HARO originally started as a Facebook group, and now connects over 30,000 journalists with 100,000 sources. Public relations professionals can register for a three-times-a-day e-mail featuring queries submitted by journalists looking for sources on specific topics or stories. All you do is reply to appropriate queries, keeping in mind that you're in competition with lots of other people pitching the same thing.

Cooperation Is the Key

Whether or not your message is delivered to your target audience depends a great deal on the cooperation of the mass media. It is in your best interest to foster a professional relationship with media representatives whom you deal with regularly. If they respect your professionalism in meeting their (and, by inference, their audiences') needs, you will be rewarded with cooperation—and that is a major step in the right direction.

KEY TERMS

consequence	hard news	media kit
interest	soft news	digital media kit
timeliness	media list	electronic media kit
proximity	placement agency	online newsroom
prominence	format	webinar

CHAPTER

6

Writing for Web and Social Media

In This Chapter, You Will Learn

- The basics of writing for the Web, including Web 2.0.

- How to create and maintain a blog for a client.

- How to effectively use such tools as Twitter.

THE CHANGING LANDSCAPE

Changes in new technology have allowed organizations to reach out to their constituencies in ways never before imaginable. They have expanded the scope of both internal and external communications far beyond that of traditional media. The role of everything from the news release to the corporate magazine has been broadened by the ability to make what was once a static delivery system interactive. The digital revolution has removed many of the barriers that once stood between public relations writers and their publics. A study by the Institute for Public Relations shows, for example:

- Nearly two-thirds of public relations practitioners (65 percent) indicate the increased information the new technologies have provided has strengthened the professional ties between journalists and public relations people.

- More than half (53 percent) say the increased information the new technologies have provided has strengthened the personal rapport and relationships between journalists and public relations people.

A separate study by the Society for New Communications Research shows that "social media power users" (communications professionals with a deep knowledge and heavy usage pattern of social media tools) showed the following tendencies: 78 percent use blogs, 63 percent use online video, 56 percent use **social networks,** and 49 percent use podcasts in their organization's communications initiatives.

With the advent of **Web 2.0,** the environment has changed again—this time, radically. Public relations executive and social media expert Brian Solis says,

> It is no longer just about audiences. . . . And, most notably, it's not about technology. This time it's about sociology and the interaction with people.[1]

According to Solis, the end users of information are now the "new influencers," with access to the Web and all its social tools. With these, they can publish, share experiences and perceptions online, and evoke emotion that can positively or negatively affect even the most seemingly invincible brand.[2] No longer is the conversation between public relations practitioners and their publics one-way. Now it's a collaboration with companies and clients pushing their brands and ideas across a complex social network, creating relationships directly with individual consumers, often bypassing traditional media entirely. Solis says that Web 2.0 is "humanizing companies, brands, and the products that define them."[3]

[1] Brian Solis, www.webpronews.com/blogtalk/2007/05/23/pr-in-the-face-of-web-2-0-and-social-media.

[2] Brian Solis, "Web 2.0 and the Reinvention of Marketing and PR," Web 2.0 Expo New York, TechWeb & O'Reilly Conferences, September 16–19, 2008, New York. http://en.oreilly.com/webexny2008/public/schedule/detail/4754.

[3] Ibid.

Essentially, Web 2.0 is the second generation of Web development and design. Its key characteristics are the sharing of information rather than the generation of it, and the collaborative nature of the designs that make that sharing possible. The advent of Web 2.0 has resulted in a number of "communities" in which this sharing takes place. Notable among them are social networking sites (Facebook, LinkedIn, etc.), wikis (Wikipedia being the most well known), blogs, and video-sharing sites (YouTube, Google Video, etc.). Most Web 2.0 sites include features such as *search capability; links* designed to guide users to other relevant information, often on other sites; *tags,* which categorize content by simple, one-word descriptions to make searching (and finding) easier; RSS technology that can notify users quickly of content changes and updates; and the ability to author and constantly update content cooperatively among users. One of the newer communication technologies on the Web is **RSS.** This variably stands for rich site summary, really simple syndication, and so on. RSS allows people to place news and other announcement-type items into a format that can be pushed to RSS readers and Web pages. Users can subscribe to the RSS news feeds of their choice and then have access to the updated information as it comes in. RSS is used for all kinds of purposes, including the news itself and announcing new content on **Websites.**

Although much of Web 2.0 is about programming, at least part of every aspect is also about writing. We will cover the most common writing issues here, realizing that the technology will continue to change rapidly, while the need for concise, well-constructed public relations writing will not.

A Quick Word about Writing for Websites

Although Web 2.0 has altered the look and function of the **Internet,** huge numbers of companies and individuals still maintain standard Websites. As long as there are Websites, there will be a need for writing correctly for that form. Briefly, then, let's cover the basics of "old-fashioned" Web writing.

The most glaring difference between the more traditional forms already covered in this book and Web writing seems to be the huge amount of "chatter" on the Internet. Fortunately, this is mostly confined to chat rooms, blogs, and e-mail (and now, Twitter); however, a casual perusal of Websites will quickly alert you to the inability of many site owners to write or, seemingly, express themselves in any coherent manner. The lesson is this: Don't succumb to the temptation to be chatty. Public relations writing is professional writing, even on the Internet. Follow the dictates of good writing no matter what vehicle you are using, and you can't go wrong.

Crawford Kilian's book *Writing on the Web* offers some sage advice for those who would like to engage in that practice. First, he cites well-known Internet guru Jakob Nielsen as saying that Web readers read 25 percent slower than print readers. Kilian concludes, "If we read 25 percent slower on screen, then perhaps we owe our readers 25% less text."[4]

---

[4] Crawford Kilian, *Writing for the Web* (Bellingham, WA: Self-Counsel Press, 1999).

Although he cautions that Website-writing rules should be taken with a grain of salt because they are constantly evolving, here are Kilian's six general principles about writing for the online medium:

1. Web writing requires orientation, information, and action. That is, provide background information and navigation aids, provide the information itself, and provide a way for a reader to respond.

2. Web writing should be understandable at first glance.

3. Web writing should be the least that you can possibly present to effectively deal with the subject. Excess information is a disservice to the Web reader.

4. Web writing displays a positive attitude toward problems. Even if you are writing about a negative topic like injustice, you may suggest ways the reader can deal with it constructively (taking advantage of the interactive nature of the online medium).

5. Web writing presents facts and ideas in terms of the reader's advantage. A smart Web writer seldom uses *I* and *we* and instead uses *you* and *your*.

6. Web writing displays correctness, clarity, and consideration—correct organization, format, names, addresses, spelling, and grammar; appropriate language, proper tone, concision, coherence, and consideration of the reader's needs.

Do these rules sound familiar? They should. They are basically what this book is all about, and they pretty much bolster my long-held argument that good writing is good writing, no matter where you read it.

Kilian also reminds us not to forget to know our target audience. Is it sophisticated about the topic? If so, we can use jargon common to the subject; if not, we must avoid using potentially confusing terms. Similarly, some audiences will need a more straightforward design with easy "signposts" leading from one place to the next, whereas other, more sophisticated audiences may respond easily to a more complex design. As with any other publication, suit your design to your audience.

The single, glaring message that Kilian brings home is that we shouldn't let technology overbear the message. Much the same as design done for the sake of design will probably deter the serious seeker of information, a technologically stunning Website may hinder your task of communicating successfully. The warning is well timed. I increasingly counsel students who are whizzes at Website design but who still can't write a coherent paragraph on their job prospects. Sadly, they continue to believe that knowing the technology is all they need.

Remember: The difference between writing for a Website and writing on the computer is that the computer is a writing tool, just like a typewriter or a pen, whereas a Website is a communication vehicle, just like a newsletter. A well-written piece of communication is what you get paid to produce as a public relations writer. Ultimately, you will be judged by how well you write.

OK, Let's Get on with Web 2.0

Journalist and media relations consultant David Freedman has called the Internet "the new prime time."[5] It is now used for entertainment and information more than any other medium, and because most of the new "publics" are online, that's where public relations needs to be. Freedman says that Americans typically join the Web 2.0 conversation in a number of ways. Anyone in public relations wanting to get in on the conversation would do well to mimic this trend.

- Participate in social networking Websites like MySpace, Facebook, LinkedIn, Biznik, hi5, and Plaxo. You can even create your own social network now with sites like Ning. Or you can add social networking features to your Website using the Google Friend Connect gadget.

- Blog and comment on other people's blogs. It's easy to set up a blog on any of the number of free services (Blogger, WordPress, etc.) or on a "micro-blog" (Twitter, Tumblr). You can also build your own niche micro-blog community with Twingr and Yonkly.

- By commenting on others' blog posts, you can generate relationships, extend the conversation, and set yourself up as an expert, or "thought leader," on a subject.

- Use wikis to collaborate with colleagues, clients, or any membership group, thanks to simple, free wiki-building tools like Wikispaces, WetPaint, and Google Sites.

- Review, rate, forward, share, bookmark, and tag online content with tools such as Digg, Delicious, and Yahoo! Buzz.

- Publish original, rich (multimedia) content such as articles, white papers, photos, and videos, either on their own Websites or blogs or on citizen journalism and community media sites such as Newsvine, iReport, Flickr, and YouTube.

You don't have to jump in with both feet, though, just to get started. Freedman suggests that you start by listening to the conversation, and discover what your clients are talking passionately about. Read a few industry- or profession-related blogs each week. Search for blogs on Technorati, Icerocket, or BlogPulse, and look for opportunities to contribute comments. Join a professional networking site like LinkedIn, and participate (don't just wait for something to happen).

After a while, you can begin publishing useful content on your own Website or blog. And, if you use plug-in tools like "digg this" and "share this," visitors can **hypersyndicate** your content for you (pass it on virally to multiple publics). However, you don't need your own site or blog to participate and have your

---

[5] The following is from "Web 2.0 Basics for Public Relations & Marketing, Social Media" by David M. Freedman. http://www.freedman-chicago.com/web2.html#FOOT. Freedman is a freelance journalist and media relations consultant in the Chicago area. Used with permission.

ideas hypersyndicated. You can post thoughtful comments on other people's blogs, forums, online communities, and professional networking sites. In some cases your comments will be commented on, shared, referred to, discussed, and virally disseminated. Providing your e-mail address with your comments offers opportunities for audience members to contact you. Providing your Website URL (which some blogs allow) invites people to visit your site and may improve its search-engine ranking.

Finally, monitor what is being said about you and your firm on blogs and especially Wikipedia (using monitoring tools like Google Alerts and Factiva). If you find inaccurate information or defamatory claims, be careful how you respond. Work quickly and diplomatically to correct factual errors, but approach the process as a collaboration in which you are a participant rather than an enforcer. If you threaten or try to take control of the conversation, you will be overwhelmed by indignant, irreverent, intentionally disruptive hordes and your efforts will backfire. Remember, opinions are usually protected by the First Amendment.

Above all, your contributions to the Web 2.0 conversation should be authentic. Don't pretend to be someone you're not, and don't use a surrogate (another, secondary blogger) to convey your message for you in an attempt to appear unbiased.

And remember, we still live offline. The landscape may be changing, but it would be a mistake to focus all your PR strategy on **social media.** Before you invest in a social media campaign, integrate it into your strategic marketing plan.

BLOGS AND BLOGGING

Believe it or not, **blogging** is a relatively new phenomenon that has managed to catch on very quickly. According to recent studies, the use and impact of blogging on public relations and corporate communication is phenomenal.[6] Blogging takes many forms. We'll discuss only those pertinent to public relations here.

In what has become known as conventional blogging, anyone can write anything he or she wants at any time. It has become a haven for the verbose, highly opinionated, and often uninformed. Obviously, this is not what blogging in public relations should represent. The key difference is that public relations people don't represent themselves. Rather, they represent their clients and/or organizations. In addition, public relations messages have to be economical, to the point, and, above all, accurate.

There are several useful ways in which blogging can be added to the mix of media used in any public relations project or campaign. According to James Horton, founder of online-pr.com, blogging can initiate and maintain a "stream of news and organizational viewpoints of the organization at large that would

---

[6] Donald K. Wright and Michelle Hinson, "Weblogs and Employee Communication: Ethical Questions for Corporate Public Relations," Paper Presented to 9th Annual International Public Relations Research Conference March 10, 2006, Miami, Florida, p. 2.

take too much time to process through the communications system."[7] In other words, blogging can be a less formal way of keeping people informed than many other media options. However, this lack of formality can also lead to a lack of reference points, especially given the transient nature of most blogging. Unless there is a concerted effort to archive blogs, information can be lost to those who wish to reference it in the future (the bane of most Internet-based information). Horton sees blogging as a low-cost publishing tool that has the advantage of being able to get company news out quickly. Unlike e-mail, blogging is literally "broadcast" simultaneously to anyone who wants to read it. It is also egalitarian in a way that much of public relations communication is not. Blogs allow for instant responses, multiple conversation threads, and a sort of accessible history of issues that can be referenced, added to, and corrected at any time.

According to long-time Web-content guru Gerry McGovern, "Traditionally, public relations was about honing a silvery message that communicated exactly what the organization wanted us to hear. Now, we can hear all sorts of voices on the subject. It's true democracy at work."[8]

- Blogs have potential to help the organization develop stronger relationships and brand loyalty with its customers because they interact with the "human face" of the organization through blogs.

- Blogs, in an **intranet** environment, can be an excellent way of sharing knowledge within the organization.

- Blogs can be a positive way of getting feedback and keeping your finger on the pulse, as readers react to certain pieces, suggest story ideas, and so on.

- Blogs can build the profile of the writer, showcasing the organization as having talent and expertise.

What to Blog About

Obviously, you can blog about your client or employer or anything related to the company such as products or services, or the industry. But where do you start? Actually, there are a number of things you can do to stimulate your creativity and get you started blogging.

- Try searching for your company, product, or even a competitor's name in any of the myriad social networks, to see how they're being discussed. This will give you some idea of what others are saying and what interests them. If they're talking about you, you should be in on the conversation.

- Read others' blogs both in your industry and in other industries. To save time, use an RSS reader so you don't waste time manually surfing.

---

[7] James L. Horton, "Blogging and PR," at online-pr.com.

[8] Much of this is excerpted from an article by Gerry McGovern, at www.gerrymcgovern.com, in the DevWebPro online newsletter, August 23, 2004, at www.devwebpro.com/devwebpro. McGovern has recently authored a book on writing for the Web, *Killer Web Content*, from A & C Black Publishing. Used with permission.

- Ask a question on LinkedIn. This social network is specifically for professionals. For example, ask what are the best print newsletters, e-zines (electronic magazines), blogs, discussion forums, and Websites that target people who want to promote a product, service, cause, or issue related to your client.

- Ask the same question on Facebook and Twitter and any other social network you think will be composed of potential target publics and other professionals in your field.

- Do a Google search for keywords and keyword phrases and see what you can find.

- Search Technorati. This search engine is designed specifically for bloggers, and it will let you know exactly who is discussing your topic.

- Create Google Alerts for your topics. This is a Google service that notifies you as soon as something appears online about your area of expertise.

- Search for electronic newsletters. New-List.com lists almost 9,000 e-zines.

Basically, find out what's already on the blogosphere and join the conversation.

Writing Blog Posts

It's still about writing, but there are some things that make blogging unique, and some advice that can make it successful. Keep in mind that blogging takes time—time to write and time to read. The average visitor to your site might spend as little as 96 seconds per blog.[9] In addition, only a very small percentage of readers read everything word-for-word, and comprehend just over 50 percent of that. According to blog guru Darren Rowse, for that reason you need to make your blogs scan-friendly.[10] This includes:

- Using lists with lots of bullet points. They are quickly scanned by readers, get your point across succinctly, and are easy to link to.

- Using short, declarative sentences, and keeping your posts short. Some bloggers write stream of consciousness. Remember, you're a public relations writer. Stick to the point and make every word count.

- Using bolding, capitals, italics, and underlining to emphasize key points. But don't overuse them. They can add to clutter and frustrate readers.

- Using headings and subheadings. They break up the copy and allow readers to find their interest points more easily.

- Using pictures. Almost all forms of writing benefit from graphics. If done properly, relevant images can expand on your topic and actually add to your point.

[9] Darren Rowse, "How long should a blog be?". Rowse is an Australian blogger and avid expert on the subject. You can find his home page at www.problogger.net/archives/2005/01/06/about-darren/.

[10] Darren Rowse, "Scannable Content," www.problogger.net/archives/2006/02/20/scannable-content.

- Using boxes and block quotes to get attention. Sidebars are also useful for related thoughts, asides, and links to other topics.

- Using short paragraphs broken up by some of the above elements and white space. Clutter doesn't look good, especially on a blog site. Web 2.0 didn't kill design, it just put it to a new purpose.

- As they say in journalism, don't bury the lead. Make your main points early and clearly.

In addition to being "scannable," blogs need to appear on search engines, and as close to the top as possible. That means using search engine optimization (SEO). SEO basically means inserting information and words into your blogs that will show up readily on the major search engines. This begins with the title.

First of all, keep it simple. As with almost all other forms of public relations writing, to-the-point is best. Brief, but clear, titles grab attention and direct readers to your post. Most experts agree that 40 characters is maximum if you want your entire title to appear in a search engine result. Nothing's as frustrating as that partial title that you can't quite decide whether to investigate further or not. Sorry, now you've lost them.

Use active words to grab attention. An exciting title will get them interested. Just make sure you pay up when they get to your post. Don't inflate the importance of your information by overdoing the title. They won't fall for that again.

Anticipate reader needs. You aren't targeting everybody, just the readers who are seeking information you can provide. Imagine what you would be looking for and use that as the hook. Often, readers are looking for advice or help. If you can provide that, say so. Seed your blog titles with "how-to" phrases or use a question format such as "How do I know when my heat pump needs replacing?" If a reader asks a question about heat pumps, this will show up on his or her radar via search engines.

Make sure your titles describe exactly what readers will get when they click on your post. This isn't the place for cute references or vague allusions. Keep it clear and concise. Use the keywords that describe what you are blogging about. Put them up front in your title. Exhibit 6.1 gives tips for making the most out of your blogs.

When it comes to the blog post itself, litter it with keywords. Imagine what words people might be using to search for this information. Put those words in the text and in the heads and subheads. Don't force it, though. It should seem natural within the context. When a reader gets to your blog post, she doesn't want to be reading a list of keywords. Remember, you're not just writing for machines. You're ultimately writing for people.

How to Write Comments on Blogs

Some of the more influential blogs are regularly "trolled" by journalists and others in your industry looking for new ideas, developing trends, and sources. If you want to become known as a thought leader, you'd better comment frequently.

Exhibit 6.1

Tips for Making the Most of Your Blog Posts

1. Never use someone else's content without crediting him or her. If you don't, it's plagiarism. You are a professional, after all.

2. Use correct grammar and syntax—and no typos and misspellings. There is a tendency, perhaps fallout from sloppy e-mail habits, to ignore standard grammar and style in blogs. That's a huge mistake, especially for a professional. A blog represents not only your client, but also you and your skill as a writer. Impress with your writing. It will always pay off.

3. Be conversational in tone, keeping in mind that you are a professional and represent not yourself, but your client. A blog is basically an informal medium, but your readers will see you as an expert most of the time. Don't be afraid to be one. The only caveat is keep the jargon out and keep the concepts clear and as simple as possible.

4. Post frequently, but keep your posts short. This will maintain your visibility and keep the ideas new. We've all read blog posts that run for pages, with lots of informal, and needless, commentary along the way. Keep it brief and to the point. You don't have to write a long essay each time you post to your blog. All you need to do is show your knowledge on a subject by being pertinent. Many of your posts may simply be links to other related and interesting posts or articles. A sentence will usually suffice in these cases. Also remember, the more you post, the more content you are creating—and content draws search engine attention.

5. Most expert bloggers agree that the best time to post is the morning when people are going through their subscriptions. Most public relations professionals tend not to blog on weekends because readers generally check their RSS reader during typical workday hours. In other words, it's your job. Don't become obsessed.

6. Organize your blog. One of the downfalls of many blogs is disorganized, seemingly endless lists of past postings running down the side of the page. The best way to organize is by categories, not necessarily chronologically. Often keywords can be the key to a category. Thoughtful titling of each blog also helps. Bloggers often use "granular" blogging to help search engines find them more easily. This means keeping each blog to a single topic and then clustering the individual blogs under a relevant category. If a search engine picks up one, it will link to the others.

7. For a more detailed reference, you can use tags. Tags are basically labels that say what your post is about and allow it to be linked quickly to other, related posts. Unlike categories, which are more general, tags allow a much finer definition. For example, you could have a category labeled "audio software." A tag might be labeled "audio software for podcasting." Bloggers with well-defined categories often choose external tagging (Technorati, Flickr, Delicious, etc.).

This allows for external exposure. Others, seeking more internal coherence and relatedness, rely on internal tagging. This relates information internally and in a finer or more granular fashion. For internal tagging, you have to acquire a bit of software such as Ultimate Tag Warrior from WordPress.

8. Link frequently to related information on other Websites, other blogs, other articles. If you read something interesting online, tell your readers about it, then post a link to it. Don't make them Google it on their own. Sure, it will take them away from your blog site, but if you're a good blogger, they'll be back. Make a habit of providing extra "resources" with each of your posts. Your readers will thank you for it.

9. Engage in your own discussion. Invite your readers to respond, and provide a comments section for them to join the conversation. Allowing readers to interact and take part in the discussion will popularize your blog. After all, blogging is a dialogue, not a monologue. And respond to comments when you get them. If the commenter leaves a link, follow it to his or her blog. If you find something useful or engaging, leave a comment (see below).

10. As with everything else written in public relations, you need to be the contact person. Make sure you include as many contact points as possible, including your e-mail and Twitter addresses. And, because you work for a client or employer, make sure people know who that is. You're not anonymous if you're a professional.

A comment should help build a conversation by saying something new, providing more information, or suggesting other relevant posts or stories. Your goal is to provide useful, factual information so that, over time, it becomes clear to other blog readers that you know what you are talking about. But remember, unless you work for yourself, you represent someone else. Both of your reputations are on the line when you comment, so credibility is the objective. Following are some simple guidelines for commenting:

- You should always sign your posts, with your real name and affiliation. Anonymity is not a particularly professional approach to writing. You're also generally asked for your e-mail address and URL, if you have one. After all, you do want them to check out your own blog.

- Don't comment randomly. If you have something important to offer to a conversation, by all means contribute. But don't get a reputation for butting in to every conversation. Choose your entry points strategically.

- Keep it professional. Bloggers are free to reject inappropriate posts including, but not limited to, overt solicitations and personal attacks.

- Be accurate and complete in your quotes and always attribute, including a link if possible.

- Comment early on the original post. Comments have a short life span. If you want to be read, strike while the iron is hot.

Micro-Blogging and Twitter

Twitter is a Web 2.0 service that allows users to perform **micro-blogging,** communicating in messages of no more than 140 characters (known as "tweets"). A Twitter subscriber can choose to receive notifications of others' updates via the service's Web interface, cell phone text message, or online instant messaging service. Tweets can be broadcast publicly or shared only with the user's personal network, at the subscriber's discretion. The speed and simplicity of Twitter make it appealing to a wide range of individuals and organizations. Twitter allows users to organize impromptu events, share opinions quickly, and keep up with trends and information. From a personal brand building and networking standpoint, the key is not to look at micro-blogging as individual posts, but to think of the overall impressions and value that can be created over time. Each 140-character-or-less entry serves as a seed of an idea for an overall objective.

Remember, Twitter is a tool and is limited as far as writing goes. What you write on Twitter, therefore, is basically an exercise in brevity and a test of your ability to communicate important matters in an extremely limited format.

How to Write Twitter Posts

We'll assume that you will be using Twitter as a professional, writing posts that inform, break news, engage, or raise thoughtful questions. The other option, of course, is to tell your followers what you're having for lunch, or when you're going to work out, or some other personal tidbit that's interesting only to you and perhaps your mother. So, with the *professional* approach in mind, here are some suggestions:

1. **Keep it short.** Twitter gives you 140 characters to get your message out. That doesn't seem like much, but don't feel obligated to use every space. Keep it as brief as you can and still have it make sense. Add a URL to the post for details. One of the most common uses of Twitter is sharing links. But remember, you have only 140 characters to work with, so instead of taking up precious characters with a long URL, use one of several URL-shortening services to shrink it, such as tinyurl.

2. **Be clear.** Anything other than the clearest of messages wastes space and readers' time. You are in the business of public relations. Practice being concise and informative.

3. **Focus on keywords.** Identify the most important words from the article and put them in your Twitter-optimized headline. Try to imagine you're a news consumer looking for a certain story; what phrases or words would you Google to find it? Those are your keywords.

4. **Don't try to do too much in one tweet.** Use one tweet for each subject. Don't confuse people by putting two or three different subjects into a single post. Remember, Twitter is much more unobtrusive than other new media, like text messaging. It's all right to put out a lot of content in separate posts as long as it's pertinent and helpful to readers.

5. **Categorize your tweets for added visibility.** If you're tweeting about a particular subject, putting a # (called a "hash mark") in front of the subject makes it easy for others to find your tweet. For example, when Motrin ran a YouTube viral ad implying that baby carriers (the ones that place the baby in front of the parent carrying it) hurt moms' backs, a groundswell of objection came from thousands of moms all over the country, and #motrinmoms became a popular tag and search term for several weeks.

6. **Share pictures.** If you've got a product to push, images can often help. Don't be afraid to post them by using services like TwitPic, which lets users easily upload its photos and post them directly to Twitter.

7. **Tweet from your phone.** Twitter allows you to update your status and receive updates via text message. Under Settings, go to the Devices tab and enter your phone number to start sending and receiving mobile tweets. If your incoming tweets/texts are overwhelming you, disable this option by going back to the same panel and following the instructions.

8. **Pick a good desktop client.** With desktop clients such as TweetDeck, Twhirl, and TwitterFox, you can receive tweets in a much more manageable fashion, especially if you follow a number of people, respond often, and use direct messages frequently. TweetDeck, for example, allows you to create specific groups, if you want to split your feed into individual columns.

9. **Download a mobile client.** If you have a BlackBerry, an iPhone, or another smartphone with Wi-Fi or 3G access, a mobile client might be a better option than using text messages. Mobile Twitter clients worth checking out include Twitterific, TwitterBerry, PocketTweets, and Twidroid.

Finally, here's a short list of Do's and Don'ts if you plan on using Twitter as a marketing tool:[11]

- Do use Twitter to sell your products, ideas, offers, insights, and so forth.

- Do advertise your Twitter account on your Website, business card, and marketing literature.

- Do create a conversation. Add your users to your Twitter account. Let those who listen to you, talk to you.

- It's tempting to post something just to get it off your chest. Don't.

- Don't spam. You don't have to post everything to Twitter—your important messages will get lost amid the junk. If yours is a high-volume Twitter channel, let users know beforehand.

- Don't rely on Twitter 100 percent. Use Twitter as just one more tool in your social media toolbox.

---

[11] Taken in part from Carlos Granier-Phelps, http://red66.com/2007/10/using-twitter-as-a-marketing-tool/. Phelps is the CEO of Red66.com, providing digital media strategy consulting services to television networks, helping them understand and adapt to the Internet and the new media landscape.

- Don't let the shorthand you develop to conform to the 140-character style on Twitter carry over to your other writing. For instance, don't get in the habit of using @ for "at" or *BTW* for "by the way," or any number of other abbreviations that make using Twitter (and instant messaging) easier. Remember, professional public relations writers are multilingual, but they know when to use what language to communicate with which audience.

KEY TERMS

social networks	hypersyndicate	intranet
Web 2.0	Internet	Twitter
RSS	social media	micro-blogging
Website	blogging	

CHAPTER

7

News Releases and Related Materials

In This Chapter, You Will Learn

- What a news release is and why it is important to public relations professionals.

- How to write various forms of news releases, including publicity releases, product news releases, broadcast news releases, and digital news releases.

- What a backgrounder is and how to write one.

- What a fact sheet is and how to write one.

The news release has been called the workhorse of public relations. Every day, thousands of news releases are sent out all over the country to newspapers, magazines, and radio and television stations. Some newspaper editors receive as many as a thousand a month. Of these, only a minuscule number are ever used, and most of these are severely edited. Why, then, do public relations professionals and the people who employ them continue to use news releases? Because they remain effective. They are still used by newspapers and trade journals to pass along information about events and occurrences that reporters might not otherwise have the time or the inclination to cover.

The key to effective news releases is not so much in the writing, although we certainly concentrate on that, but in the placement. As we saw in Chapter 5, knowing when something is newsworthy and when it is not and knowing your contacts in the media and their schedules and guidelines are the most important elements of news release writing.

As a writer of news releases, you will become a reporter. It is essential that you understand journalistic style to present your releases in the proper format. Remember that reporters and editors are used to seeing one style of writing on a daily basis. That style fits their papers, and they are unlikely to print anything that doesn't conform. Remember, too, that although the reporter is responsible only to his or her editor, you are responsible to both the editor and the people you work for. This means that you must accommodate both the style of the newspaper and the needs of your employer. It is not an easy fence to walk, but as a public relations practitioner you have to try to keep your balance.

WHAT IS A NEWS RELEASE?

A **news release** is information that you wish released to the Media. Although all news releases have format in common, there are different emphases:

- Basic **publicity releases** cover any information occurring within an organization that might have some news value to local, regional, or even national media.

- **Product releases** deal with specific products or product lines. These are usually targeted to trade publications within individual industries. They can deal with the product itself, consumer use of the product, or a particular business or marketing angle.

- **Financial releases** are used primarily in shareholder relations; however, they are also of interest to financial media. Many local, regional, and national general media have financial highlights sections.

One of the most important points to remember is that all news releases should contain at least three elements: publicity, angle, and story. These elements may overlap or be quite distinct from one another, but they are all there. The **publicity** value of a news release is sometimes hidden whereas the story is the perceived reason for writing the release, at least from the media's point of view. The **angle,** by contrast, may be simply the hook that attracts media attention.

Often it is the same as the story but not as often the same as the publicity value. The reason is that most media aren't interested in your organization receiving publicity; they are interested in a story their audience wants to know about.

WRITING A NEWS RELEASE

The style of the news release is that of the straight news story: It begins with a lead, expands on the lead, and proceeds to present information in decreasing order of importance. This style, known as the **inverted pyramid style,** allows an editor to perform his or her job—that is, to edit—from the bottom up. A good news release also utilizes accurate quotes.

The Lead

The **lead,** or opening sentence of the news release, is all important. As every journalist knows, the lead is the hook that entices the reader into your story. For the public relations practitioner, too, the lead is a hook to entice the editor into running your release. Don't ever get the notion that any news release that you send out will automatically be run or that it will even be run the way you wrote it. The fact is, even if you have written the most appealing news release ever seen at the *Daily Planet,* most editors feel an obligation to edit. Indeed, you will be lucky to have the information in your release placed at all. This should not deter you, however, from writing a good release. You have to sell the editor first before your release will ever be seen by anyone else, and that's where a well-written lead comes in.

Editors often take less than 30 seconds to peruse a news release. Their decision to run the message depends a lot on how you present yourself in the headline (title) and the lead. Most editors use several measures to determine whether your release will be used. Who you are, in terms of your past record of providing only legitimate news, is the first important consideration. Once past that, your headline or title should tell them whether your release is important to them (more on this later). Finally, your lead should summarize the relevancy of your story.

The **summary lead** is by far the most common type of news release lead. A good summary lead will answer the key questions: who, what, when, where, why, and how. The **delayed lead** is used to add drama to a news story; however, this type of lead is usually reserved for feature stories and is not appropriate for straight news. Thus, we concentrate here on summary leads.

Before you write the lead, you must first decide on a theme. Try to determine what is unique about the event covered by your release. Although news releases should generally be considered as straight news stories and must be informative, they don't have to be boring. To illustrate, look at the summary lead from a release distributed by the Electronic Products Producers Association:

> "The present condition of the software market is such that companies involved in software development should be able to capitalize on current economic trends. This means that new product development should allow the earliest investors a significant niche in the market." This statement was made by Mr. James L. Sutton,

President of Associated Products Corporation, during a speech at the fall convention of the Electronic Products Producers Association held in Syracuse, New York.

Now consider this revised version of the same lead:

A leading electronics industry executive declared today (October 21) that the computer software market is wide open to new investors.

"The present condition of the software market is such that companies involved in software development should be able to capitalize on current trends," said James L. Sutton, president of Associated Products Corporation. "This means that new product development should allow the earliest investors a significant niche in the market."

Sutton's prediction of a dynamic market was made in a speech given at the fall convention of the Electronic Products Producers Association in Syracuse, New York.

Notice how the second lead has broken up the quote and used the proper journalistic form for **attribution** ("said James L. Sutton"). The opening paragraph has been rewritten to include most of the pertinent information:

Who? A leading electronics industry executive.

What? Declared a wide-open computer software market.

When? Today (October 21). Notice the inclusion of the actual date in parentheses. This is to let the editor know that the "today" you are speaking of is October 21. If the paper receives the release on October 20 but doesn't publish the information until October 22, it will need to correct the copy to read "yesterday."

Where? Left until the final paragraph. (It isn't always necessary to squeeze all of the information into the first paragraph.)

Why? Included in the explanatory paragraph following the lead. Of all the information, "why" is the most likely to be left out of the lead because it usually takes the most explanation and invites the interested reader to look further.

How? In a speech. Also left for the final paragraph.

Remember that you are responsible for the ordering of points in your lead and in your news release. The more interesting you can make the information by order of presentation, the better it will read. Notice also how much shorter the sentences seem in the revised version. In fact, there is only one more sentence than in the original, but because the quote is broken up and the attribution is placed in the middle, the sentences seem much shorter. Although it is wise to present most of the key information early in the release, only the most important elements need appear in the lead. The rest can follow in logical order.

A publicist's lead is likely to differ from one written by a reporter. The following examples, written for a local newspaper, illustrate the difference:

Publicist's Lead

Francis Langly, former Director of Research and Development at Rogers Experimental Plastics Company, will be awarded the prestigious Goodyear Medal on June 6 in Indianapolis at a banquet held in his honor. Awarded by the American Chemical Society, the Goodyear Medal is the premier award for work in the field of specialty elastomers.

Reporter's Lead
Francis Langly, 24 Cedar Crest Drive, will receive the Goodyear Medal at the annual meeting of the American Chemical Society. The conference is being held in Indianapolis on June 6.

Although neither of these examples is particularly original—public relations releases rarely are—the differences in content and style exist for a reason. Consider these questions:

- Why is the address left out in the publicist's lead?
- Why is Langly's title included in the publicist's lead?
- What is the difference between the phrases "will receive" and "will be awarded"?
- What is the significance for the publicist in pointing out that the Goodyear Medal is the premier award in the field?

Answers to these questions illustrate the differences between hard news and publicity and between the publicist's and the journalist's objectives.

Quotations and Attributions

Quotations add interest to your news release. It is always good to obtain usable quotations and then to place them at appropriate spots throughout the release. It is never a good idea to begin a news release with a quote. Because news releases are considered straight news stories, a quote fails to come to the point soon enough. As was illustrated above, quotes need not be written as complete sentences followed by the attribution; they can be broken up by the attribution. You don't need to follow every quotation by an attribution, especially if it is understood that the same person quoted earlier is still being quoted. A good rule is to repeat an attribution if more than one paragraph has elapsed since it was last given. Of course, if you change the source of the quotation, you will need to designate the change by a new attribution. Don't be afraid to work with the form of attribution and don't use the same form each time. Consider the following:

> Johnson, a long-time trucker, doesn't like the strike. "This layoff has really affected my family," he said. The strike has been in effect for 3 months. "We're down to eating beans out of a can," he said. Johnson has three small children and a $500 a month house payment. "I don't know what I'm going to do about my bills," he said.

Although the form of attribution ("he said") is correct, its repetition is monotonous. There are a number of ways of attributing a quotation that can add variety to releases. For example, you can paraphrase points of the quote, combine quotes, or simply use one attribution between two quotes. Look at this revised version:

> Johnson, a long-time trucker, doesn't like the 3-month-long strike. "This layoff has really affected my family," he says. "We're down to eating beans out of a can."

Johnson, who has three small children and a $500 a month house payment, says he doesn't know what he's going to do about his bills.

Notice that the tense of the attribution has also been changed to the present. News releases need to sound as timely as possible, which includes using the present tense in attributions. If you are dealing with a story that is obviously past, then the attribution must reflect this.

Most news-writing classes and most journalists adhere to the rule of using only the last name in an attribution. News releases, by contrast, must follow the conventions set by the originating organization. In most cases, even if you do insist on attributing a quotation to "Mr. Jones" or "President Smith," the news editor will delete the honorific. You will have done your job by using the conventions of your employer. In the long run, that is all you are expected to do.

The accuracy of quotations is obviously important, but even though reporters must be absolutely accurate, public relations writers can have some leeway. An illustration will help explain. Suppose you work for Rogers Experimental Plastics Company (REPC). You are writing a release on a new product line and are quoting the company president. You have interviewed the president, and she knows that you are writing the release. She is also aware of what she said; however, because she will probably be reviewing the release before it is sent out, she will correct anything that she doesn't like. As a writer and an employee, you have the creative ability and leeway to "invent" a quotation as long as she approves it. No employer will fault you for putting well-written words in his or her mouth. Suppose in your interview the president had said,

"I don't think anything like this new plastic has ever been seen—at least not around this area of the world. It may be the greatest thing since sliced bread and who knows how much money we'll make from it."

You may write in your release,

Paula Johnson, president of REPC, is excited about the new product. "We've come up with a totally new concept in plastic," she says. "I expect that the market for 'Plagets' in the West will be tremendous."

All you've done is tidy up the quotation and make it more interesting. Remember that you may doctor only quotations that will be checked for accuracy and approved by the party to whom they are attributed. It is a good rule to make sure that anyone you interview receives a copy of the finished release before it is distributed. There is nothing like a libel suit to sober up a writer! Another legitimate way of presenting unclear or clumsy quotations is to paraphrase or use indirect attribution. This is fine for news stories written by reporters, but news releases can benefit a great deal from well-written quotations.

Finally, if you want to help prevent serious editing, or even elimination, of your quotations (and your sources' names), you must learn to protect your quote. In other words, learn to use information that is vital to the understanding of the story as quotes rather than the fluff quotes often provided by those giving you the assignment. For example, consider the following:

"This is an exciting day for all of us," says Delphi CEO Robert Altus.

Any self-respecting editor would edit out this nearly meaningless quote. It's painfully clear that it was included to get the CEO's name in the release. Instead, you could write this:

"The merger of Delphi and TransAmerican airlines will more than double the workforce available to both companies currently," says Delphi CEO Robert Altus.

Although it may still be clear that this quote provides for mention of the CEO's name, it has a greater chance of staying because it provides important information. Used in this way, quotes can be placed strategically, based on the level of importance of the information. Fluff quotes, of course, belong at the end of the release—if used at all.

Local Interest

Local media outlets like local stories. For most public relations writers, news releases can almost always be oriented to a local audience. The real problem is finding just the right local angle—the one that will entice the newspaper into running the story. Some basic guidelines will help you in your placement:

- If you are releasing a story with national as well as local interest, try to construct your release so that any local information is interspersed throughout the release. This way, it will be difficult to cut out the national information, which might not be of interest to a local editor, without harming the local angle.
- Avoid commercial plugs. Editors recognize advertising instantly and will simply round-file (trash) your release. Keep your local angle newsworthy.
- If you are sending only to local media and you reference a local city in your release, omit the name of the state.
- Above all, don't strain to find a local angle where there is none.

Suppose that you are assigned to write a release that has national importance and you want to target it for a local paper, the *Seattle Times.* You know from your interview with William J. Hoffman, chief systems engineer of Associated Products Corporation of Syracuse, New York, that he went to high school and college in Seattle. Based only on this little bit of knowledge, the piece can be localized. In addition, you could try to place a version of the release in the *Lincoln High Review* and another version in the University of Washington *Husky* (the alumni paper). Your leads might look like this:

For the Seattle Times
William J. Hoffman, Seattle native and chief systems engineer for Associated Products Corporation (APC) of Syracuse, New York, has been credited with developing a revolutionary educational software line.

For the Lincoln High Review
William J. Hoffman, a Lincoln High School graduate and former president of the LHS Electronics Club, has been credited with developing a revolutionary educational software line.

For the University of Washington Husky

William J. Hoffman, a University of Washington graduate with honors in engineering, has been credited with developing a revolutionary educational software line.

You might think that the Lincoln High School angle is too much of a strain. If you do, don't use it. Every angle, however, is worth at least some consideration. You'll be surprised how your placements can multiply if you ask the right questions in your interviews and construct the right angles from the answers.

Remember, though, that the focus of your release isn't always the local angle; that is only the hook. Don't slight your real story in favor of the local angle, no matter how interesting it is. In the samples above, for instance, Hoffman is the angle, but the software is the story. The trick is to lead with the angle, move to the story, and keep the two so intertwined that any editor will have difficulty separating them.

NEWS RELEASE FORMAT

Although public relations practitioners often incorporate the conventions of their organization into their news releases, a standard news release format exists. Exhibit 7.1 provides a sample news release, with all format elements in place.

- News releases typically are written on plain, white bond paper with no decorative border.
- Margins are 1 to 1½ inches on all sides.
- The address of the sender is placed in the upper left-hand corner of the first page. This identifying block should include the complete address, name of the contact person (usually the person who wrote the release), and telephone numbers. It is especially important to include a night telephone number as well as a daytime number. Remember, newspapers don't shut down at night, and if an editor wants to use your release but needs further or clarifying information and can't reach you, the release may get dumped.
- The release date appears on the right margin, slightly lower than the bottom of the address block. This portion provides the editor with exact information concerning the appropriate timing for the release. (More will be said later about release dates.)
- The body of the release begins about one-third of the way down the page, allowing some white space for comments or notes from the editor. If there is to be a title—and titles are entirely optional—it should come between the address block and the body of the release, flush left. Typically, the title does not extend beyond the address block by more than a few characters, which usually means that it will be stacked (broken into two lines on top of each other). The title should be in all caps, single-spaced, with the last line underlined.

Exhibit 7.1

News Release Format

Company or Client Name
and Address Here
Contact: (Your Name)
Day Phone:

Night Phone:

Release Date and Time

THE TITLE GOES HERE, ALL UPPER

CASE AND UNDERLINED LIKE THIS

    The Point of Origin Dateline Goes Here -- The body of the release should begin one-third of the way down the page to leave enough room for the editor or copy person to write remarks.The release proper should be all double spaced for ease of readability and editing.

    Be sure to use normal indents and consistent spacing between paragraphs. It is not necessary to triple space between paragraphs. All information should be presented in descending order of importance, ending with the least important items in case last-minute editing results in the bottom of your release being lopped off.

    Remember to leave at least one-inch margins all around, but resist the urge to leave huge right-hand margins in order to stretch your information.

    When you arrive at the bottom of the first page, leave at least a one-inch margin and indicate either the end of your release (-30-) or that more information follows (-more-). If more information follows, try not to break paragraphs or sentences in the middle. Never break a word and complete it on the next page.

.-30-

- The body of the news release is double-spaced. Never single-space a news release. Paragraphs usually are indented with normal spacing between paragraphs. Some companies prefer no indention and triple-spacing between paragraphs, but the standard is indented.
- If the release runs more than a page, the word *more* is placed in brackets or within hyphens at the bottom of the page.
- Following pages are identified by a slug line (abbreviated title) followed by several dashes and the page number at the top of the page, usually either flush left or flush right.
- The end of the release is designated in one of several ways. Use the word *end* or the number 30 either in quotation marks or within hyphens, or the symbol #####.

Timing and Dating Releases

When do you want your release to be published or broadcast? If you have just written a release about an important meeting that will be held tomorrow (January 23) but you don't want the information that will be presented at that meeting to reach the public prior to the meeting, you will have to say so on your release. Although it is wise not to send out releases too far in advance of an event, it is also wise to be as timely as possible—which means getting your release to the media outlet beforehand.

Release dates and times can be designated in a number of ways. Regardless of which method you choose, the time and date belong just slightly below the address block, flush right. The most common designations are as follows:

- *Release with no specific time frame.* This type of release is by far the most widely used and is usually designated by *For Immediate Release.* Other phrases include *For Release on Receipt* or *For Release at Will.* It is unnecessary to add a date to this type of release statement.
- *Release with specific date.* An example of this type of release designation would be *For Release January 23 or Thereafter,* or if you need to be even more specific, *For Release January 23, 10:00 p.m. or Thereafter.* Other options are *Hold for Release, Friday, January 23, 10 a.m.,* or *For Release after 10:00 a.m., Friday, January 23.* This type of release statement could be used, for instance, if you want all the media to carry it at one time or if the event is occurring at a future date but you want to release the information early.

Datelines

Datelines are used to indicate the point of origin of your news release if, for some reason, that is important. Datelines are important to foreign correspondents to enable readers to appreciate that a story originated at the location where it happened. For public relations practitioners, a dateline may serve the same purpose. It alerts the editor that your release concerns an event either reported from or happening at a certain geographic location. Datelines should be placed immediately preceding the opening of your release proper, on the same line:

> Springfield, OH—Rogers Experimental Plastics Company (REPC) has announced the development of a versatile new plastic widget that has the potential for use in a number of industries from automotives to electronics.

If the city is well known, there is no need to include the name of the state (for example, New York and Los Angeles). If the name of the city may be popular in a number of states, designate the state (as in the example above, to differentiate Springfield, Ohio, from Springfield, Oregon, or Springfield, Kentucky, or any number of Springfields). However, if the release is intended for a statewide press only, you can get by with just the name of the city. Also, if any confusion might arise from use of the city name only, include the state (for example, Moscow, Idaho, or Moscow, Russia).

Exclusives and Specials

If your release is an **exclusive** (intended for only one paper), make sure that the editor knows it. Remember that an exclusive can be sent to only one publication. A **special,** by contrast, is a release written in a certain style, intended for a specific publication but being released elsewhere as well (see Exhibit 7.2). Both designations should be noted immediately below the release information as follows:

> For Immediate Release Exclusive to the *Daily Planet*
> For Release February 24 or Thereafter Special to the *Daily Planet*

TYPES OF NEWS RELEASES

Don't imagine that one-size-fits-all when it comes to news releases. Although the inverted pyramid approach is usually the best for most releases, there are a number of different types that may or may not benefit from that approach. Some of the differences among the various types of news releases are obvious, some more subtle. What follows are brief descriptions of some of the most common types of news releases, along with a few examples that should give you an idea of how different they are.

Product Releases

Product publicity often has little or nothing to do with advertising. In its strictest sense, advertising refers only to the purchasing of time or space in which to run a message. Product publicity is not paid for; it is a far more subtle art. You must be able to construct informative passages concerning a given product without

Exhibit 7.2

Exclusives and Specials

Deer Point Development, Inc.
Box 1387
Deer Point, Michigan 72493
Contact: Warren Bailey
Day Phone: (714) 555-6635
Night Phone: (714) 555-1765

For Immediate Release
Special to the Deer Point Sentinel

NEW PLANT TO OPEN IN DEER POINT

A new plant designed to manufacture high tech components for automobiles is scheduled to be opened in late July according to Eleanor Maston, president of Deer Point Development, Inc. (DPD).The two-building facility will encompass over 55,000 square feet and be housed on a five-acre plot near the Doe River. Maston's company was instrumental in the planning, acquisition of land, and contracting of firms for the construction of the new plant. The plant will be owned and operated by Auto-Tech, Inc. of Albatross, Maine—a long-time member of the automotive peripherals industry.

Maston predicts that over 800 new jobs will be created by the plant's construction. "Auto-Tech has assured us that they intend to hire the majority of their plant workers from the local community," she says. "They plan to bring in only a bare-bones management crew from the outside to begin with, and train local people from the ground up."

According to Maston, DPD first learned of the scheme last December when Auto-Tech president Wilson Klatchki contacted her. The New England-based company was seeking to expand into the high-tech industry and needed a plant close to the major automobile manufacturers in Detroit. Deer Point seemed like the perfect solution.

"Auto-Tech felt that our proximity to Detroit was ideal," Maston says. "They wanted to be close without having to build in the city itself."

The site was chosen for its availability and scenic location, according to Maston. "Because high tech is basically a 'clean' industry, being located near Doe River poses no environmental problems," she says.

Construction of the plant began in February and is expected to continue through the summer.

-30-

actually pitching the product. This is not an easy task. The minute an editor detects a sales pitch, the release gets thrown out.

Most product publicity goes through several stages: product introduction (usually via news releases to trade media), articles in which the product is reviewed after testing (written by the trade publications themselves), and user articles (submitted by the public relations writer focusing on actual users of the new product). This section covers only product introduction releases.

Product releases serve a multitude of purposes, from providing pure information about a single product to publicizing other companies and other products. It is common to mention contributing manufacturers in a product release. For example, if you develop a basic plastic that is then used by a leading headphone manufacturer in its product design, it is usually acceptable to mention that company's use of your product. There is always the chance that the headphone manufacturer will reciprocate. In fact, many such joint arrangements are formalized when products are publicized. Consider the release in Exhibit 7.3 about a new water fountain.

Can you tell whom the publicity is for? From the address block, you learn that the company that manufactures the fountain is sending out the release; however, a second company is also mentioned. The manufacturer of the ice maker is given some free publicity. In many cases, this is a good thing to do. Of course, you don't want to give your competition a helping hand, but it never hurts to help your friends. Often, it's difficult to determine the real publicity point in a product release. If the release in Exhibit 7.3 had been written and distributed by an agency or by FREON, Inc., then the bottom-line publicity would be for the ice maker, through publicity for the fountain. This approach is not uncommon in product publicity and is not usually considered unethical.

Product news releases are arranged slightly differently from other releases. Although they certainly follow the normal inverted pyramid style of decreasing order of importance, they are quite obvious in their inductive approach to the product definition. In other words, product releases usually proceed from a general statement concerning the product (often an announcement that the product is on the market) to specific information about the product's attributes, characteristics, and applications. The end of the release is usually reserved for company background—full name, relationship to parent or subsidiary companies, and branch locations or the location at which the specific product is made.

A number of industries don't use the inverted pyramid style for news releases. These industries typically use a more feature-oriented style, usually owing to the media outlets to which they typically send the releases and also because of the nature of the industries themselves. For example, the clothing and fashion industry has developed a feature-oriented media. So have the food and beverage industry and the entertainment industry. News releases produced for these and some other industries will usually be constructed more like features.

Exhibit 7.3

Product News Release

Tall Drink of Water, Inc.
435 Lasado Circle
Watertown, NY 10056
Contact: Myrna Hofman
Phone: (121) 555-1222

For Immediate Release

NEW FOUNTAIN DISPENSES

COLD, HOT, AND ICE WATER

Watertown, NY —-A new water fountain that dispenses cold water, hot water, and ice has been marketed by Tall Drink of Water, Inc. (TDW) of Watertown, NY. The new fountain, which already is appearing in offices across the country, operates on an entirely new system for compartmentalizing water supplies.

According to TDW president and co-founder, Willis Reed, the new fountain represents four years of hard work. "We spent a lot of time on this new fountain," he says. "It's a whole new concept in water fountains. We did some initial research on office water consumers and found that they wanted not only cold water, but also hot and iced water as well."

The new fountain uses a system of valves that pass the water from the building plumbing system through the fountain in a series of stages. The incoming water is captured first in a central reservoir. From this central pool, the liquid is siphoned off to the cold water tank. This tank feeds the main drinking spout for normal water needs. Ice is produced in a refrigerated tank located next to the cold water reservoir and dispensed through a separate opening in the side of the fountain. On the opposite side of the fountain is the hot water dispenser, which feeds off a heater tank located above the main reservoir.

"It's the addition of the ice maker that makes our fountain unique," says Reed. "We use a Handy-Ice III manufactured by FREON, Inc. in Asbury Park, NJ," he says. "The Handy Ice III produces ice at a rate that far exceeds anything else on the market today. A number of other manufacturers already make dual purpose fountains, but ours covers the entire range of drinking needs."

Reed indicates that the new fountain will probably be marketed in areas with noticeable seasonal
-more-

shifts. "We expect that areas that have pronounced seasonal temperature fluctuations will have the greatest need for our fountain," he says. "But almost any office where people have different tastes in beverages is a potential market." Reed explains that in any given office environment, 75 percent of the staff will be satisfied with just plain water; however, the other 25 percent will use a fountain for making hot drinks such as tea and soup in the winter and iced drinks in the hot months. He also expects that the very availability of such a fountain will increase its usage.

# # # # #

Some interesting hybrids are born of a combination of industries. For example, the release in Exhibit 7.4 is from computer industry giant Intel, but it is targeted to a different type of audience than the company usually focuses on. It could be seen as a combination of both product and feature release. Exhibit 7.5 is the first page of an Intel release that is even more feature oriented in its lead.

Event Announcements

Special events aren't just the domain of nonprofits (although they are used a lot in that area, especially for fund-raising). Pretty much anything your company is doing that is public is an opportunity for an **event announcement.** It could be a grand opening of a new site, an open house, or a press conference on an important topic. The primary goal of an event is the generation of publicity. Because of this, it's important to make the event seem important enough so that media outlets want to cover it. This generally means making it important to their constituents (readers, viewers, listeners)—then, it's automatically important to the news media.

There are two things that need to happen with event announcements: the event itself needs to be publicized to the public, and the media need to be encouraged to attend to cover the event itself (see Exhibit 7.6). The public announcement (news release) often takes the form of a bulleted outline, stating clearly the who, what, when, where, and why information. That will take care of alerting the public. Alerting the media to attend is usually taken care of with a media advisory (see below) prior to the event and a press kit about the event itself to be handed out to the attending media.

Personnel Releases

All companies experience personnel changes. These are usually promotions (especially if it's a high-level promotion), or the hiring of new people in important positions. **Personnel releases** are a good opportunity to present more

Exhibit 7.4

Feature-Oriented Release

Intel Corporation
2200 Mission College Blvd.
P.O. Box 58119
Santa Clara, CA 95052-8119

News Release

CONTACT: Sam Smith
(555) 123-2190
s.smith@intel.com

INTEL GOES INSIDE HOLLYWOOD FOR A NEW GENERATION OF FILMMAKING

**Visual Effects Leader Industrial Light & Magic
Using Intel Technology at the Core of its Desktop Workstations**

SANTA CLARA, Calif., July 22, 2002 – Hollywood has found an unlikely ally in its efforts to lower costs in the increasingly complex world of digital filmmaking: Intel Corporation.

Industrial Light & Magic* (ILM), a division of Lucas Digital Ltd. LLC, today revealed its latest Intel technology deployment of 600 Pentium® 4 processor-based animation workstations. ILM is one of many studios adopting Intel technology to assist with the future of filmmaking.

"The visual effects industry has traditionally been a land of proprietary systems and software," said Cliff Plumer, ILM's chief technology officer. "At ILM, we're increasingly using Intel-based systems to expand our range of software choices for animation and compositing. In fact, having Intel at the core of our desktop systems provides greater quality and productivity because the technology can handle more iterations with greater frequency. We can now run any operating system we want."

ILM began using Intel-based systems on "Star Wars: Episode II -- Attack of the Clones," and then with "Men in Black II" and "Minority Report." They are currently employed in the development of "Star Wars: Episode III," "Harry Potter and the Chamber of Secrets," "The Hulk" and "Terminator 3: The Rise of the Machines."

-- more --

Intel/Page 2

Use of Intel technology is on a rapid rise in Hollywood because of the convergence of four key factors. First, the performance of Intel-based systems over the past two years has consistently surpassed that of proprietary systems, while system costs have come down. This has led to significant savings for studios. Next, major studios are increasingly outsourcing the rendering of digital effects to "render farms" that use large banks of small servers, and in that model Intel's high-volume, high-performance, low-cost, any-software approach makes sense. In addition, studios are now using a variety of operating systems, and Intel technology provides them the most flexibility. Finally, the results of Intel's multi-year effort to make movie software more Intel-friendly has borne fruit. Applications from such companies as Adobe*, Alias/Wavefront*, Digital Domain*, Discreet*, Macromedia* and Softimage* have reached critical mass.

Large studios are now using or have recently used Intel technology to help create some of Hollywood's leading movies. DreamWorks*, which used Intel-based systems in the Academy Award*-winning "Shrek" and recent hit "Spirit: Stallion of the Cimarron," continues to expand its Intel-based work, and is now testing Itanium® 2-based systems. Weta Digital Ltd.* recently announced it is using hundreds of Intel® Xeon™ processor-based servers for its work on the "Lord of the Rings" trilogy. The first movie of the trilogy, "The Lord of the Rings: The Fellowship of the Rings," won four Academy Awards, including Best Visual Effects. Walt Disney Pictures* recently disclosed plans to use Intel-based Hewlett-Packard* workstations and data-serving computers for work in its animation division. Digital Revelations, a Hollywood studio owned by actor Morgan Freeman, is utilizing mostly Intel Architecture in its development of "Rendezvous with Rama," scheduled for release in 2003. Sony Pictures Imageworks recently used more than 600 Intel processors in creating visual effects and animation for the recent "Spider-Man" blockbuster and "Stuart Little 2," in addition to evaluating Intel® Itanium®-based systems.

"Imageworks chose Intel-based systems for its newest server farm due to the open, scalable nature of the technology and its superior price-performance," said George Joblove, vice president of technology, Sony Pictures Imageworks.

Intel, the world's largest chip maker, is also a leading manufacturer of computer, networking and communications products. Additional information about Intel is available at www.intel.com/pressroom.

-- 30 --

Intel, Intel Xeon, Pentium and Itanium are trademarks or registered trademarks of Intel Corporation or its subsidiaries in the United States and other countries
* Other names and brands may be claimed as the property of others.

Exhibit 7.5

Feature-Oriented Release Lead

Intel Corporation
2200 Mission College Blvd.
P.O. Box 58119
Santa Clara, CA 95052-8119

Feature Release

CONTACT: Jill Brown
GCI Group
(555) 123-8094
HYPERLINK: jbrown@gcigroup.com

Carry Jones
Intel Corporation
(555) 123-0146
c.jones@intel.com

HOME MOVIES GET THE STAR TREATMENT
Powerful PCs Help Families Create, Enhance and Preserve Home Movie Memories

NEW YORK, Dec. 2001 – Consumers may not realize that their VHS and 8mm home movies can degrade to the point of being unusable within 15 years.[1] Ralph Bond knows this only too well.

When Bond watched a 16-year-old VHS videotape of his children's first steps, he was shocked – not by how much they had grown, but at how close he had come to forever losing a precious video memory.

Damaged by the passing of time, the tape's crispness was gone, a dark band was creeping from the edge of each frame to the center of the action, and a pink hue tinted the true colors of the entire tape. Bond, consumer education manager at Intel Corporation, learned from personal experience – and just in time.

Home Movie, Meet the PC

The key to preserving precious home movies is to make them digital, and a powerful personal computer is an invaluable tool to ensure that every special moment is captured in time – not destroyed by it.

"Powerful home PCs coupled with a digital camcorder, new software applications and CD or DVD recorders give consumers a gateway to creative freedom and fun with their home movies," Bond said. "Whether it is creating new home movies or preserving memories filmed many years ago, digital video is a hot application for PC users and all the necessary tools are widely available."

-- more --

Exhibit 7.6

Event Release

John Mitchell, Event Coordinator
Phone: (541)-354-9723
E-mail: JM@home.com

<u>FOR IMMEDIATE RELEASE</u>

Cooking Up the World's Largest Bowl of Chili at Autzen Stadium

On September 26, 600 local Oregonians will participate in the grandest charity chili cookoff of all times. They'll be attempting to break the *Guinness Book of World Records* by assembling the largest bowl of chili ever made—right in the middle of Autzen Stadium at the University of Oregon. More than a thousand bowls of chili will be served to attendees of the event.

WHO: Six-hundred local Oregonians, along with help from UO faculty and staff and Roger O'Neil, founder and CEO of Ireland's Best line of soups and stews (event cosponsor)

WHAT: The "Great charity chili cookoff"

WHEN: Saturday, September 26, 2009

WHERE: Autzen Stadium, Eugene, Oregon

WHY: To break the *Guinness Book of World Records* for the largest bowl of chili. All proceeds will go to five local charities. Ireland's Best has also generously donated $10,000 toward the proceeds.

Questions regarding the event should be directed to John Mitchell, Event Coordinator, (541)-354-9723, JM@home.com.

#####

detailed biographical information on company personnel and on the company itself. It's entirely appropriate to include a photo of the person being featured as part of the release.

As with any good news release, it's important to highlight *who* is being featured, *what* he or she will do for your company, *why* the person's appointment is important, and *what* he or she did previously. And don't ignore the opportunity to multiply your potential placements. People have home towns, professional affiliations, and other ties that make their personal successes important to more than just the local media. Get as much mileage as you can from this type of release (see Exhibit 7.7).

Tips/Hints Releases

Tips/hints releases are easy to write because they typically use an outline format with plenty of bulleted items. The objective is to position you or your company as an authority on the subject. As with other types of releases, keep your writing focused and organized, and restrict yourself to a two-page maximum. Examples might be a wedding planner listing 10 tips for planning the perfect wedding; or a carpet manufacturer explaining how to remove spots easily; or the local sports outlet listing the top fishing spots in the state. Remember, this may seem like a lightweight approach to publicity, but people do love their lists (see Exhibit 7.8 and 7.9).

WRITING NEWS RELEASES FOR BROADCAST

Radio is meant to be heard, and television is made to be seen and heard. That means you have to write for the ear or for the ear and eye. Simplification is the key to broadcast writing. Because it is harder to absorb the spoken word than the written word, concepts need to be pared down to the bare bones. Sentences must be shorter, speech more colloquial, and complex issues distilled to their essence. One of the major advantages of using broadcast media is repeatability: Listeners may hear or see a message many times in the course of a single day or a single week. Even so, you must learn to write as though your audience will hear or see your message only one time.

Consider the differences between the following leads written for two different releases: one meant for print, the other for radio.

Print
INDIANAPOLIS, June 6—Francis Langly, former director of Research and Development for Associated Products Corporation (APC), today received the American Chemical Society's (ACS) Goodyear Medal—ACS's most prestigious award—for his work in the field of specialty elastomers.

Radio
At an awards luncheon in Indianapolis today, a Wilmington native received the highest honor of the American Chemical Society. The prestigious Goodyear Medal—awarded for work in the field of specialty elastomers—went to Francis Langly, former director of research and development for Associated Products Corporation.

Exhibit 7.7

Personnel Release

Associated Products Corporation

Contact: Alex Cohen
　　　　Elastomers Division
　　　　(555) 540-0998
　　　　alex@APC.org

FOR IMMEDIATE RELEASE

Associated Products Names New Vice President of Development

WILMINGTON, DE, Oct. 2009—Associated Products Corporation (APC), manufacturers and designers of custom elastomer products, has named Francis Langly its new vice president of development.

Langly, who had been assistant director of research and development, will enter his new job with over 15 years of experience at APC. He will be in charge of managing and increasing APC's network of research sites around the country. Associated Products, which has focused exclusively on the Northwest, is in the process of expanding its efforts nationally. Langly will spearhead this drive.

"There is no surprise in development," Langly says. "We understand the properties of the products we are developing and we're sure that markets will eventually open up." His goal is to bring three new research sites online within the next 12 months.

Langly's background in organic chemistry led to his initial hire at the Organic Chemicals Department at APC's Johnson Laboratory in Stillwater, Oklahoma, where he discovered the first light-fast yellow dyes for cotton, During the next 10 years he led the task force that developed dyes for the new synthetic fibers that are fast becoming a mainstay of American fashion.

Langly recently won the prestigious Goodyear Medal of the American Chemical Society for his work in the field of specialty elastomers.

He has a PhD in organic chemistry from Cornell and an MBA from Princeton. He and his wife Laticia live in Newark, Delaware.

-30-

Exhibit 7.8

Tips Release

Marilyn Milne
Public Relations Services
mm@prpr.com
(888) 797-6051/ (541) 498-3200
Fax: (541) 498-3212

Build Business Plan with Bricks for Solid Home-Based Success

Just like the pigs' houses in "The Three Little Pigs", business plans will get blown down if they aren't built right. "The best business plans are built of three types of solid bricks: specificity, realism, and simplicity. Otherwise, they fall down," says Tim Berry, internationally known planning expert and principal author of Business Plan Pro™, a leading business plan software.

The big bad wolf is the real world. It gets in the way of completing and using a plan, according to Berry. The best way to succeed in a home-based business is to build a brick foundation and maintain the plan's structure with follow-up.

Start with specifics. Does the plan set concrete, measurable objectives? For example, a specific sales increase percentage or gross margin is measurable; statements like "being the best" or "optimizing customer satisfaction" are not measurable. Fill your plan with names and dates. Every business activity needs a person in charge whose work depends on the activity's success or failure. Assign real responsibilities to real people, attaching names, deadline dates, and budgets for later follow-up. "Even if you're a one-person business," Berry stresses, "assign tasks so you can track yourself."

The second brick is realism. Are the forecasts and expenses realistic? A company that has steadily sold $50,000 per year and is growing at 10 percent per year should not expect to sell $200,000 next year. When business plans are based on common sense, the results can be tracked. Also, no one will feel obligated to achieve the objectives if they seem unattainable. To develop objectives, check with similar businesses or look at the company's past results.

The third brick is simplicity. "This is a business plan, not a doctoral thesis," explains Berry. "Don't show off." A simple plan can be grasped immediately and is easy to track and update. Stick to the main points, explain them simply, and summarize well.

When a plan is built with the right bricks, the business is off to a good start. But Berry cautions plan writers to revisit the plan every month. "Compare your planned results to the actual results and follow up on any changes. Make revisions as needed and continue to manage. What you want in the end," Berry says, "is results, not just a plan. Your brick foundation will get you there."

#####

Exhibit 7.9

Tips Release

Appleton Fire and Rescue
Jimmy Bolton, Public Information Officer
(541) 498-5944
pio@afr.org

How to Fire proof Your Home

A fire can destroy all the things you worked so hard for. Thanks to home owner's insurance, you will be able to replace some of them. But there are things that you cannot replace; things, that have no financial value but mean the most to you. Here are a few strategies that you can do to fireproof your home:

- Install smoke detectors in your home. Make sure there is one outside your bedroom. Test your smoke detectors once a month and change the batteries every fall and spring. Mark these dates on your calendar so you'll remember.

- Make sure there is a fire extinguisher on every floor, including the basement. The extinguishers should be located in a visual spot that has easy access. Take the time to learn how to use the extinguisher, and teach your children how to use it.

- Make sure each bedroom has two escape routes. Practice with your kids so that they know where the second escape route is and how to use it.

- Clean out old boxes, magazines, newspapers, and soiled cloth that may be piled up. It's easy for these items to ignite, and you never know what you will find beneath them.

- Never leave candles burning unattended. Make a habit of blowing out the candles when you leave the room whether you are leaving the house or not.

Electrical Appliances
- All electrical appliances and tools should have a testing agency label. If an appliance is accidentally exposed to water, service it before you use it. Don't overload power adapters, and check electric wires for worn and frayed wires, especially cords that run under rugs. Turn off computers when not in use. Check appliances periodically.

(continued)

(continued)

- Clean out dryer lint every time you use the dryer. Check periodically behind the dryer for lint that may have accumulated.

Wood Stoves
- Make sure your stove is installed properly. It should have adequate clearance from combustible surfaces, and proper floor support and protection.
- Have the chimney inspected annually and cleaned if necessary, especially if it has not been used for some time. Do not use flammable liquids to start or accelerate any fire.

The Fireplace
- Keep a glass or metal screen in front of the fireplace opening to prevent embers or sparks from jumping out and unwanted materials (or people) from going in.

When There Is a Fire in Your Home
1. Get out immediately. Don't try to take your possessions: they can be replaced; you can't.
2. Crawl under the smoke; don't try to run through it. You should "stop, drop, and roll" upon leaving the burning house or building if your clothes have caught on fire. Teach these tips to your children.
3. Your family should have a predetermined place where you all know you should go if there is a fire in your home. That will make it easy to do a head-count and determine who is missing. It would be tragic if someone went back to the house to look for a person who was already outside, and got stuck in the fire.
4. Call the fire department. Don't assume your neighbors did. During your call, give your physical address as well as information about what is burning.

With proper maintenance and periodic checks, your home will be safer. Teach your children to check items as well. Make this a family event.

Although both releases are approximately the same length, noticeable differences exist that raise some interesting questions:

- Why doesn't the broadcast release start with a dateline?
- Why not use the abbreviations *ACS* and *APC* in the broadcast release?
- What is the reason for beginning the broadcast release with the location rather than the name, as in the print release?

Datelines are not needed in broadcast releases because they won't be read. The point of origin usually becomes clear through the narrative. Abbreviations are too confusing when heard on the air. It is always advisable to use the entire name, unless the abbreviation has become commonplace usage. Finally, beginning with location in broadcast helps set the scene. This approach is peculiar to broadcasting and is a carryover from drama, in which a scene is set prior to any dialogue.

Use the medium to your advantage. If you are using radio, set the scene first, then populate it with real people and easy-to-understand facts. Remember, a news release for radio or television is just that—news. It is intended for the same purpose as a print news release—to be used as news. The closer to acceptable news style it is, the better your chances of getting it broadcast. Prepare your releases for broadcast media using the same format that you would use for a print release. Exhibit 7.10 illustrates a broadcast release.

After reading the release in Exhibit 7.10, consider these questions:

- Why is paraphrase used instead of direct quotation in this release?
- Does the lead establish a sense of place prior to coming to the point?
- Can you locate all the elements of a lead within the release?
- Are they where they should be in order of importance?
- If you were a news announcer, what additional information would you want to have before you ran this story?

Remember, no matter what the type of news release, it is still information that you will lose control over once it is sent out to the media. They are your primary audience. You must learn to write for them first. To the extent that you do this, your releases will have a greater chance of reaching any other audience.

PITCH LETTERS AND MEDIA ADVISORIES
Pitch Letters

A **pitch letter** is a brief (usually no longer than a single page) introduction to a subject you intend to cover in more detail in press releases, backgrounders, or other publicity pieces. It is generally intended for a media audience (reporters, editors, news directors, etc.) and not the general public. The idea is to pique the media's interest in your story and get them to ask for more information. Following are some guidelines.

Getting Started

- *Keep it short and get to the point quickly.* Just like press releases, pitch letters need to capture the reader's attention immediately. If it doesn't accomplish that, you might as well not write one.
- *Know your audience.* Ideally, you should write a different letter for each medium you're trying to reach with your story. A pitch letter to a TV station will necessarily contain information on potential, on-camera interviews, whereas a pitch letter for a trade publication might only need to indicate how to be reached for a phone interview.

Exhibit 7.10

Broadcast Release

Society for Needy Children

4240 Welxton Avenue

Newhope, MN 78940

Contact: Lucille Bevard

Day Phone: 555-8743

Night Phone: 555-9745

For Immediate Release

A little girl stood for the first time today to receive a new teddy bear and a check for $75,000 from the Society for Needy Children. Eight-year-old Mary Patterson accepted the check on behalf of the children at the St. Mary Martha's Children's Hospital. The money represents the culmination of a year-long fund-raising drive by the Society.

The money is earmarked for a new ward to be devoted exclusively to the treatment of crippling diseases in children. One of the first beneficiaries will undoubtedly be little Mary, who has been disabled by congenital arthritis since birth. Along with her new teddy bear, Mary and the other children at the hospital will be using a new physical therapy center donated through a matching grant from the Friends of St. Mary Martha's.

Hospital Administrator Lois Shelcroft says that the check and the new therapy center are just the first step, and that the Society for Needy Children has promised to continue their fundraising efforts on the hospital's behalf in the coming year. Society spokesperson Jane Alexander says that the next fund-raising drive, scheduled to begin in September, will provide funding for a new lab.

# # # # #

- *Know your medium.* Read the publication or watch or listen to the show. Become familiar with the types of stories the medium covers and the kind of people it interviews.

- *Target precisely.* Send your letter to the right person. Don't send a lifestyle pitch to the business editor. Use your media contact list.

- *Offer a newsworthy topic.* Keep an eye out for what's happening in the community or in the news to see if what you have to offer matches what's of interest right now.

- Follow the publicity guidelines for each medium. If the local newspaper requires a specific format, use it. If it doesn't, it probably won't even look at it.

- *Don't send attachments.* That's what your follow-up information is for.

Format

Try to limit yourself to three succinct paragraphs. Use a standard business letter format with your name and contact information at the top. You may use a title (headline), as with a press release, but it's not always necessary. Use plain, white stationary (or letterhead) with 1-inch margins all around. And make sure you spell the name of the person you're sending it to correctly.

Just like a lead for a press release, the first paragraph should introduce your story and provide the hook that will make it of interest to the media. Use the same inverted pyramid style as you would in a release—all the relevant information up front. The second paragraph should explain why the medium you're querying should use your information, either as an interview or as an article in its publication. Keep it relevant to the specific medium and to the locale. If it's local, provide a local angle, even if the story is national in scope. If needed, reference the larger scope or trend you are playing off of in your local angle. Proximity is as important here as in a press release. In addition, make sure you emphasize the importance of your information to the medium's target audience. If it's not relevant to your medium, it just isn't relevant.

The third, or final, paragraph explains how you can be reached and/or how the medium can connect with your source. For example, if you're pitching a visiting speaker, let the medium know her availability and how to book her for an interview or attend her presentation. Be sure to provide your phone number, e-mail address, and any other contact information. Finally, say you'll be contacting the medium personally about this story, and indicate when, specifically.

Remember that the media are always looking for news. If you can provide it, they'll use it—as long as you make it easy for them. Respect their needs, their deadlines, and their power. Publicity runs off the media engine. Without it, we might as well be writing for ourselves (See Exhibits 7.11 and 7.12 for examples of pitch letters.)

Exhibit 7.11

Sample Pitch Letter

John Mitchell, Event Coordinator
Phone: (541) 354-9723
E-mail: JM@home.com

Dear [Name of media contact]:

On September 26, 600 local Oregonians will participate in the grandest charity chili cookoff of all times. They'll be attempting to break the *Guinness Book of World Records* by assembling the largest bowl of chili ever made—right in the middle of Autzen Stadium at the University of Oregon. More than a thousand bowls of chili will be served to attendees of the event.

The University of Oregon has donated its football stadium for the event, and faculty and staff volunteers will be handling ticket sales, crowd control, and cleanup.

The record-breaking event was the brainchild of Roger O'Neil, the founder and CEO of Ireland's Best line of soups and stews, which is cosponsoring the event. Ticket fees will be nominal ($5 per person, children free) and all the proceeds will go to five local charities. Ireland's Best has also generously donated $10,000 toward the proceeds.

Roger will be available to discuss the big event and his role as cosponsor on Thursday, September 24, or Friday, September 25. If you would like to book Roger for an interview, just call the number above.

In the meantime, I'll be in touch within the next few days to discuss a possible interview.

Sincerely,

John Mitchell

Media Advisories

A **media advisory** alerts the news media to upcoming items of interest to their constituents. It's one of the best ways to let them know what's happening and why they should be paying attention. An advisory might alert them to an upcoming special event your company is hosting, a grand opening of a new store, a press conference, the availability of a spokesperson for a new product or service, or basically anything the public might be interested in knowing about. The goal of a media advisory is not to give reporters everything they need to write the story, but rather to get them interested enough to mark their calendars. Here are some guidelines.

Exhibit 7.12

Sample Pitch Letter

Tim Brown
Crime Team
The Oregonian
1321 S.W. Broadway
Portland, OR 97201

Re: Criminals and Addictions

Recovery Row's Straight Facts, in Salem, works with prisoners and parolees who have drug
and/or alcohol addictions but would not succeed in traditional treatment centers. Straight Facts is
unique in its work as an outpatient program that successfully addresses criminality and
addictions.

"We do just as much lifestyle work as on alcohol and drug education," says Ellie Merskin, the
director. Ellie, who was in the criminal justice system, founded the program in 1996 with Marion
County Corrections. The county funds it, along with grants and the Oregon Health Plan.

Statistics from Straight Fact's 2007–2008 programs show that success rates ranged from 68 to
79 percentage. Since then, Straight Facts has tripled the number of clients it serves.

In 2006, Straight Facts became part of Recovery Row. Recovery Row is a licensed specialty
hospital and is included in the book *The 100 Best Treatment Centers for Alcoholism and Drug
Abuse*. It is headquartered in Eugene, with facilities and outpatient programs throughout
Oregon.

You are welcome to attend groups and talk to counselors and clients. If you would like to explore
Straight Facts, please call me (888) 959-8143 or use my e-mail: tb@pcc.com.

Thanks for your time.

Sincerely,

Tim Burton
PR representative for Recovery Row/Straight Facts

- Keep it short, typically no more than one page. This will be easy on reporters and allow them to parse the most relevant information quickly. An outline format is often best.

- Start with a short summary of your event. It should quickly convey what the event is, why you're holding it, and why the issues covered are relevant to your (and the medium's) constituency, which will, by default, explain exactly why it is newsworthy.

- Follow with all the details of the event: what it is, where it is taking place, the day and time it will begin, and who is participating. If you're using a well-known spokesperson, be sure to cite how individual interviews can be set up between him or her and the local media.

- Remember to include a contact name, a telephone number, and an e-mail address that reporters can use to ask questions before or after the event.

The basic media advisory uses the traditional five Ws.

What: The event itself or a brief description of what's going on.
Who: Speakers, celebrities, representatives of the event, and so on.
When: Date and time.
Where: Location of event.
Why: Background information about the event, directions to the event, if necessary, and, if you really feel it's necessary, the company boilerplate. This is especially useful if the tie between the company and the event isn't apparently clear, or you're just not that well known.
Contact Information: That's generally you, but can be other people connected with the event as well.

It's usually a good idea to send out a media advisory about a week before the event and then redistribute it the day before the event as a reminder. Keep media deadlines in mind when planning and make it easy on reporters to attend and still have time to do their story. Remember, breaking news may trump your event. That's why it's important to try to make this a "must attend" occasion (see Exhibit 7.13).

THE DIGITAL NEWS RELEASE

Traditional news releases were targeted to the media. First, you had to sell the editor before your release would ever be seen by anyone else. Most of that has changed with the move to reach publics directly, often through social networks using social media releases. However, a well-written news release is still a great way to get the word out about your client. There are several categories of news releases that could be said to be "digital," "electronic," or "Web releases."

The *standard news release* today helps both reporters and bloggers build their *own* stories based on yours. This type of release must still be well written, providing legitimate and relevant information to those who will be using it. The old "canned" quote should be thrown out and replaced, if necessary, by authentic

Exhibit 7.13

Sample Media Advisory

<u>FOR IMMEDIATE RELEASE</u>

Contact Julie Smith
(555) 567-5888
November, 1, 2009

Save a Life, Learn CPR

According to the American Heart Association, About 75 to 80 percent of all out-of-hospital cardiac arrests happen at home, so being trained to perform cardiopulmonary resuscitation (CPR) can mean the difference between life and death for a loved one. Effective bystander CPR, provided immediately after cardiac arrest, can double a victim's chance of survival.

As part of National CPR Training Week, Hopkins United Hospital will be offering a day of free CPR training at its Bayside Clinic, November, 21, 2009.

WHO: Staff of Bayside Clinic (a unit of Hopkins United Hospital).

WHAT: A day of basic CPR training, free and open to the community.

WHERE: Bayside Clinic, Hopkins United Hospital, 205 Elm Street, Hopkins, MN.

WHEN: 10 a.m. to 4 p.m., Saturday, November, 21, 2009. Each training session takes about a half-hour. Sessions will begin on the half-hour throughout the day.

WHY: The event will highlight the importance of basic CPR training for everyone and demonstrate how easy it is to learn. "Heart-Healthy Living" guides will be distributed to everyone attending the training sessions.

Janice Panitoni, the head of the Bayside Clinic, will be available throughout the day for press interviews.

For more information contact Julie Smith, Community Relations Liaison, Hopkins United Hospital, at the above number, or by e-mail: jscrl@hopkins.org.

voices that provide real value as a cited source. The standard release should be focused on the needs of the receiver—in this case journalists and bloggers. According to social media expert Brian Solis, "The best releases are going to be outward-focused and reflective of the state of the market, how you fit in it, and what's in it for the potential stakeholders (customers)."[1] Solis suggests that the best of these releases "read like the article that you would ultimately like to see" instead of the traditional release format and structure. Keep it short—between 400 and 500 words *or less*. Remember, this type of release is the basis for a more detailed and nuanced story that will ultimately grow organically through the input and pass-along of your target public.

Standard Release Format

A standard news release is electronic and, as such, is not as restricted by time and space constraints as for-print releases are. That doesn't mean you can ramble. If you think of this type of release as more of a teaser, you'll probably succeed. The goal might simply be to get reporters and bloggers to your Website for more information. With that in mind, try the following.

A common approach these days is to develop the "elevator pitch"—how you'd describe the story to someone on a 30-second elevator ride. Keep the lead paragraph to about 40 words with no more than 6 to 10 of those describing what the company (or client) does. Additional material can follow in subsequent paragraphs. Not unlike traditional releases, the lead should be able to stand on its own. Look at a typical story in the online *New York Times,* for example. How does the *Times* capture your attention and tell you what the basic story is about? It manages to tell what each story is about in a sentence or two. Keep your release to no more than five short paragraphs of a couple of sentences each organized around the standard who, what, when, where, and why.

That's pretty much it. Remember that you want to gain attention, but you also want to write it well enough that it's useful both for providing information and for guiding users back to you.

Search Engine Optimized Releases

Search engine optimized (SEO) releases are designed specifically to register on search engines and are typically released to wire services. Among the largest and most popular of these news release distribution Websites are PRNewsire, BusinessWire, and MarketWire. These sites distribute to a vast number of other sites, and their content (including your news release) is constantly being scanned by search engines. By working with large distribution sites such as these, you'll be making sure that your search engine optimizing efforts are being used to their fullest. Integrating keywords and phrases and embedded links optimizes the

---

[1] Brian Solis, "The Evolution of the Press Release," for techcrunch.com, www.techcrunch.com/2008/05/11/the-evolution-of-the-press-release.

chance that your release will show up near the top in searches. What this means is that you have to load your release with **keywords.**

Before you start to write, however, you must identify the keywords you are optimizing for (using to attract search engines). These are the words most likely to be used by those searching on Google, Yahoo!, or the myriad other search engines. One way to start is by using Google Adwords keyword search. You simply enter the keyword you'd like to use, and you'll get a listing of various combinations using that word (which is helpful for broadening your keyword placements without seeming redundant). The list is broken down by monthly local and global search volume, so you can see at a glance how many people search that word on Google. You also see the level of competition for that word (others who use the same keyword in their releases or on their sites). For example, entering "comic" and "comic book" will net you "comic book maker," "online comic book store," and "comic book news," among dozens of others. Among those, the most searched is "comic book," but the highest competition is for "online comic book store." You just go through the list and pick out the words and phrases that will work to get you a higher ranking on search engines, and incorporate those into your SEO release. Following are some suggestions on how to optimize your press release:

- Include your most important keywords toward the top of the release, especially in the headline/title, subhead, and the opening paragraph. Keep the title to less than 80 characters and make sure it's in bold type. Search engines seem to pay more attention to the natural bolded words as well as the repeated words toward the top of press releases.

- If your distributor asks for a summary of your release, make sure your keywords appear there as well; however, try to make them different from title keywords to broaden the subject a bit.

- Choose up to three words to repeat throughout the release—especially in the body. It's also extremely helpful to use those keywords as clickable text to link back to strategic locations on your Website, but don't overdo it.

- According to experts, keyword density, the number of times a keyword or phrase appears compared to the total number of words in a page, should be optimized between 2 and 8 percent. That means a 400-word press release might contain between 8 and 32 uses of keywords. Somewhere in the middle is probably best.

- Be sure to include industry and product names and categories in place of generic descriptors such as "the product," "the solution," and "the company" throughout the release. Remember, you are pushing someone or something specific. You're not just selling generic services. You want people to know who you are.

The goal of an SEO release is to get users to your site. If you want to deepen your information output, then the *social media release* may have everything you need. See Exhibit 7.14.

Exhibit 7.14

Online News Release

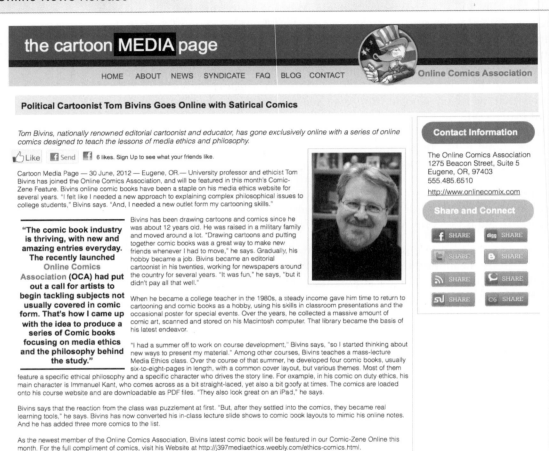

In this online release the keywords *online comics, comics, online comic books,* and *Online Comics Association* all appear several times in the banner, headline, sub-head, and first paragraphs. Additional anchor links appear throughout the release, and a separate section allows visitors to "share" the release on their own social media sites.

Social Media Release

Social media releases (SMRs) use social media. That may seem obvious, but to get the most out of an SMR, it needs to be designed in a way that only Internet users could benefit from. In other words, SMRs are literally multimedia-packed pieces that can be used as a digital touchstone for anyone seeking information about your client, product, or service. They provide bloggers and online journalists with all the information they need in a single package to more effectively write a rich media post or online news story.

Traditional press releases and, to an extent, the more current standard press release provided basic information designed to tease a journalist into asking for more, which was then provided by backgrounders, collateral pieces like brochures, and an invitation to an interview or two. SMRs provide that follow-up information and more, all in a single package. Today's social media release "should contain everything necessary to share, discover, and retell a story in a way that is complementary to your original intent and context."[2]

SMRs don't need to be distributed via wire services because they are meant to be "social"—that is, distributed through social networks. A client or company blog site dedicated to SMRs or a link to some other social network site from an online press room would be better.

How to Write a Social Media Release

The headline on a social media release from SHIFT Communications in 2006 read:

> SHIFT COMMUNICATIONS DEBUTS FIRST-EVER TEMPLATE FOR "SOCIAL MEDIA PRESS RELEASE"

The subhead followed with:

> The "Re-Mixable" Press Release Provides Relevant Context & Content in a Hyperlinked Format for Journalists, Bloggers.

With that introduction, a new age in press release writing was born.

Todd Defren, the principal of SHIFT, had developed an answer to the question, Is the press release dead? His answer was a resounding "NO—but it has changed." The SHIFT template was made available, free, to anyone wanting to use it. Defren explained the purpose of the template this way:

- SHIFT Communications believes that journalists and bloggers are now fully adapted to using the World Wide Web for research purposes. The social media release merely facilitates their research by using the latest tools (social bookmarking, RSS, etc.) to provide background data, context, and ongoing updates to clients' news.

- The social media release is also distinctive for tying together various multimedia elements in one place, enabling the journalist to view and/or "re-mix" media elements. For example, the journalist can learn more about the client's story via a demo video, or adapt the multimedia content for their own stories.[3]

A social media release has to offer the social media ingredients that will allow those reading it to utilize its message and information in a way best suited to *their*

---

[2] Ibid.

[3] Todd Defren, SHIFT Communications, SHIFT in the News, May 23, 2006, www.shiftcomm.com/Web20Releases/5232006.html.

needs. In short, a social media release should contain everything necessary to share and discover a story in a way that is complementary to your original intent while, at the same time, useful to your readers and enabling them to share and broadcast it. Giving everyone what they need in the best format for them to use it requires a different approach. Exhibit 7.15 is an aggregate of several SMR templates. As such, it pretty much covers the range of possibilities. Exhibits 7.16 and 7.17 show the first two iterations of the SHIFT template. Compare them with the information in Exhibit 7.15.[4]

Todd Defren discusses the purposes of his latest iteration of SMR template this way:[5]

- To highlight the importance of engagement: Version 1.5 includes a permalink to the newsmaker's online newsroom, which should be powered by a blogging engine to enable moderated comments and trackbacks. While a handful of wire services already enable comments, the best place for people to discuss the news is at the newsmaker's own site, which is not only an "official" spot for conversation but also aggregates any directly related posts via the trackbacks/pingbacks (a.k.a. "blogs that link to this news").

- To account for technology changes: The universal "Share This" widget (many variations exist) are great ways to allow end users to post/share information in *their* preferred format. In addition, since the publication of Version 1.0, we've seen services like Twitter and Facebook make a big impact on the social networking scene. While such social networking stars are only beginning to achieve true mainstream adoption, it's exciting to envision a day when we could not only read an executive spokesperson's official quote, but also have the option of following him or her via twitterstream or personal blog.

  Additionally, the inclusion of an OPML (outline processor markup language) feed allows the reader to instantly subscribe to all of a company's official blogs. As the Blog Council asks, "What do you do when hundreds or thousands of your employees have personal blogs?" At least one answer is: make it easy to find and track them all.

- To provide greater context: It's one thing to offer trackbacks, since those links clearly are relevant to the news release. But to provide even *more* value to the reader—especially to writers who may want to draft a big article or blog post—why not offer a "Sphere It" link? Sphere offers readers a chance to look at related news from the blogosphere and mainstream news sources. The Sphere Related Content Widget connects with an icon link at the end of a blog post. When a reader clicks on the icon link, he or she will find blog and media articles related to your blog posts.

- To tighten things up: Another challenge for Version 1.0 was the tendency of some companies to overdo it in terms of "relevant links." Thus, partly in

[4] For an excellent online example of an SMR, see http://smr.newswire.ca/en/cnw/cnw-group-launches-new-social-media-tool.

[5] Todd Defren, "Social Media Release Template, Version 1.5," at PR-Squared, www.pr-squared.com/2008/04/social_media_release_template.html.

Exhibit 7.15

SMR Template

- **Headline**—Keep it short, bold, uppercase, and use keywords.

- **Intro paragraph**—Make it rich with keywords, relevance, and context. Not everything can be pared down to bulleted lists. An intro paragraph presents the highlights of the SMR in paragraph form, allowing more room for tonality and perspective.

- **Supporting facts**—Short and to-the-point statements comprise the important takeaways that are the reason for the release. There is no technical limit on these highlights, only practical limits of brevity. These can be bulleted.

- **Quotes**—These are an easily identifiable and widely used element of the traditional press release. Calling out quotes as a unique field (sidebar, box, etc.) is good way to get them noticed. If a quote is necessary, there are a couple of ways to implement it into the SMR.

  - *Corporate quote:* Don't start with "We are excited . . ." or "We are thrilled . . ." Keep the quote on target explaining why this is a significant milestone.

  - *Expert or customer quote (if necessary):* Keep it related to the news and how the product/service benefits customers in real-world applications.

- **Embeddable video, audio, and other images**—Use existing RSS protocols for creating enclosures that enable practitioners to include logos, photos, audio clips, video, and other similar content along with the release. One of the best ways to link to images is to use social media photo sharing services such as flickr or zooomr. The best part about social media is the ability not only to share your photos with bloggers and reporters, but with the right tags, the pictures can also make their way onto the desktops of anyone searching for similar products/services for consumption and sharing.

- **RSS for the company and product information**—This can be a couple of sentences or just information on where to find and subscribe to all releases from the company, client, and product/service. The URL for this feed may exist on the company site or at a third-party location such as FeedBurner or PR Newswire. Additionally, it may serve as a location for all feeds from the company's blog or just the specific feed for the company's e-releases.

- **Technorati tags**—Technorati tracks the number of links and the perceived relevance of blogs, as well as the real-time nature of blogging. Technorati allows users to search by "tags" or keywords to help identify who's talking about areas of interest. With social media releases, readers also have access to your news—if tagged and published correctly.

- **Widgets**—These embedded links allow visitors to move around, print, share, archive, bookmark, or perform practically any other function. They often

(continued)

(continued)

appear as icons. Both the icons and the functionality can be obtained from a number of sources including widgetbox, KickApps, printfriendly, and ShareThis, among others.

- **Post in**—Post on the social network of your choice—Facebook, MySpace, LinkedIn.
- **Blog this**—Provides links to blogging platforms.
- **Share**—Feature on Twitter, Jaikue, Pownce or Tumblr
- **Bookmarks**—It's important to give readers a way to save the link, using their favorite tools. The idea is that you provide a means to enable social bookmarking which allows other people to find and share favorite things on the Web.
- **Relevant links**—Anything you think is important or can expand on your information in a positive way, including other company blog posts or Websites.
- **News Sharing**—This includes Digg, Reddit, and other relevant news aggregators and communities.
- **Comment**—You might also include a link to a hosted network on Ning or even a discussion forum on Tangler or Google Groups.
- **Contact**—Says how to contact you on hcard, vcard, LinkedIn, Facebook.

recognition to the tight editing enforced by services like Twitter, a good idea would be the optional inclusion of "3 Links That Matter" to give readers more info, context, and so on. If you get only three links, you'll be forced to make them *good* links.

Finally, remember that SMRs are only one way to tell your story. After all is said and done, Brian Solis reminds us that the same tools that help you expand visibility can also set you up for failure. Wire services edit only for typos, not for content. This means that you can publish a release riddled with hyperbole, spin, buzzwords, and hype that will only confuse and dissuade your customers from doing business with you. It will send them to your competition. And, as Todd Defren, the man who started it all, says,

It's important to understand that the Social Media News Release is not intended as a replacement for the traditional news release. It's an evolution. [Its] core function is simply to allow creators of news to leverage the Web familiarity that is now ingrained in consumer audiences. With 50+ percent of consumers now creating and sharing content online (Pew Research), it just makes sense to democratize access to corporate news and multimedia assets to anyone (reporters, bloggers, laypeople) who might be interested, and, to create a forum for community and context that—to date—has been unavailable via old-world press releases.[6]

[6] Todd Defren, quoted at www.socialmediarelease.org/2006/11/03/how-to-write-a-social-media-release-for-everyone-involved-in-pr-marketing-and-communications·

Exhibit 7.16

Social Media Press Release Template, Version 1.0

SHIFT
communications

SOCIAL MEDIA RELEASE
TEMPLATE, VERSION 1.0

CONTACT INFORMATION:	Client contact	Spokesperson	Agency contact
	Phone #/skype	Phone #/skype	Phone #/skype
	Email	Email	Email
	IM address	IM address	IM address
	Web site	Blog/relevant post	Web site

NEWS RELEASE HEADLINE
Subhead

CORE NEWS FACTS
• Bullet-points preferable

 LINK & RSS FEED TO PURPOSE-BUILT DEL.ICIO.US PAGE
The purpose-built del.icio.us page offers hyperlinks (*and PR annotation in "notes" fields*) to relevant historical, trend, market, product & competitive content sources, providing context as-needed, and, on-going updates.

PHOTO	MP3 FILE OR PODCAST LINK	GRAPHIC	VIDEO
e.g., product picture, exec headshot, etc.	e.g., sound bytes by various stakeholders	e.g., product schematic; market size graphs; logos	e.g., brief product demo by in-house expert

MORE MULTIMEDIA AVAILABLE BY REQUEST
e.g., "download white paper"

PRE-APPROVED QUOTES FROM CORPORATE EXECUTIVES, ANALYSTS, CUSTOMERS AND/OR PARTNERS
Recommendation: no more than 2 quotes per contact. The PR agency should have additional quotes at-the-ready, "upon request," for journalists who desire exclusive content. This provides opportunity for Agency to add further value to interested media.

LINKS TO RELEVANT COVERAGE TO-DATE (OPTIONAL)
This empowers journalist to "take a different angle," etc.
These links would also be cross-posted to the custom del.icio.us site.

BOILERPLATE STATEMENTS

 RSS FEED TO CLIENT'S NEWS RELEASES

"ADD TO DEL.ICIO.US"
Allows readers to use the release as a standalone portal to this news

 TECHNORATI TAGS/"DIGG THIS"

Exhibit 7.17

Social Media News Release Template, Version 1.5

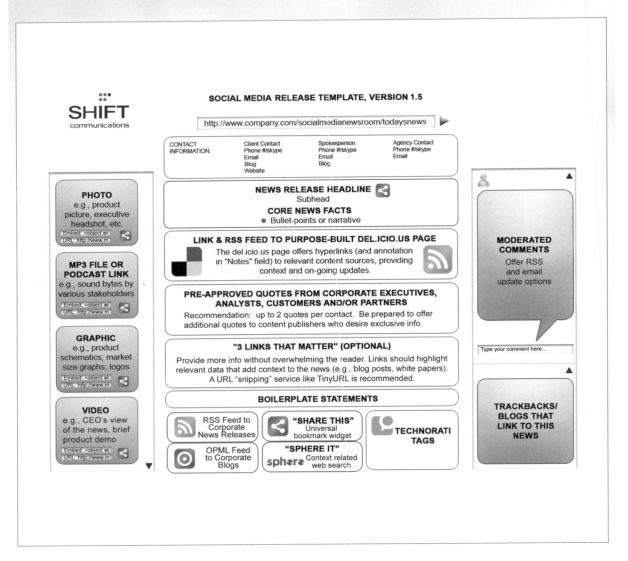

The Inbound Marketing News Release

HubSpot, a company that specializes in online marketing software, disputes the notion that the Social Media News Release (SMNR) is the best way to garner attention. Based on some pretty solid research, they have come up with a concept they call the "Inbound Marketing News Release" (IMNR). The idea is that, although the

SMNR is a good first step in adapting the traditional news release to the new Web format, it's limited for use in wire service distribution delivery systems. The problem seems to be with news release syndication. **Syndication** is the act of distributing your news release through web feeds, such as those provided by wire services. Much of the success of syndication is based on keywords picked up by search engines. The idea is to get those keywords, embedded in your published-in-full release (complete with links), on as many sites as possible in order to build "inbound" links to *your* site. These other Websites are called "portals" because they act as a gateway to your site. HubSpot suggests that concentrating on Search Engine Optimization (SEO) should be the main focus when attempting to build inbound links, because it will ultimately result in a better ranking on search engines such as Google.

Their research shows that traditional releases faired better than SMNRs over multiple wire distribution services. For example, traditional releases syndicated 20 percent more often than SMNRs. In addition, links contained in those traditional releases were syndicated 14 percent more often. They claim the problem is that many portal sites syndicating releases in full don't support such multi-media elements as anchor links, embedded video, photos, or audio—thus, those elements are wasted. They recommend the following "best practices" when crafting a news release:[7]

- Conduct keyword research to discover your best keywords. Use Google"s Keyword Tool to help you decide on which keywords to focus. Then use those keywords in your release, especially in anchor text. This will help in terms of SEO.

- Use a descriptive headline, limited to 80 characters or fewer. Lengthy headlines often get cut off on portal sites. In addition, because search engines treat a news release's headline as an H1 (Header) tag, it's beneficial to also make your headline keyword-rich.

- Limit your release to 300-500 words. All wire services HubSpot spoke with during their research agreed that this was the ideal length for a release. A longer release is a sign of verbose content, and a lengthy release also hinders its ability for syndication.

- Don't use formatting such as bullets, italics, and bold type. It may not transfer successfully when syndicated, and it complicates the coding.

- Don't embed multimedia elements. Instead of embedding a video or photo directly into the release, publish it somewhere on your own Website (such as on your company blog), and link to it in the release. This will save you money as well as drive traffic to and centralize interaction on your own Website. Regarding Links:

  - Put the most important link at the beginning. Some portal sites will automatically cut off your release after a certain word count. For the best chance of generating traffic back to your site, include the link to which you want to generate the most traffic early on in the release.

---

[7] This is an edited version of information appearing in HubSpot's free e-book, *How to Leverage Social Media for Public Relations Success*, downloadable at http://www.hubspot.com/Portals/53/docs/hubspot_social_media_pr_ebook.pdf. Hubspot's main site is located at http://www.hubspot.com/?source=social-media-pr-ebook.

- Always use anchor text (text that acts as a link to another site or resource). Not all portal sites will syndicate anchor text links, but for the ones that do, you'll receive maximum SEO benefit from inbound links utilizing anchor text.

- Use full URLs next to anchor text links for important links. Don't do this for every link, but do use it for the one to which you really want to drive traffic. This will ensure that the URL still gets pulled in when portal sites won't syndicate anchor text.

BACKGROUNDERS

Backgrounders are in-depth information pieces. As the name implies, they provide background information for anyone wishing it—reporters, ad copywriters, speechwriters, and editors. Backgrounders are almost always prepared by the public relations staff. A good backgrounder is comprehensive, yet concise. It should never be used to espouse company policy or philosophy—that is reserved for controlled media, such as ads and editorials.

Backgrounders frequently accompany news releases in media kits. They usually supply enough information to fill in any gaps left by the release. Often, they are just insurance against getting called in the middle of the night by a reporter who is editing your news release and in need of some background. Other times, they are important sales pieces, setting up a historical need for a new product.

To make a backgrounder comprehensive, the public relations writer must research as many sources as possible, including old articles, brochures, reports, news releases, and materials published outside the organization. Backgrounders can also benefit from personal interviews. As with news releases, backgrounders are more readable if they contain firsthand information.

A backgrounder should begin with a statement of the issue being addressed. Because it is not a news story or news release, it need not be presented as a lead nor need it follow the inverted pyramid style. Most backgrounders, however, do follow a basic pattern:

1. Open with a concise statement of the issue or subject on which the accompanying news release is based. Try to make it as interesting as possible. This opening statement should lead logically into the next section.

2. Follow the opening with a historical overview of the issue. You should trace its evolution—how it came to be—and the major events leading up to it. It is permissible here to use outside information. For instance, if you were writing a backgrounder on a new surgical technique, you would want to trace briefly the history of the technique's development and tie this in with information on techniques that had been used in the past. It is advisable to name your sources in the body of the text when appropriate. Readers of backgrounders want to know where you got your information.

3. Work your way to the present. This is the meat of your backgrounder. You want to explain the issue you opened with and its significance. Be factual. Remember, a backgrounder is an information piece, not an advertisement or the place to sell your company's philosophy.

4. Present the implications of the issue being discussed and point the direction for future applications. Even though a backgrounder is a public relations piece, it needs to be carefully couched in fact-based information.

5. Use subheads where appropriate. Subheads negate the need for elaborate transitions and allow you to order your information logically. Subheads need to be carefully chosen and should contribute to understanding.

6. Most backgrounders are four or five pages in length. Let your information dictate your length; however, don't become long winded or pad your document. Editors will recognize fluff immediately. The object of a backgrounder is to provide information and answer anticipated questions, nothing more.

The backgrounder in Exhibit 7.18 was used as an accompanying piece to a news release touting the advantages of fire-resistant latex foam for use in upholstered furniture and mattresses. After you have read it, consider the following questions:

- How does it follow the recommendations for writing a backgrounder?

- How does it differ?

- Does it trace the history of the issue adequately?

- Does it bring the reader up to the present and cover the current status of the issue?

Can you tell from reading this backgrounder that it was meant to sell a product? Probably not, unless you knew in advance that it was part of a product-related press kit. The object of a backgrounder is to provide background, not to sell anything. In this particular backgrounder, information is provided concerning fire safety and the need for purchasers of upholstered furniture to be aware of the dangers of fire.

The next step is to present readers with a suggested action. This can and often does come in the accompanying product news release. Thus, the trick to writing backgrounders is to make them relate to your subject without actually pushing your product, philosophy, or service.

FACT SHEETS

Fact sheets contain just that—facts—and nothing more. If you have several figures, a few charts that help explain your topic more easily, or a number of itemized points that you want to make, then a fact sheet is the form to use. A fact sheet is usually only one page, sometimes printed on both sides. It should elaborate on already presented information, such as a news release, and not merely repeat what has already been said.

For example, if you have written a news release about the relocation of a facility to a new site, the news release undoubtedly discloses the newsworthiness of the event with particulars on when the move is to take place, for what reasons, and the like. A fact sheet, however, can elaborate in

Exhibit 7.18

Backgrounder

CONTENTS, NOT STRUCTURE, POSE THE MOST FIRE HAZARDS

Losses to fires are costing billions of dollars and claiming thousands of lives each year in the United States. The National Fire Protection Association handbook states: "Fire resistive construction is an important life-safety measure. However, severe fires may occur in the contents of fire resistive buildings, and highly combustible decorations and interior finish materials may more than offset the value of noncombustible structurals." In fact, of all the contents common to residential, commercial, and institutional occupancies, the most often underestimated is the hazard from burning upholstered chairs and mattresses.

Although the many desirable features of a fire resistive building cannot be overlooked, there is no such thing as a "fireproof" building. Regardless of the construction type, there are always combustibles within the building. Generally, contents fires present a greater life safety hazard to building occupants than the eventual ignition of the structure. In fact, the cause and early stages of fires are related to the building contents and interior finish materials and not the structure.

No matter what the construction type, the contents fire must be controlled in order to achieve life safety. A parallel may be drawn between a contents fire in a fire resistive building and a fire in a furnace. The contents are the fuel and the building is the furnace.

Statistics Show Furniture Fires on the Rise

The Consumer Products Safety Commission recently stated that last year there were about 62,000 bedding fires which caused 930 fatalities. Another 35,000 fires in upholstered furniture took 1,400 lives, prompting the Commission to declare that these materials are the "biggest killer of all the products under the jurisdiction of the agency."

The National Bureau of Standards had earlier reported that mattresses, bedding, and upholstered furniture were involved in 45 percent of the fatal fires they reviewed where the materials first ignited could be identified. They concluded that "any inroads that can be made into the furniture problem promises greater fire-death reduction than any other type of strategy."

Building Design Not the Answer

As for building design, recent well-publicized fires have resulted in new provisions to building fire codes; however, over 90 percent of the buildings that will be in use in the year 2000 have already been built. Reliance on these new fire codes for personal safety may, in fact, be unwarranted.

Although building design and fire protection devices are important, they do not guarantee the

-more-

safety of the occupants. Many fires develop too rapidly for fire systems, such as sprinklers, to control. Fires can spread past a sprinkler head to another area before the sprinkler head operates. Another fire might smolder for hours, producing deadly smoke and gases but not enough heat to cause operation for the sprinkler system. In addition, property loss is most closely related to fire-resistant building materials which would have to be incorporated into future structures. Building contents most strongly affect human safety.

<u>Fire Reduction Not Yet a Reality</u>

A decade ago, the National Commission on Fire Prevention and Control reported that fire was a major national problem, ranking between crime and product safety in annual cost. They were appalled to find "that the richest nation in the world leads all the major industrialized countries in per capita deaths and property loss from fire." The efforts of this commission focused attention on fires and resulted in the establishment of a goal to reduce the nation's fire losses by 50 percent in the next decade. That goal has not be realized.

Recent fire loss data from the National Fire Prevention Association suggests that we have performed poorly in our efforts to reduce the nation's fire losses. Multiple death fires, killing three or more people, have increased 70 percent in the past decade. In fact, fatalities in this group rose 37 percent between 1972 and 1980, and fires in this category are increasing at an average rate of 7.5 percent a year.

The estimated property loss from just building fires in the United States last year was about $6 billion, an increase of almost 7 percent from the year before. Further analysis of the estimate for fire loss data this year shows that:

— Educational facilities lost $184 million, an increase of 82.2 percent over last year's figures.

— Institutional facilities lost $38 million, up 52 percent.

— Areas of public assembly lost $356 million, up 9.2 percent.

— And residential occupancies, such as hotels, motels, and apartments, lost $3.3 billion, up 7.1 percent from last year.

Judging from this data, it is apparent that the goal of reducing fire losses by 50 percent has not been met. In fact, fire losses are steadily increasing in most cases. Why? In answering this question,

(continued)

(continued)

some important points must be taken into consideration:

— Contents may more than offset the value of noncombustible building materials, and

— The flammability properties of the contents are critical to life safety.

Although most new buildings are constructed in accordance with a national building code such as the National Fire Protection Agency (NFPA) 101 Life Safety Code or a similar code, no national code regulates upholstered seating or mattresses. And although a Federal mattress flammability standard exists, its effectiveness has been questioned by both the Consumer Products Safety Commission and the National Bureau of Standards. As a result, a concrete fortress could be built according to code and filled with furniture that burns like gasoline. Larger buildings can contain tons of such furniture.

The Burden of Safety Is on the Buyer

In the absence of codes specifically meant for furniture, the burden of safety falls on the person selecting furniture for a residence, commercial structure, or installation. Greater care must be taken to select the most fire-resistant furniture available for a particular need. In judging these needs, the hazards to which the furniture might be exposed should be considered, such as the likelihood of cigarette burns, open flames, proximity of fuel or other combustibles, and population density. For example, in areas with a high level of vandalism, materials with a good open flame resistance might be needed, while furniture prone to accidental ignition may only need to be cigarette resistant.

The ultimate test of any furniture is, of course, how it will perform in an actual fire. It is obvious that fire-resistant structures are not enough to ensure life safety. If the nation's fire losses are to be reduced, then the potential hazards of furnishings must be considered.

-end-

interesting ways. For example, you might want to itemize costs, break out major donations made toward the move, or elaborate on size of facility with square-foot comparisons.

Take a look at Exhibits 7.19 and 7.20. These fact sheets are slightly different, but each contributes to forming a more complete story. The first fills in the numbers on a museum move, and the second supports a product press kit for a line of vitamins.

Exhibit 7.19

Fact Sheet

University of Northern Washington

Museum of Natural History Fact Sheet

The University of Northern Washington Museum of Natural History will move into a new building on the east side of campus by March of 1996. The museum is being relocated as part of the university's $45 million project to expand and modernize its science facilities.

Future Location:
On the northwest end of a university-owned parking lot on East 23rd Avenue, between Renton and Box Streets. The parking lot is being redesigned so that no parking spaces will be lost as a result of the new building.

Construction timeline:
Five months, beginning in late summer.

Cost:
$635,000

Fund-raising goal:
$150,000 to complete and equip the building.

Balance left to be raised by mid-August:
$72,500

Pledges to date: $77,000

- $32,500 from former UNW football coach Arlyss Thompson to build the storage area for the geology collection.

- $22,500 on a one-to-two challenge match pledged by Thompson for construction costs.

- $22,500 from Seattle philanthropist Frazier Crane, to match half of the Thompson challenge, on the condition that the rest of the money be raised from other sources.

Other funding sources:
$485,000 allocated by the university from the $8.1 million Department of Energy grant for the first phase of the capital construction program to build modern science facilities on campus.

Square feet:
11,000 with a 9,100 square-foot courtyard. Total square footage of existing building is 10,689.

Special features:
Air-conditioned and climate-controlled to protect the highly fragile collections.

Advantages:
Improved public access and increased public parking.

# # # # #

2900 Provender Drive · Alderdale, Washington 99304 · (206) 345-8749

Exhibit 7.20

Fact Sheet

VITAMIX VITALSTATS

Vitamix International
P.O. Box 9234
Westphalen, Ohio 76456

Vitamix Vital Statistics

- About 2/3 of U.S. households reported making dietary changes in the past survey year for reasons of health or nutrition. Of these, 43% cited weight control as the primary reason for the changes.

- 53% of the adult population surveyed have tried to control weight during the past year by "staying away from fattening foods and/or eating less"—up from 48% the year before.

- 18% of the adult population surveyed this year reported the use of "low-fat" food/beverage options as part of weight control strategy.

Population Overweight/Obese

- According to the data collected in the most recent Health and Weight Loss Survey (HWLS), 32% of the men and 36% of the women aged 20-27 were 10 percent or more above their desirable weight.

- 14% of the men and 24% of the women were 20 percent or more above their desirable weight in the same HWLS survey.

- 7 million Americans are classified as extremely obese.

- 30% of all males and 49% of all females surveyed by the National Center for Vital Statistics said they considered themselves overweight.

- More than half of those surveyed in a recent Aerobic 4 National Fitness Survey said "it would be beneficial to lose weight."

Weight Control Diets

- At any given time, at least 20% of the population are on some kind of weight-loss diet.

- 33% of those surveyed in the Aerobic 4 National Fitness Survey said they are dieting either to lose or maintain weight.

- 56% of women aged 25-34 said they were dieting in a recent Nielsen Survey.

# # # # #

KEY TERMS

news release	delayed lead	media advisory
publicity release	attribution	Search engine
product release	dateline	optimized (SEO)
financial release	exclusive	releases
publicity	special	social media
angle	event announcement	releases (SMRs)
inverted pyramid style	personnel release	syndication
lead	tips/hints release	backgrounder
summary lead	pitch letter	fact sheet

CHAPTER

8

Controlled Publications

In This Chapter, You Will Learn

- The various types of newsletters and why they are used.
- How to research, write, and design a newsletter, both digital and traditional.
- The purpose of house magazines and how to create them.
- How to write in the feature style.
- How to plan, write, and design a brochure.

- How to plan, write, and design flyers and posters.
- The differences among brochures, booklets, and hybrids.
- What a nonprofit annual report is and how it differs from a corporate annual report.
- The contents of a typical nonprofit annual report.

Controlled publications are those over which the writer, editor, and client/ organization have nearly complete control. This generally means that everything from the research to the actual publication of the piece is in the hands of those who produce it. Unlike news releases or news conferences, the end message is unaltered by pass-along gatekeepers, such as the media. Controlled publications may take any form, including those covered in this chapter. Using controlled publications ensures that your message will be received exactly as you wrote it. Sometimes, you just don't want to be edited.

NEWSLETTERS

Every day in the United States, thousands of **newsletters** are published and distributed to hundreds of thousands of readers. Despite the rise of digital publication, thousands of print newsletters are still produced each year in this country. Most newsletters are internal publications in the sense that they reach a highly unified public—employees, shareholders, members, volunteers, voting constituencies, and others with a common interest. In fact, if you ask any self-respecting communication professional for the most effective means of reaching a primarily internal audience, the response will most likely be the newsletter.

Types of Newsletters

Newsletters are as varied as the audiences who read them; however, they do break down into several different types:

- *Association newsletters* help a scattered membership with a common interest keep in touch. Profit and nonprofit associations and almost every trade association in the United States publish newsletters for their members, often at both national and regional levels.

- *Community group newsletters* are often used by civic organizations to keep in touch with members, announce meetings, and stimulate attendance at events. The local YWCA or Boys Club newsletter might announce their schedules, whereas a community church group newsletter distributed throughout surrounding neighborhoods might be a tool for increasing membership.

- *Institutional newsletters,* perhaps the most common type of newsletter, are usually distributed among employees. Used by profit and nonprofit organizations, they are designed to give employees a feeling of belonging. They frequently include a balanced mix of employee-related information and news about the company.

- *Publicity newsletters* often create their own readers. They can be developed for fan clubs, resorts (some resort hotels mail their own newsletters to previous guests), and politicians. Congressional representatives often use newsletters to keep their constituencies up-to-date on their activities.

- *Special-interest newsletters* developed by special-interest groups tend to grow with their following. *Common Cause,* for instance, began as a newsletter and has grown into a magazine representing the largest lobbying-interest group in the United States.

- *Self-interest or "digest" newsletters* are designed to make a profit. The individuals or groups who develop them typically offer advice or present solutions to problems held in common by their target readers. These often come in the form of a sort of digest of topics of interest to a certain profession. In the public relations profession, for instance, you'll find *PR Reporter, PR News, Communicate, O'Dwyer's Newsletter, Communication Briefings,* and many more.

Why a Newsletter?

Why indeed? Most newsletters address an internal public, with the exception of those that target single-interest groups—such as professionals and executives—outside a formal organizational structure. The goal of most newsletters, then, is communication with a largely internal public (see Exhibit 8.1).

Downward and Upward Communication

In the ideal organizational structure, communication flows both vertically (upward and downward) and horizontally. The newsletter is a good example of **downward communication.** It fulfills part of management's obligation to provide its employees formal channels of communication. **Upward communication** provides employees a means of communicating their opinions to management. Ideally, even downward communication channels such as newsletters permit upward communication through letters to the editor, articles written by employees, surveys, and so forth. Newsletters can also provide horizontal communication (that is, a newsletter that covers a whole industry and is distributed among similar organizations), but this type of newsletter is rarely produced within an organization; rather, it originates from outside.

Newsletter or Something Else?

Why a newsletter instead of a magazine, booklets, bulletin boards, or (heaven forbid) more meetings? You can ask yourself several questions when deciding whether a newsletter is the publication that best suits your purpose:

- What is the purpose of the publication? Is it to entertain? Inform? Solicit?

- What is the nature and scope of the information that you wish to present? Longer information is probably better suited to a longer publication such as a magazine; shorter, to brochures or folders. If your information is strictly entertaining or human interest in nature, it may also be better received within a magazine format.

Exhibit 8.1

Newsletter Examples

EWEB NEWS YOU CAN USE

SPRING 2003

Pipeline

EWEB cuts budget to shield customers from lingering effects of energy crisis, BPA electricity rate increases

RATES UPDATE

ike other public utilities in the Northwest, the Eugene Water & Electric Board gets most of its electricity from the Bonneville Power Administration.

This federal agency is responsible for marketing hydroelectric power generated at three dozen dams in the Northwest. The BPA supplies Northwest homes, businesses and schools from Everett to Ashland with almost half the electricity they need.

For decades, EWEB and other public utility customers have enjoyed the benefits of plentiful, ultra-cheap power produced by these hydroelectric dams. EWEB currently buys almost 70 percent of the power it needs from Bonneville (the rest comes mainly from EWEB's own hydroelectric facilities).

But as every electricity consumer in the Northwest knows, power isn't so cheap any more. Bonneville, rocked by a financial crisis brought on by the 2001 energy crisis, increased the price of electricity it sells to utilities by almost 50 percent in October 2001. These local utilities, including EWEB, were forced to pass on those higher costs to consumers.

Generators convert water into electricity at Bonneville Dam, which was built in 1938.

But while the West Coast energy "crisis" has begun to fade from memory, its impact on electricity costs has not. Since late 2001, Bonneville has continued to increase the price of the electricity it sells to Northwest utilities and has announced it may raise rates by another 15 percent or more again this October.

EWEB's elected commissioners, well aware that the poor economy has put financial hardships on many customers, have been wrestling with these ever-increasing Bonneville-related power costs, which will reach almost $10 million by early fall.

Fortunately for customers, EWEB has cut its budget substantially and has found a number of one-time cost savings to avoid raising electric rates so far. These $9 million in cuts and other savings include freezing wages and salaries, reducing the work force by 6 to 10 employees, putting off new vehicle purchases, cutting conservation services and reducing the hours EWEB offices are open to the public.

"EWEB commissioners have worked hard to minimize rate increases by cutting the utility's budget

continued on page four

EWEB

OPPORTUNITIES to speak to the elected Board that guides EWEB.

Founded in 1911, the Eugene Water & Electric Board is one of the oldest publicly owned electric utilities in the Northwest. Today, EWEB is Oregon's largest customer-owned utility.

The citizens of Eugene elect a five-member Board of Commissioners, which retains full control of the utility and sets policies that guide its operation.

Commissioners meet on the first and third Tuesdays of every month, beginning at 7:30 p.m., in the North Building at 500 E. Fourth Ave. Time is reserved at each meeting for you to speak to the Board on any utility-related issue.

In This Issue

FEATURES

Rates Update

ENERGY STAR®

Slow the Flow

New Board Member

HIGHLIGHTS

Earth Works

Quick Read

McKenzie Currents

(continued)

(continued)

WINTER ISSUE 2000

FRESH AIR

JOURNAL

Windpower and Wildlife

In terms of the environment, no energy resource is entirely benign – even windpower. A key issue for windpower is the potentially negative effect on both resident and migratory bird populations, particularly raptors such as eagles, hawks and other birds of prey.

Since the Foote Creek Rim wind project in Wyoming included the Bonneville Power Administration, the federal National Environmental Policy Act (NEPA) required a formal Environmental Impact Statement (EIS). Part of this extensive on-site assessment included surveys and field studies of resident and migratory bird populations, as well as other wildlife.

Because of the rural nature of the Foote Creek Rim environment, a variety of birds were identified during a number of site surveys. Specifically, the EIS noted the presence of several native species of raptors and other birds that are on — or are candidates for — the Endangered Species Act (ESA) list. The list included bald eagles, peregrine falcons and mountain plovers.

In addition to their listing as a threatened species under the ESA, bald eagles are also afforded protection under the Bald Eagle Protection Act. While some bald eagles were sited during the surveys, no nests were found within the project area.

At the time of the surveys in 1994, peregrine falcons were listed as endangered under the ESA. However, while a small number of these birds were reported in the project area, no nesting sites were identified. In 1999, the U.S. Fish and Wildlife Service removed the peregrine falcon from the list of threatened and endangered species. Even though the peregrine falcon is no longer on the list, the bird's recovery rate will continue to be monitored.

At the same time, the mountain plover was considered a "species of concern," but was not formally listed. Today, however, the mountain plover is proposed for listing as a threatened species, and mature birds and nesting sites were found at the project site.

A Peregrine Falcon (Falco peregrinus)

Wind Turbine Design Focuses on Protective Measures

Once the EIS was completed, the permit focused on a number of "reasonable and prudent measures" that the developer, SeaWest Energy Corporation, could integrate into the design of the project to reduce the impact on these birds. SeaWest also consulted with other federal agencies, including the Bureau of Land Management and the Wyoming Game and Fish Department. As a result, the project designers incorporated a number of protective measures into the design of the facility to keep the impact of the wind machines on bird species to a minimum.

For example, a key measure was to locate the wind turbines away from the edge of the rim, where resident raptors tend to soar on wind currents while hunting. Another design feature was to paint the turbine and blades with an ultraviolet coating to make them more visible to birds.

see BIRDS page 2

Fresh Air Journal is a publication of Eugene Water & Electric Board for EWEB customers who support energy resources that are renewable, sustainable and have minimal impact on the environment.

EWEB
Windpower.

Once a newsletter is deemed a successful way to reach constituents, many companies use them for multiple purposes. Here we see two different uses of the newsletter format from the same company. *Pipeline* is the regular quarterly newsletter of the Eugene (Oregon) Water and Electric Board. It is large (11 × 15½ inches) and is printed in full color. Its general focus is news about how to save energy and its associated costs. *Fresh Air Journal* contains information specific to wind generation of power. It is a more standard 8½ × 11 inches in size and is also printed in full color.

- Who, exactly, are you trying to reach? All employees from the top down? A select few (the marketing department, the credit department, the vice president in charge of looking out windows)?

- How often do you need to publish it to realize the objectives that you set in answering the previous questions? Newsletters are best suited to situations requiring a short editorial and design lead time.

Newsletters are best for small publication runs and information that needs a quick turnover. They handle information that is considered necessary but disposable (much like a newspaper, which in a sense the newsletter mimics). However, this is generally but not universally true. Many fine newsletters are designed to be kept. Health and financial newsletters, for instance, are often hole-punched so that the reader can save them in ring binders. For the most part, though, they are considered disposable.

Content

To determine a newsletter's content, you must first know your audience. Is it totally internal or a combination of internal and external? Your audience and its interests will dictate, to a large extent, the topic and direction of your articles.

Depending on the type of newsletter that you are publishing, the focus will be broad or narrow. For example, when you write for an internal, employee public, you must carefully balance information with entertainment. You must please management by providing information that it wants to see in print, and you must please the employees by providing information that they want to read. Otis Baskin and Craig Aronoff, in their book *Public Relations: The Profession and the Practice*, present a rule of thumb for an appropriate mix in an internal publication (not necessarily a newsletter) aimed primarily at an employee audience:

- 50 percent information about the organization—local, national, and international

- 20 percent employee information—benefits, quality of working life, and so on

- 20 percent relevant noncompany information—competitors, community, and the like

- 10 percent small talk and personals

Given that most newsletters are fairly short, such a complete mix may be impractical; however, a close approximation will probably work. Remember, though, that this mix is appropriate only for publications such as institutional newsletters.

By comparison, most horizontal publications tend to focus on items of interest to a more narrowly defined target public. For example, a newsletter for telecommunications executives may concentrate on news about that industry, omitting human-interest items, small talk, or industry gossip. In fact, almost every newsletter targeted to executives contains only short, no-nonsense articles. The reason, of course, is that busy executives simply don't have the time to read the type of article that interests the average employee.

Objectives

Newsletters, like any well-managed publication, will achieve best results if objectives are set and all actions follow logically from them. Objectives relate to your publication's editorial statement. Editorial statements shouldn't be pie-in-the-sky rhetoric; they should reflect the honest intent of your publication. If your intent is to present management's story to employees, then say so up front. An editorial statement can be an objective, or it can serve as a touchstone for other objectives.

For example, from the editorial statement in the previous paragraph, you could reasonably derive an objective such as "To raise the level of awareness of management policies among all employees by X percent over the next year" or "To provide an open line of upward and downward communication for both management and employees." Whatever your objectives, make sure they are measurable. Then, you can point to your success in reaching them over the period of time you specified. You should also have some means by which to measure the success of your objectives. If your objective is simply "To present management's message to employees," how will you measure its success or failure? Don't you want to find out if just presenting the message was enough? How will you tell if employees even read your message or, if they did, whether they responded in any way?

Make your objectives realistic and measurable, and once you have set them, follow them. Use them as a yardstick by which to measure every story you run. If a story doesn't help realize one of your objectives, don't run it. If you just can't live without running it, maybe your objectives aren't complete enough.

Scheduling and Budgeting

Scheduling and budgeting for newsletters and magazines are similar, except that magazines are longer and a bit more complex, so the schedule will necessarily be longer and the budget larger. Other than that, the same elements that were called for in general budgeting in Chapter 3 applies here. Take a look at Exhibit 8.2 for a generic scheduling format for both newsletters and magazines.

Articles

Most newsletters are journalistic in style. They usually include both straight news and feature stories and range from informal to formal depending on the organization and its audience. Usually, the smaller the organization, the less formal the newsletter will be. Large corporations, by contrast, often have a very formal newsletter with a slick format combining employee-centered news with company news.

The responsibility for writing the newsletter is almost always handled in-house, although some agencies produce newsletters on contract for organizations. In-house personnel tend to be more in tune with company employees and activities. Sometimes the writing is done in-house, and the production—including design, layout, and printing—is done by an agency.

Exhibit 8.2

Production Scheduling Form

Sample Production Schedule

The basic work of determining target audiences, basic design and format, paper and ink, budget, printing process, and frequency and distribution is assumed to have been accomplished prior to beginning the actual production process. What remains is the sequence of events common to the physical production of each issue.

Activity	Responsibility	Date Accomplished
Decide on basic content for current issue.		
Determine number and type and approximate length of stories.		
Make up dummy layout for current issue.		
Gather information and/or interview appropriate sources.		
Write first draft.		
Obtain critiques and edit first draft.		
Create artwork for each story (photos taken, illustrations created or obtained, charts/graphs created, and so on).		
Write final draft.		
Obtain critiques, edit final draft, and copy-fit articles to dummy.		
Write headlines, captions, pull quotes, and copy-fit to layout.		
Fit artwork to layout.		
Finalize and proof layout.		
Send to printer.		
Check proofs.		

If you produce your own newsletter, you are limited only by expense and imagination. A standard newsletter is usually 8½ × 11 inches or 11 × 17 inches folded in half. It averages in length from two to four pages and is frequently folded and mailed. Many are designed with an address area on the back for mailing.

Article length varies. Some newsletters contain only one article, whereas others include several. An average four-page newsletter uses about 2,000 words of copy. Depending on the focus of the newsletter, articles can range in length from digest articles of less than 100 words to longer articles of 600 words for newsletters that cover only one or two topics per issue. The trend today is toward shorter articles, especially for the newsletter aimed at the businessperson or corporate executive. Even for the average employee, newsletter articles usually need to be brief.

Because newsletters inform and entertain, articles should be written in an entertaining way. Usually, news about the company or strictly informational pieces utilize the standard news story style, except that there is no need to use the inverted pyramid because newsletter stories are seldom edited for space from the bottom up. Employee-interest pieces tend to use the feature story style. Feature-type articles for newsletters should be complete, with a beginning and an ending (see more detailed discussion of feature writing later in this chapter).

Story Ideas

There are many ways to come up with acceptable ideas for articles. Sometimes you might receive ideas from employees or management. Sometimes a news release or a short piece done for another publication will spark enough interest to warrant a full-blown newsletter article. Whatever the source of the idea, you must evaluate the topic based on reader interest and reader consequence.

If you're familiar with your audience members' tastes, you can quickly determine their interests. To evaluate consequence, ask yourself what they will learn from the article. Although light reading is fun for some, an organizational publication isn't usually the place to engage in it.

Every newsletter editor will tell you that getting story ideas isn't all that hard. Finding someone to write the stories is. There are several methods for enlisting writers. If you are putting out an in-house publication, try assigning beats like at a newspaper. If you're lucky enough to have a staff, assign them to different types of stories perhaps by department or division or by product or service. If you don't have a staff, rely on certain people in each department or division to submit stories to you. Sometimes the simple promise of seeing their name in print is enough inducement.

You can also send employees a simple request form, spelling out exactly what you are looking for. The information you get back will be sketchy, but you can flesh it out with a few phone calls (see Exhibit 8.3). This is an especially good method of gathering employee-related tidbits that don't deserve an entire story but should still be mentioned. One method for organizing your shorter stories is to group them according to topic. For example, group all stories relating to employee sports, employee community involvement, employee promotions, and so on.

Exhibit 8.3

Employee Information Sheet

Employee Information Form
For Newsletter Articles

Employee Name: _____

Department: _____

Position: _____

Do you have any information pertaining to promotions, awards, service recognition, etc. that might be of interest to fellow employees? If so, please give details below.

Do you have any story ideas for the employee newsletter?
Please list your suggestions below.

If you are directly involved in any of the above information, would you be willing to be interviewed?

Would you be willing to write any or all of an article relating to any of the ideas mentioned above?

Please return this form to the Corporate Communications Department, #302.

Of course, if your publication is a narrowly focused horizontal publication, you may end up doing most of the research and writing yourself. Many such newsletters are truly one-person operations. Because desktop publishing allows a single person to act as reporter, editor, typesetter, and printer, this type of publication is enjoying a rebirth.

Whatever system you use to gather stories, as editor you will probably be doing most of the writing as well as the editing.

Researching Stories

If you write most of your own stories, you know that every topic must be researched thoroughly. The first step in a normal research process is to do a literature search to determine whether your article has already been written. If it has, but you still want to explore the topic for your specific audience, then try another angle.

Next, gather background information. Try to get specifics. You can't write about something you don't know a lot about personally. It also pays to get first-hand information. Interview people who know something about your topic. You will not only get up-to-date information but also may end up with some usable quotes and some new leads. (see Chapter 3 on interviewing tips.)

Believe it or not, you can't find everything on the Internet. Don't forget the library. Many a fine article has been written based on a library visit. Library research is among the most valuable and one of the cheapest forms of research. In any event, most articles will be fairly complete and accurate if you do a little background research and conduct an interview or two. Because newsletter articles are usually short, this is about all the information that you can use.

Design Considerations

No discussion of newsletters would be complete without some mention of design. Most people who engage in newsletter writing and editing today also lay out their own newsletters. With the plethora of publication design software now available that job has become increasingly easy.

We've already seen how most newsletters are simply 11 × 17-inch pages folded in half, giving us four panels, or pages, to work with. However, once we include the design elements that will make our newsletter attractive enough to be picked up by readers, there's not all that much room left for words. Exactly how much room will depend on your design capabilities.

What most designers especially love about newsletters is the wide variety of available formats. Just picking one can be a challenge. A newsletter can take on any number of disguises, ranging from the standard 11 × 17-inch format folded down to a four-page 8½ × 11-inch size, to a lengthy magazine-like format folded and stapled, to a tabloid newspaper, to a tabloid-sized magazine-type format known as a magapaper. Audience needs and cost are the most important deciding factors in picking a format for your newsletter.

No matter what format you ultimately decide on, you will be stuck with it for quite some time. If you are going to have enough information to fill a 12-page magazine format four times a year—good, use a magazine format. If not, try something smaller. If you need to insert your newsletter in a monthly billing envelope, try something even smaller. If size is what attracts your audience and you usually don't have to mail your newsletter, try a magapaper or a tabloid (even these can be mailed—they just cost a lot more).

Whatever you decide, remember that your design elements must fit your format. Large formats call for larger artwork. Small formats call for shorter articles. White space is an extravagance in a bill stuffer but not in a tabloid. Folding and mailing differ immensely among the various sizes. Suit your format to your needs.

The well-designed newsletter won't shout "look at my look." Instead, it will simply say "pick me up and read me." More than anything else, the design that you choose and the skill that you use in implementing that design will be nearly subliminal to the message you impart. As mentioned earlier, the nonverbal message imparted through choices of paper, color, and format is as important as anything you have to say. If you fail to entice your readers through these subtle nuances, you may not have any readers.

To get the most out of a newsletter, you must design it with your target audience always in mind. Are they a conservative, business executive group? Shouldn't your newsletter reflect that conservatism? Are they an artistic, easygoing audience? Shouldn't your newsletter appeal to their sense of freedom of expression? In fact, your newsletter has to appeal to your readers' sense of what is correct for them—both in the information that you provide and in the packaging providing that information.

Take a look at Exhibit 8.4 for some of the essential elements of a newsletter front page. Although there isn't time or space to cover newsletter design in detail here, refer to Chapter 9 for more information on design and working with printers.

Style Sheets

To maintain consistency in your newsletter from issue to issue, you will need to develop a style sheet. A **style sheet** is a listing of all the type specifications that you use in your newsletter. It should be as complete as possible, and every member of your staff should have a copy. Style sheets are especially important if you are sick or on vacation and someone else has to produce an issue or two of your newsletter. It will tell at a glance what it probably took you hours to determine when you first started. As you can see from the simple style sheet shown in Exhibit 8.5, you'll have to make numerous design considerations as editor of your own newsletter. The fun is in the experimenting. Don't give up until you have it the way you want it.

CREATING A DIGITAL NEWSLETTER

Although writing for newsletters hasn't changed much, how the newsletter is "published" and distributed has. Digital newsletters have become by far the cheapest method of distributing organizational information, and depending on how much effort you want to put into design, possibly the easiest to lay out. A digital, or electronic, newsletter can be emailed, posted on your Website or social media page, and can reach your constituents the minute it's published. How you decide to distribute your newsletter will dictate how you construct it.

Exhibit 8.4

Newsletter Front Page

This illustration shows some of the more important design elements of a typical newsletter. (1) The banner, or name, of your newsletter. Make sure that it neither overpowers your front page nor is overpowered by other elements on the page. (2) The headline. Typically, there should be only one major head on the front page. Make it large enough to draw attention but not so large as to overpower your banner. (3) Photos and illustrations. Don't scrimp on size. Draw attention to your stories with large photos and illustrations. Just make sure that they are of a quality worthy of the attention. (4) Body copy. Flush left, ragged right if columns are wide (two or three columns); justified if narrow (four or more columns). (5) Table of contents. Don't assume that it has to be boxed. Try an open format for a change. (6) Rules and boxes. Use them to delineate your columns or to set apart items.

Exhibit 8.5

Newsletter Style Sheet

As you can see from this simple style sheet, you'll have to make numerous design considerations as editor of your own newsletter. The fun is in the experimenting. Don't give up until you have it the way you want it.

Style Sheet: <u>On Line</u>

Newsletter of the Public Relations Student Society of America, University of Oregon Chapter

<u>Page size</u>—11 × 17 inches, one-page, printed front and back, vertical tabloid layout. Margins 3/4 inch on all sides. Folded in thirds for mailing. Self-mailer on bottom third of back page. Sixty-pound white, semimatte finish.

<u>Grid</u>—Five columns for normal text layout. Four or five columns for boxed or feature items. One pica between columns with a hairline rule.

<u>Body text</u>—10-point Times, auto leaded, flush left, first indents 1/4 inch.

<u>Captions</u>—9-point Times italic, flush left, run width of photo, 1/2 pica beneath photo.

<u>Lead article headline</u>—24-point Optima bold, set solid, reversed on 40% screen. Run full width of page (five columns).

<u>Two- and three-column heads</u>—18-point Optima bold, leaded 19, flush left running width of article. Reversed on 40% screen.

<u>Pull quotes</u>—14-point Optima italic, centered, one- to three-column width as needed. Two-point line 1 pica above and 1-point line below as needed to fill space.

<u>Masthead copy</u>—9-point Optima, flush left, one-column width.

<u>Ink color</u>—Black ink run on preprinted blanks with banner in PMS 4515.

You have basically two options: You can send it via e-mail or you can build it directly on your Website. If you e-mail it, it can be in a PDF downloadable format or an HTML (Hypertext Markup Language) format.

Online Versions

- An e-mailed PDF newsletter requires that recipients have either e-mail or Internet access and Adobe Acrobat Reader (which is a free download) installed on their computers. PDF newsletters can be laid out just like traditional print newsletters, which gives you a chance to show off your design skills. The downside is that, depending on the compression rate you choose to save the finished layout, it can download very slowly, which can be annoying to readers. This type of newsletter can also be placed online and downloaded. See Exhibit 8.6.

Exhibit 8.6

Digital PDF-format Newsletter

This association newsletter is designed in a typical layout program and converted to PDF format for distribution. It can be sent via e-mail as an attachment or downloaded directly from a Website. It can also contain links to online resources which will open on a Web browser when clicked.

- An HTML e-mail will reach anybody with an e-mail account, but they'll need Internet access and an HTML-capable Web browser. When a reader opens the e-mail in HTML format, it looks just as it would online, complete with your layout and graphic elements.

- A Web-based newsletter will give you the opportunity to upload your newsletter to your site, in any format you like but readers must have Internet access, and they must access your Website to read or download it. If you put it online, it's also easy to archive (see Exhibit 8.8). An online HTML newsletter will show up the same as any other element on your Website. A PDF newsletter will have to be downloaded from your site, and has the same issues as an e-mailed PDF newsletter.

E-mail Versions

If you opt for an HTML newsletter that will be e-mailed, you'll need a template. Fortunately, there are plenty of free, downloadable templates online. Of course, if you can code in HTML, or know someone who can, you could develop your own template. Most HTML templates have at least two columns. All you do is select the column and enter your information. You can also copy and paste from a word-processing program right onto the template. An HTML newsletter also allows you to embed links that can take readers to information related to the article they're reading, or to other resources that may be available on our Website. Typically, HTML templates include a table of contents where you can enter the titles of your articles along with brief descriptions that link directly to the articles. As with a traditional newsletter, you'll want to set up a design and style that will become familiar to your readers, and stick with it. The template is reusable. See Exhibit 8.7.

If you decide on e-mail distribution, you'll need a mailing list—either one you've compiled yourself or, more typically, one that is purchased from an e-mail marketing service. Most of these services charge by the number of addresses. And, even if e-mail is your primary distribution method, it's always a good idea to post the newsletter to your Website.

If you decide to put your newsletter exclusively online, you have at least two options: a 100 percent online newsletter (typically in HTML format) or a downloadable PDF format. Both will allow you to embed links. The only difference is that if you provide links in a PDF downloadable format, every time a link is selected, your Web browser will have to open to display the link.

Whichever method you choose, feedback is important. Select a measurement tool that will provide you with numbers of people who opened your e-mailed newsletter or accessed your online newsletter. Include a way to collect information on what they read and what links they clicked on. This will help you to determine what was of most interest and allow you to adjust in subsequent issues to their needs and interests.

Some Writing Tips

Most of what was covered under writing for traditional newsletters is true for digital newsletters. Keep your articles short. Keep your headlines brief and on point. However, for digital newsletters, you have the potential to increase readership by using the same Search Engine Optimization (SEO) techniques covered under digital news releases and other digital forms elsewhere in this book. This means that key words are important if you want to drive traffic to your newsletter via search engines.

Exhibit 8.7

An Online HTML Newsletter

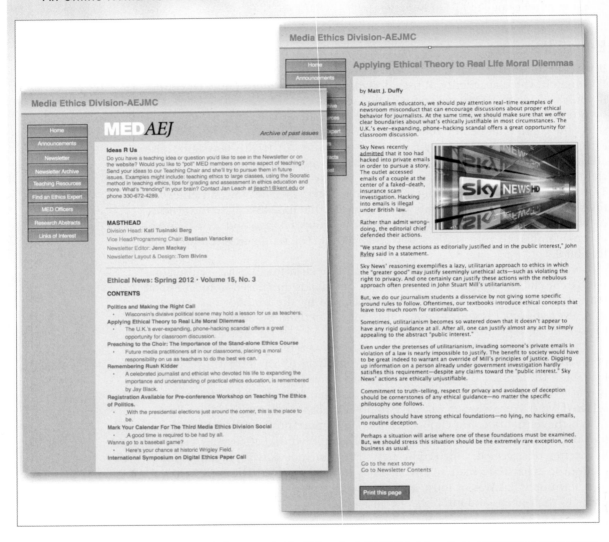

This online newsletter succeeded the PDF version in Exhibit 8.6. It is easier to put together, easier to change copy and make corrections, instantly accessible, provides more opportunity for linking to other information, and easily archived online for access to earlier issues. The "cover" contains the table of contents which contains anchor links to the stories' individual stories. Each story page contains a link-back to the contents page and link-forward to the next story.

Exhibit 8.8

HTML Pages Saved as PDF Files

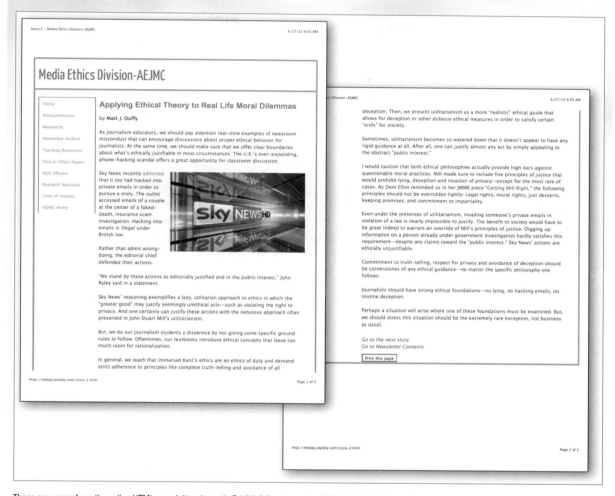

These are pages from the online HTML newsletter shown in Exhibit 8.7 and saved as PDF files, which allows for easy archiving. An additional benefit is that the links on the saved PDF remain active.

Your lead story and lead paragraph are the places to embed your keywords. What you put at the top of your newsletter will receive the most attention, and the links you place there will usually get the most clicks. However, because a newsletter is composed of a number of different articles, often on different, yet related, subjects, don't forget to scatter keywords into each article, close to the top, and especially in headlines.

MAGAZINES

When we speak of magazines, most of us think of our favorite consumer publication (for example, *Time, Newsweek, National Geographic,* and *Atlantic Monthly*); however, we are speaking primarily but not exclusively of the house publication. Recent research has shown that house publications are the least looked to form of organizational communication. Guess what's first? Face-to-face communication. That's not surprising, but it doesn't mean that the house magazine is dead (although it has taken on some new forms in the computer age). What it does mean is that the magazine should contribute to open communication rather than be relied upon as the sole source. It also plays another role. Unlike most print media an organization that might have access to, the house publication is a totally controlled medium—that is, the organization producing it has sole editorial control. The company can go on record through its house organ, state its position on a controversial issue, or simply tell its story its way. In other words, the house organ is still a good public relations tool.

The typical house organ is meant for an internal public—usually employees, shareholders, and retirees. Sometimes, though, it is offered to the external public. A publication like *Weyerhaeuser Today* stresses a broader emphasis with articles often dealing with the industry as a whole and subjects of interest to those outside the company. Because the house organ is, at bottom, still a public relations piece, its thrust remains company oriented. Even a seemingly unrelated story will, in some way, eventually relate to the organization.

The house publication is usually in either magazine or newspaper format (or sometimes in the hybrid magapaper format). Both communicate with their various publics efficiently. Unless the company is large enough to produce a slick in-house publication, the house organ will be sent out to an agency for design and printing. Sometimes the agency will even provide writers to work up the stories; however, the best articles still come from writers inside the company who know and work with the people they write about.

Content and Format

Like their smaller cousin, the newsletter, house magazines usually present the following editorial mix:

- 50 percent information about the organization—local, national, and international
- 20 percent employee information—benefits, quality of working life, raises, and so on
- 20 percent relevant noncompany information—competitors, the community, and so on
- 10 percent small talk and personals

How you organize these elements is important. You should lead your reader through your magazine in a logical order that is pleasing and interesting. There is no single organizational format for house magazines. What is important is that you find a place for all relevant information, a place inclusive enough to house similar information from issue to issue.

Before you even start (or if you're overhauling an existing publication), you need to set some objectives. To make sure that your reasons for publishing a house magazine are realistic, ask yourself some questions:

- Are my goals and objectives consistent with the goals and objectives of the organization itself? What am I really trying to get out of this? The temptation is very real, especially for creative people, to produce a magazine for simple ego gratification. Don't succumb to it. Have good, solid reasons for publishing.

- Can I attain these objectives through another, more effective method? Can I achieve good downward communication through an existing newsletter or more frequent meetings?

- Can I attain these objectives in a more cost-effective way? House magazines are expensive to produce. As usual, budget restrictions will have the final say.

Once you have answered these questions and you have satisfied yourself that your prospective audience will benefit from your publication, you can decide on its proper organizational format.

Most house magazines contain very much the same type of editorial information as newsletters. The following items are listed in the approximate order in which they might appear (allowing for overlap in the case of articles):

- *Table of contents.* Usually runs on the front page.

- *Masthead.* Gives publication information (for example, editor and publisher) and usually runs on the table of contents or second page.

- *Editorial.* Can be in the form of a "President's Column," a signed editorial from management or the publication's editor.

- *Letters.* If the publication is designed for two-way communication, a letters column is a common addition.

- *News notes.* A quick (and brief) look at what's happening around the organization. You can get a lot of these in two or three pages. This is a good place for employee information as well.

- *Articles.* News and feature articles make up the bulk of the magazine and should have a consistent order of their own. For instance, the cover story should always appear in the same approximate location in each issue.

- *Announcements.* Usually boxed but sometimes run as regular columns for job placement, promotions, and so on. This is another good place for employee-interest pieces.

- *Calendar.* Upcoming events of interest to readers.

Remember, there is no hard-and-fast rule for formatting your magazine, but stick to whatever method you choose. Your readers look for consistency. If the format changes every two issues, you'll quickly lose your readers.

Types of Articles

House publication articles range from straight news to complete fiction and include everything in between. Most, though, are either straight news or feature. A vast array of writing styles can justifiably be called magazine writing. Articles or ideas for articles that don't seem to fit one particular magazine format or even one section of a magazine may well fit into another. For example, let's say that you interview an employee on a job-related topic such as benefits. In the course of your conversation, you discover that he builds model ships for a hobby and in fact has won several competitions. You gather enough information for a how-to article on building model ships as well as enough for a feature on the employee. Neither of these ideas may fit into the story that you originally set out to do; however, they may fit into another section on employees or one on hobbies. The lesson, of course, is never discard information just because it doesn't fit into your present assignment. Even if the tone or style of the article or information doesn't seem to fit one category, it may well fit another.

Articles for house publications tend to be shorter than those for consumer magazine articles or even trade journals (dealt with next). The average length of most house publications in magazine format is around 12 pages. Article length runs about 1,000 words or less for features (about 4 typed pages). Considering that magazine column width is about 14 picas for a three-column spread and that articles are usually accompanied by photographs or artwork and headlines, subheads, and blurbs, a 750-word article may cover several pages.

TRADE JOURNALS

Trade journals are a valuable source of information for those who work within a specific industry. They provide news and stories dealing with the concerns and products of that industry. Trade journals accept product news releases readily and are an excellent target for placement. They usually have a section devoted specifically to new products and will usually place your release, edited, of course, in this section.

For those desiring more attention, trade journals also accept articles written on products, concepts, and services of interest to their specific audiences (that is, the industries that they serve). These are normally submitted in the manner of any freelance magazine article. First, you query the journal by letter explaining that you have an article idea, what it is, and why you think it might fit the journal's format and be of interest to its readership. If you receive a positive response, send the article, carefully following the journal's editorial style. Trade journals, like consumer magazines, often have author's guidelines explaining their style, average length, manuscript requirements, and so on. Follow these guidelines explicitly if you want to get published or get your client the publicity you were hired to provide.

The variety of trade journal articles is immense. They can range from feature-type articles using human interest, through straight news stories on products and services, to light-fluff articles on travel and entertainment. To determine what style best fits your idea and their magazine, obtain a copy of the publication and read it thoroughly. Never submit an article to a magazine that you haven't read.

Get a copy of one of the numerous media directories that list all of the publications by industry (see Chapter 5). For my money, *Standard Rate and Data Service* provides the most comprehensive look at trade publications of any on the market. Almost every industry has a trade journal, sometimes a number of them. For instance, there are trade journals for golf course groundskeepers, racetrack owners, thoroughbred breeders, paper manufacturers, supermarket owners, food servers, bartenders, railroad workers, airline workers, and almost every other trade imaginable. One or more of these will fit your needs.

FEATURE WRITING FOR NEWSLETTERS AND MAGAZINES

We have seen that much of what public relations writers produce is in so-called straight news format, or inverted pyramid style. This is always true of news releases and can be true of anything written that is deemed straight news as opposed to a feature. We now know what straight news is, but what is a feature?

A feature can be construed as almost anything that isn't straight news. In fact, *feature* has several meanings. As used in the term *feature story,* it simply means the main story or cover story in the publication. In its broader sense, it means an article that features something as its central point or theme. This something may not necessarily be the message of the story or its publicity angle. It is most often the story itself. For example, you've been asked to do a story on a new product—say, a plastic lining that can be used as a bed for soil or sod to keep it from eroding or slipping. Instead of doing a straight news story on the product itself, you opt to do a feature story on a user of the new product. Maybe you find a golf course that's using the new underliner to rebuild its greens, and the focus of the story becomes the golf course. The publicity angle or the message about the new product becomes almost secondary. Featuring the golf course adds an extra dimension to your product story and sets it in context. In fact, the most useful element of a feature story approach is that it presents a context. Not every straight news story can do that.

Feature Style

Feature style is usually less objective and provides less hard information than straight news style. Features generally take a point of view or discuss issues, people, and places. The style is more relaxed, more descriptive, and often more creative than straight news style. Read over the straight news story in Exhibit 8.9. Next, look at the opening paragraphs of the feature story in Exhibit 8.10. This story is on the same topic as the straight news example, but the approach is quite different.

The facts are still here, but the focus is on creative information presentation. The lead is a question (a typical delayed lead strategy). Answering that question becomes part of the story itself. Quotes are used liberally. They not only validate and lend credibility to the subject discussed but also add human interest.

Exhibit 8.9

Straight News Story

Newsletter
AMHCA story
Page 1 of 1
Counselors' Association "Hires" PRSSA

The American Mental Health Counselors Association (AMHCA), a representative association for community counselors, has hired the Public Relations Student Society of America (PRSSA) to develop and implement a series of communication projects. The projects began last spring when a committee of five PRSSA members developed a public relations plan for AMHCA. The comprehensive plan is targeted at present and potential members. The two main objectives of the plan are to strengthen AMHCA as a membership organization and to create awareness of AMHCA among its target audiences.

After receiving approval for the plan from AMHCA board members, PRSSA was asked to develop more specific projects. This fall, a committee of eight PRSSA members worked on two projects. The first was to develop a logo and slogan for AMHCA to be used on all informational materials. The logo, now finished, symbolically represents the safety and shelter of a hearth, utilizing a stylized Hebrew symbol for home and well-being. The second project involved redesigning an existing AMHCA brochure. The committee developed a whole new layout and cover design.

The committee will also continue to develop projects during the winter and spring terms. The main project will be a series of brochures for AMHCA. The brochures will range from information on membership to information on mental health counseling. Other upcoming projects include writing a series of public service announcements to be broadcast nationally for Mental Health Week in March.

"Overall, the project has been a great experience for all of us involved," said committee chairperson Wendy Wintrode.

Human interest is a key characteristic of much feature writing. It can be simple inclusion of the human voice in a story, or it can be an entire profile featuring a single person. Although the term *profile* usually refers to a feature story done on a person or on one aspect or issue relating to a person, individual companies or products may be profiled as well (discussed in more detail later).

The following is from a profile on a corporate legal department and its new head. Notice how the scene is set in the lead before the subject is introduced.

Exhibit 8.10

Feature Story

AMHCA story
Page l of 1
Clearing Up the Confusion over Mental Health

What's the difference between a therapist, psychologist, psychotherapist, psychiatrist, and a counselor? If you don't know, you're among the millions of people who are confused about the multitiered mental health counseling field.

In an effort to clear up some of the confusion, the American Mental Health Counselors Association (AMHCA) has "hired" a university student group to produce a public information campaign for them.

The Public Relations Student Society of America (PRSSA) at the University of Oregon has been retained by the association to develop a program of information that will better define the various roles contained under the umbrella term "mental health counselor." Jane Weiskoff, regional director of AMHCA, says that the confusion seems to stem from a misconception over what constitutes a "counselor." "In the mental health profession, there is a perceived hierarchy," she says. "Psychiatrists are seen as being at the apex of the field with psychologists, therapists, and other counselors falling into place under them. We'd like to clarify and possibly alter that perception."

Part of the plan, which has already been produced and approved, is to establish and maintain contact with current AMHCA members through a series of brochures and an updated and redesigned association newsletter. These informational pieces will carry the message that mental health counselors come in a variety of forms with a variety of educational and training backgrounds, and that each of these levels is suited to certain types of counseling. The goal is to establish credibility for certain counseling functions not fully recognized at this time by the general public and the mental health profession. . . .

[For illustration purposes, part of the story has been deleted here.]

If committee chairperson Wendy Wintrode has her way, the term "mental health counseling" will soon have a completely different, and definitely more expanded, definition. "We want everyone to know that professionalism doesn't begin and end with a small clique at the top—it is the guiding force behind the entire field of mental health counseling."

Sitting behind a cluttered desk, boxes scattered around the office—some still unopened—is the new head of Associated Products Corporation's Law Department, Ed Bennett. Ed is a neat man, both in appearance and in speech. As he speaks about the new Law Department, he grins occasionally as though to say, "Why take the time to interview someone as unimportant as a lawyer?" That grin is deceiving because, to Ed and the other attorneys who work for Associated Products Corporation, law is serious business.

To add human interest is merely to add the human element to a story. Information without this element is only information. With it, information becomes more interesting, more personal, and more attuned to readers' experiences. As a further example, consider the following lead:

Somewhere north of Fairbanks, long after the highway disappears into the low growth and stubby trees, Seth Browner is stalking an elusive prey—his health. Seth is one of 20 hikers involved in the inaugural "hiking for health" program. Seth hopes the program will give him an opportunity to see the outdoors up close for the first time in his life and provide him with something he badly needs right now. Six months ago, Seth's doctor told him if he didn't exercise he would die.

And, if you're trying to reach people with your message—I mean really reach them—injecting human interest is often the best way to do it.

Writing the Feature Story

Feature stories, unlike straight news stories, must have a definite beginning (the *lead*), middle (the *body*), and end (the *ending*). Developing these elements takes patience, practice, and organization. Exhibit 8.11 points out the elements of a feature story.

The Lead

Always start at the beginning. A good lead is the hook that entices the reader into reading the complete piece.

Your lead must tell the reader what the story is about. It is not necessary to cram everything into the lead; however, you must include enough information so that the reader doesn't have to search for your topic. For straight news articles, the lead needs to come right to the point with the facts up front. For a feature, the delayed lead may be used. In this type of lead, you create ambiance and then place your story within the environment you have created, but it must still come to the point before the end of the second paragraph. Consider the following leads:

For a Horse-Racing Trade Magazine
For some time now, the sound of heavy machinery has been echoing through the rolling green countryside and heavily forested groves of eastern Maryland. But that sound will soon be replaced by the sound of galloping horses as they take to the newly banked turns and straightaway at what is being billed as "the most innovative thoroughbred training and sports medicine facility in North America."

For the Hospital Industry
The scene is a standard hospital room designed with fire safety in mind: a very low fuel load, floors of asbestos tile, walls of gypsum board on steel studs, and a ceiling

Exhibit 8.11

Feature Story Structure

APC's Answer Man

You might have noticed, if you've been in the new headquarters building at Associated Products Corporation long, a rather harried figure dashing madly up and down the halls. That man with the worried expression is Dave Martin. Dave, in a sense, is the ombudsman for APC's new building. He's the man who fields all the complaints, large and small, that have to do with everything from desk positioning to major malfunctions.

Dave's official title reads: Manager, Headquarters Facilities and Services. This constitutes a promotion for Dave, who previously was Manager, Technical Services. It also constitutes quite a lot of heartburn.

The job was almost a matter of evolution for Dave, who became associated with the project through working with Bob Allen, project manager for the new building. Dave continually found himself involved with planning of space allocation because this was a natural carryover from his former job. He cites the speed at which the building was completed as one of the major factors for his almost sudden immersion in the project.

An undertaking of this magnitude usually takes years to complete. The space layout itself, which usually takes 6 to 8 months, took only 6 to 8 weeks. Dave and the planners worked night and day setting up seating arrangements for each department. These arrangements had gone through each department weeks before but had to be thoroughly scrutinized by the architects and planners before implementation.

Dave realizes, of course, that not everyone is going to be completely happy with his or her particular arrangement, but no major changes can be made until after the first of the year. There are several reasons for this. "The move itself will take up to 60 days to complete," says Dave, "during which time furniture will constantly be arriving." According to Dave, each piece has been designated for a particular spot in the new building, and last-minute changes would only serve to confuse further what will doubtless be a confusing move as it is.

Telephones have already been assigned to particular individuals and can't be moved, and the special ambient lighting fixtures built into the desks provide light for a specific grouping of furniture. Moving a desk would mean disrupting the lighting scheme for a particular area, which would affect more than just one person. All these factors lead Dave to stress acceptance of the new floor plan, at least for the time being. According to Dave, psychological adjustment to new surroundings normally takes about 30 days. A great deal of complaints handled prior to that time ia likely to be adjustment oriented. Those are the complaints he would like to avoid initially.

The lead paragraph incorporates many of the basic elements of a news-type lead, including who, what, where, and how. It also delays the discovery of the topic until the second sentence by setting the scene first.

The second paragraph is the bridge from the lead to the body of the story. It begins with a factual statement and ends with another.

Paragraphs 3 through 6 follow a sort of chronological order, based on the construction of the new building, and provide background information.

(continued)

(continued)

Paragraph 7 comes back to the subject (focusing on the human angle) and expands on position and point of view.

Dave's new position will have him on the fourth floor as part of the Industrial Relations Department, where he will be in charge of the expanded reproduction facilities as well as Office Services, which handles supplies, PBX operation, mail service, and messenger service. Dave is going to be monitoring almost every aspect of the new building. He will handle the janitorial contract, the plant contract (yes, Virginia, there will be greenery inside too), and snow removal. As Dave says, "If the building has a problem during the day, I'll hear about it first." Dave's only concern right now is that he will receive too many complaint calls like, "I don't want to sit next to Joe" or "I can't see the window from here." With all of the major problems involved in a move of this magnitude (by the way, he's also in charge of getting everybody into the building), Dave doesn't need to hear the "personal" problems each employee is bound to have.

So, if you see this man with the harried expression in his eyes rushing around the halls of APC's new headquarters building, have a heart. Remember that Dave, like a modern-day Atlas, bears the weight of six floors on his shoulders. Just say "Hi," give him a smile, and learn to live with your new desk for a while.

The closing paragraph refers to the opening paragraph as a technique for gaining closure.

of fiberglass panels. The hospital is built in accordance with the National Fire Protection Agency Life Safety Code and has received the Joint Commission on Accreditation of Healthcare Organization's maximum 2-year approval.

Late in the evening, a patient accidentally ignites the contents of his trash can, which in turn ignite the bed clothes and, eventually, the mattress. The ensuing fire is a disaster, and despite the correct operation of all fire systems, multiple fatalities occur and the entire hospital wing is a total loss. Why? There are no fire standards on the upholstered furniture in this hospital, and the mattresses meet a federal code designed to retard fires from smoldering cigarettes, not open flames.

For a New Product Aimed at Highway Engineers

You're traveling along at high speed—the familiar clackety-clack of the rails beneath your feet. But wait a minute. You're not on a train, you're in an automobile, and that familiar sound beneath your feet is the result of deteriorating pavement joints that have been repaired with the usual "hot pour" method.

For an Article for Golf Course Superintendents

Valleyview Country Club had a problem—the 12th hole was sinking again. For almost 40 years, the facilities people at Valleyview had been rebuilding the green.

In fact, it had been rebuilt three times over that period of time, but each time with the same results—in a matter of a few years, the green would begin to sag again. This time, it was almost bowl-shaped and was acting as a funnel for rainwater that was draining from its outer edges into its concave center.

Although you may not have guessed it, all these leads come from articles announcing new products or new applications for established products.

Remember, even the most mundane subject can benefit from a creative treatment. Your readers will read your story only if they like your lead.

Other techniques for beginning your story include leading with a quote and placing it in context or using metaphor, simile, analogy, anecdote, and other interest-getting devices. Although most of us forgot these literary tools the minute that we left first-year composition, we shouldn't assume that good writing can get along without them. Look over the following literary uses of metaphor, simile, and analogy and then compare them with the feature article leads that follow them:

- A metaphor says that one thing is another:

CAULIFLOWER IS NOTHING BUT A CABBAGE WITH A COLLEGE EDUCATION.

—Mark Twain

TREE YOU ARE,
MOSS YOU ARE,
YOU ARE VIOLETS WITH WIND ABOVE THEM.

—Ezra Pound

- A simile says that one thing is like another:

THOUGH I MUST GO, ENDURE NOT YET
A BREACH, BUT AN EXPANSION,
LIKE GOLD TO AIRY THINNESS BEAT.

—John Donne

IN TIME OF PERIL LIKE THE NEEDLE TO THE LODESTONE,
OBEDIENCE, IRRESPECTIVE OF RANK, GENERALLY FLIES TO HIM
WHO IS BEST FITTED TO COMMAND.

—Herman Melville

- Analogies make hard-to-understand ideas easier to grasp by placing them in reader context or, as in the following example, by making a point of view more understandable through humor:

SOAP AND EDUCATION ARE NOT AS SUDDEN AS A MASSACRE, BUT THEY ARE MORE DEADLY IN THE LONG RUN.

—Mark Twain

The following leads show even the most mundane subject is of interest to someone and deserves the most interesting treatment possible. Pay particular attention to the number of scene-setting or descriptive words used in these leads:

Leading with a Quote
"Steelhead trout are an elitist fish; they're scarce, big, beautiful and they're good fighters," says Bob Hooton, Fish and Wildlife biologist responsible for steelhead on Vancouver Island. (*Salmonid,* newsletter of the Canadian Dept. of Fisheries and Oceans)

Leading with an Anecdote

If past experience is an indication, the telephones at our Client Services Center in Laurel, Maryland, will rarely stop ringing on December 16. That day the Center begins accepting calls for appointments to review diaries from the fall radio survey. (*Beyond the Ratings,* national newsletter of Arbitron)

April 1 marks the beginning of a new era in banking—and a new dawn of satellite communications. On that day a clerk in Citicorp's Long Island, New York, office will make history by picking up the phone and dialing a Citicorp office in California. (*Telecommunications Week,* national newsletter published by Business Research Publications, Inc.)

Leading with an Analogy

You've heard the adage "two heads are better than one." What about 40? The division's plants, more than 40 of them, are "putting their heads together" in the form of a division-wide information sharing project recently released. (*Action Connection,* employee newsletter of Weyerhaeuser Packaging Division)

Setting the Scene

It's 5:30 on a Monday afternoon and you've just finished one of those days. Not only did the never-ending pile of work on your desk cease to go away, but you just received two additional A priority assignments. On top of that, the phones wouldn't stop ringing and the air conditioning wouldn't start working, even though the temperature hit 95. (*Spectra,* employee newsletter of the SAIF Corporation)

It's pretty quiet at Merwin Dam in southwest Washington. Two generators are running. The water level is down a little so folks along the reservoir can repair some docks while the weather stays nice.

For the 21 people working at the dam, it's business as usual. But, there is a subtle change. There's no longer a threat hanging over their heads that Pacific might not own or operate the dam. The court case that could have forced Pacific to give it up was finally resolved at the end of February. (*Pacific Power Bulletin,* employee newsletter of Pacific Power)

Leading with a Metaphor or Simile

Recession fears faded like presidential candidates this spring. Markets were jolted by the February employment release, which showed an increase in employment of over 500,000. . . . The mood has gone full circle as there is renewed focus on the strength of the economy with its 5.4 percent unemployment rate, and the whiff of higher inflation in the air. (*Northwest Business Barometer,* a quarterly economic review for customers from U.S. Bank)

The Body

Once the lead is conceived and written, the story must elaborate on it. If possible, make points one by one, explaining each as you go. Get the who, what, when, where, and how down in the most interesting way possible—but get to the point early. The "why" element is developed in the rest of the story.

The body of the article must support your main point, preferably already made in the lead, and elaborate on it. It should contain all the information that your reader needs to understand what you are trying to say. Obviously, it's in your best interest to present your ideas clearly. Working from an outline is the best way to ensure that you have covered all your key points in a logical order.

You should anticipate questions that your reader might have and answer them satisfactorily. Remember to use logical transitional devices when moving from one point to another. Subheads, although helpful to the reader, don't alleviate the need for thoughtful transitions. Back up your statements with facts and support all generalizations with specifics. Although magazine and newsletter feature stories seldom use footnotes, they are not completely inappropriate. Usually, however, citations can be taken care of in the body of the text. If, however, you are quoting someone, be sure to use attribution. Don't just give the person's name. A person's title or job may lend your quote authority if that person is considered knowledgeable or an expert on your subject.

In a feature, cover the news angle in a more people-oriented way. Paint word pictures to help readers hear, smell, and feel the story. If your story has a possible human-interest angle, use it. It helps your readers relate to the message through other human beings. Above all, don't be afraid to experiment with different approaches to the same topic. Try a straight news approach, then a human-interest angle or maybe a dramatic dialogue. Whatever approach you use, try to make your story specific to your audience. Remember, they are major players in your scripts, in reality or vicariously.

The Ending

The most powerful and most remembered parts of your article will be the beginning and the end. Good endings are as difficult to write as good beginnings. However, there are only a few ways to wrap up an article and bring your readers to closure (a sense that they are satisfactorily finished): Summarize your main points (**summary ending**), refer back to the beginning in some way (**referral ending**), or call for action (**response ending**), although this last type of ending is rarely used in feature article writing. Consider the following leads with their respective endings:

- Posing a question in the lead/summary ending:

  Lead
  Name the oldest civilization in North America. If your anthropological information is such that you pinpointed the Aleut peoples of Alaska, you are both well informed and correct.

  Ending
  "Intellect and knowledge, technical skills, helpfulness, and concern for the truth are still the hallmarks of Aleut culture," observes the Connecticut anthropologist, Laughlin. Such virtues are valuable assets, ever more useful as the 21st century approaches, and the bedrock on which the best that is Aleut may find permanence and continuity. (Richard C. Davids for *Exxon USA*)

- Setting the scene in the lead/referral ending:

  Lead
  For one emotion-filled moment on July 28, when the Olympic torch is lit atop the Los Angeles Memorial Coliseum, this sprawling California city will be transformed into an arena of challenges and champions. But that magic event, shared with two billion television viewers around the world, will mark more than the beginning of the XXIII Summer Olympic Games.

Ending
For GTE employees worldwide, perhaps some of that special thrill can be shared by just watching the Games on television, and knowing that whenever gymnastics, fencing, water polo, volleyball, yachting, or tennis are televised, those images and sounds will have passed through the hands of 425 fellow employees—GTE's team at the Olympics. (Bill Ferree for *GTE Together*)

- An anecdotal lead/summary and referral ending:

Lead
In 1737, Benjamin Franklin wrote in the *Pennsylvania Gazette* of an auroral display so red and vivid that some people thought it was a fire and ran to help put it out.

Ending
Although the effects of auroral activity on the lower levels of the earth's atmosphere are more apparent, the effects on the upper atmosphere are not, and we are only now beginning to understand them. With more understanding, we may eventually view the aurora with a more scientific eye, but until that day comes, it still remains the greatest light show on earth. (Tom Bivins for National Bank of Alaska *Interbranch*)

Common Types of Features

Although several standard types of feature articles are appropriate for magazines and newsletters, the most common is the profile. The **profile** is most typically a feature story written specifically about a person, a product or service, or an organization or some part of it. It literally profiles the subject, listing facts, highlighting points of interest, and—most important—tying them to the organization. Regardless of the subject of your article, you are writing for a specific organization and the article must have some bearing on it: direct or indirect.

The Personality Profile

Personality profiles are popular because people like to read about other people, whether these people are just like them (so that they can easily relate) or very different (so that they can aspire or admire). Of course, a personality profile should do more than just satisfy human curiosity, it should inform the reader of something important about the organization itself by putting it in the context of a biographical sketch. For example, this lead was written for a brief profile on an award-winning engineer:

When Francis Langly receives the Goodyear Medal this spring, it will represent the symbolic crowning of a lifetime of dedication to the field of chemistry. Awarded by the Rubber Division of the American Chemical Society, the Goodyear Medal is the premier award for work in the field of specialty elastomers—an area that Langly helped pioneer. When Langly makes his medalist's address to the gathering in Indianapolis in May, his comments will be a reflection of almost 50 years of innovation and development, which began in 1960 when he joined Rogers Experimental Plastics Company as a research chemist.

What does this say about the organization? It implies, for one thing, that the company is obviously a good one to have such a well-respected person work for it for so long. A profile like this calls attention to the merits of the organization by calling attention to someone who has something to do with it—or, in some cases, to someone who benefits from its services or products. Consider the following lead:

> Guy Exton is a superb artist. His oils have hung in galleries all over the country. But, for nearly 5 years, he couldn't paint anything. To paint, you typically need fingers and a hand, and Guy lost his right hand in an auto accident in 2003. But now, thanks to a revolutionary new elastomer product developed by Rogers Experimental Plastics Company (REPC), Guy is painting again. He can grip even the smallest of his paintbrushes and control the tiniest nuance through the use of a special prosthetic device designed by Medical Help, Inc., of Franklin, New York. The device, which uses REPC's Elastoflex membrane as a flexible covering, provides minute control of digits through an electromechanical power pack embedded in the wrist.

One of the most common types of personality profiles is the Q & A (question-and-answer) format. This style typically begins with a brief biographical sketch of the person being interviewed, hints at the reason for the interview, and sets the scene by describing the surroundings in which the interview took place. For the remainder of the piece, speakers are tagged Q or A. Sometimes, the interviewer is designated with the publication's name (for example, *The Corporate Connection* might be shortened to *CC*). Likewise, the interviewee might be designated by his or her last name.

The descriptive narrative tells the story of the individual being profiled from a third-person point of view. Naturally, quotes from the subject may be included, but sometimes a successful profile is simply a biographical sketch and won't necessarily need quotes. The profile in Exhibit 8.9 is a mixture. Although some brief quotes are included, most of the profile is simple biography.

The Product or Service Profile

Profiling a product or service means describing it in a way that is unusual to draw attention to the product and the organization. This is often done in subtle ways. For example, the personality profile on the artist Guy Exton is really a way of mentioning a product. Clearly this doesn't detract from the human-interest angle, but it does accomplish a second purpose (probably the primary purpose), which is publicity. The same techniques you use in other article types can be used in profiling products.

The Organizational Profile

In the organizational profile, an entire organization or some part of it is profiled. The organizational profile and the personality profile are accomplished much the same way, except that you need to interview a number of key people in the unit you are profiling in order to obtain a complete picture of that unit. The profile in Exhibit 8.13 looks at a department within a large corporation.

Exhibit 8.12

Personality Profile

When Francis Langly receives the Goodyear Medal this spring, it will represent the symbolic crowning of a lifetime of dedication to the field of chemistry. Awarded by the Rubber Division of the American Chemical Society, the Goodyear medal is the premier award for work in the field of specialty elastomers—an area that Langly helped pioneer. When Langly makes his medalist's address to the gathering in Indianapolis in May, his comments will be a reflection of almost 50 years of innovation and development, which began in 1960 when he joined Rogers Experimental Plastics Company as a research chemist.

Born in Brooklyn, New York, in 1935, Langly received his BA in chemistry in 1950 and his PhD in organic chemistry from Cornell in 1959. His first position at REPC was in the Chemical Department at the Experimental Station near Ravenswood, Vermont. At the beginning of the Vietnam War, he was working on the synthetic rubber program addressing the problem of an adhesive for nylon tire cord for F-14 fighter jet tires. These studies eventually culminated in the development of the vinyl pyridine adhesives so widely used today.

Langly's background in organic chemistry led to his transfer to the Organic Chemicals Department at the Johnson Laboratory in Stillwater, Oklahoma, where he discovered the first light-fast yellow dyes for cotton; and during the next 10 years, he led the task force that developed dyes for the new synthetic fibers that were fast becoming a mainstay of American fashion.

From his work in dyes, Langly moved on to work in fluorine chemical research. The small research team that he headed is credited with the discovery of a family of new elastomers. The team at that time had what Langly calls, "a very special business in fluorine chemicals" but no solid applications yet for these quickly developing products. Langly and his group knew that they had something distinctly different and new in the field of elastomers. To an inventor, of course, the invention comes first. It didn't seem to trouble him that there was little or no market at that time for these new products. "There was no surprise in development," Langly says. "We understood the properties of the products we were developing and were sure that markets would eventually open up."

Chief among these early fluoroelastomers was "Axon," a polymer that could resist extremely high temperatures, toxic chemicals, and a broad range of fluids. Other products, however, were gathering attention in industry and defense, and the company was eager to market these already-accepted materials. In fact, the Axon project was sidetracked in the early 1970s when it was thought that the Langly research team could be better utilized in work a redundant product. In a way, this turned out to be a profitable diversion. Although the proposed research turned out to be a dead end, a small pressure reactor system that had been designed to build EP rubbers was converted to make fluoropolymer and used as a pilot plant to produce Axon.

According to Langly, "You rarely have a chance to fill a vacuum with something entirely new." And Axon was entirely new. The Air Force had been searching for some time for a product that could withstand very low and very high temperatures and was impervious to oil for use as engine seals on jet aircraft. Axon fit the bill perfectly. The Air Force quickly adopted it for use in jets, and the product went commercial for the first time in 1979.

The U.S. space program provided yet another and larger market for Axon's use in rocket engine seals. Because of its ability to seal against "hard" vacuum, Axon was one of the first rubbers that could be used in space.

As the markets for Axon continued to expand—to automotives, industry, and oil exploration uses—Langly progressed through a series of promotions. When the Elastomer Chemicals Department was formed in the mid-1980s, he was transferred to corporate headquarters in Freeport as Assistant Director of Research and Development.

Until his retirement in 2005, Langly continued to develop his interest in the field of elastomers. To date, he has 35 patents issued in his name and some 15 publications. In the 30 years since the birth of Axon, Langly has seen the product grow to its present status as the premium fluoroelastomer in the world with a new plant recently opened in Belgium providing the product for a hungry European market.

Langly numbers the discovery and development of Axon as only one in a long line of accomplishments attained during his half-century of work in the field of chemistry. Since his retirement, he has remained active in the field, working in art conservation, developing new techniques for the preservation of rare oil paintings. In a year and a half of work with the City Museum in New York, he set up a sciences department for the conservation of paintings. He is currently scientific advisor for the Partham Museum in Baltimore. He continues to consult, working closely with industry. He serves as expert testimony at court trials involving chemicals. And, he has given a speech before the United Nations on rubber.

Yet, Langly remains low key about his accomplishments and his current interests. "I'm just trying to keep the fires going," he says. Despite this modesty, it is apparent to others that when Francis Langly receives the Goodyear Medal this year it will represent not a capstone but simply another milestone in a lifetime of service.

-30-

Exhibit 8.13

Organizational Profile

APC's Law Department

Sitting behind a cluttered desk, boxes scattered around the office—some still unopened—is the new head of Associated Products Corporation's Law Department, Ed Bennett. Ed is a neat man, both in appearance and in speech. As he speaks about the "new" Law Department, he grins occasionally as though to say, "Why take the time to interview someone as unimportant as a lawyer?" That grin is deceiving because, to Ed and the other attorneys who work for Associated Products Corporation (APC), law is serious business.

Questions of law are rarely debated around APC. According to Ed, when something is not legal, it simply is not legal. No vote is taken by anyone; no decision needs to be arrived at. For this reason, house counsel (those attorneys who work for and in companies rather than for individuals) are often thought to be against all suggestions—paid to say no to projects or suggestions. This isn't so, says Ed. "It just so happens that a number of things that people wish to do must meet certain requirements. In most cases," he says, "it's not a question of 'you can't do it' but rather a matter of 'you have to do it this way.'"

According to Ed, this often puts the bearer of this news in an awkward position—much like the messenger who brings the Chinese Emperor bad tidings and has his head cut off for his efforts. It is a lot better in Ed's mind to make the adjustments to a particular project now than to wait until they can no longer be made and find out that the entire project is unworkable.

In APC's Law Department, each attorney handles a specific area dealing with particular projects. Like many of the other departments in APC, Law is experiencing a period of transition. Consequently, specific areas of assignment are only tentative. Still, the four-person legal staff now employed by APC is specialized to the extent that each member has an area of expertise in which he works a majority of the time.

Dennis Silva, newly arrived at APC from work with the state, is involved primarily with local and state government matters. Gary Williams is involved primarily in contractual matters, often between APC and other large companies. Keith McGowan has been handling research and certain other issues frequently dealing with the federal government.

Ed, just recently elected vice president and general attorney, describes his role as that of a player-coach. Aside from his specific responsibilities, he must also present the legal overview of the company's actions and accept the consequences of his advice. "Along with responsibility comes accountability," he says.

Ed, who has been with APC for nearly 2 years, was assistant center judge advocate at Walter Reed Army Medical Center prior to coming to APC. He received his Juris Doctor from the University of Pennsylvania Law School and graduated from the College of William and Mary. Before coming to work for APC, Ed was a judge advocate officer at the Headquarters, U.S. Army Fort Dix, New Jersey, from 1992-1995.

Together with the three other attorneys, Ed helps comprise a relatively small department. Despite its size, it may well be one of the most important functions within the company. "The myriad of legal and regulatory requirements, particularly in a business like this, creates a jungle," Ed says. "It is impossible to get to the other shore of this particular river by rowing in a straight line. There are cross currents and tides with the wind blowing from a hundred different directions."

The metaphor may be mixed, but the point is clear. According to Ed, the various state and federal regulations governing our operations are, by no means, consistent. Neither, frequently, are the goals of the company as expressed by the input of each of the departments. Consequently, it is also the responsibility of the Law Department to make uniform, or parallel, the various desires of the company.

"The end is always the same though," says Ed. "It is not to turn out neat legal briefs, which, though often well researched and executed, are not useful if a manager can neither understand nor conform to them. It is to strike a balance between our own professional conscience and the utilitarian nature of the work."

"Of course," says Ed, "we'd like to spend 6 months on each item, carefully researching it, but by then we have lost the element of timeliness, which is often equally important."

The people who make up the Law Department are, in the highest sense, professional. In fact, they have a professional responsibility quite separate from the company. Every attorney is a member of a bar association and thus must adhere to the Code of Professional Responsibility unique to the profession. "We are not exempted," says Ed, "simply because we are 'house counsel,' from the dictates of that Code." Thus, their advice has to be correct, or as correct as it can be under prevailing circumstances. All of APC's attorneys are members of at least one bar and some are members of up to four.

The role of the APC attorney is similar to that of the "outside" attorney in that they are here to represent the company in legal matters. But APC's Law Department does more than that. It not only represents the company when it gets into difficulty but also expends a great deal of time and effort in keeping the company out of difficulty. To that end, the house counsel of APC must maintain sufficient contact with the company, its people, and its activities in order that it may render timely advice and thus prevent difficulties.

(continued)

(continued)

> In a way, modern attorneys are still much like their medieval predecessors, who, hired to represent clients on the field of combat, used every honorable device in their power to win. Perhaps the shield has been replaced by the briefcase, but the same keen edge that decided many a trial-by-combat is still very much apparent. Never draw down on an attorney. They are still skilled combatants.
>
> -30-

EDITORIAL CONSIDERATIONS FOR DISPLAY COPY

Display copy, from an editorial viewpoint, includes headlines, subheads, captions, and pull quotes. Each of these elements has to be written for best effect. Ideally, each should contribute to the article to which it refers by adding to, elaborating or amplifying on, or drawing attention to information already presented in the article.

Writing Headlines

Headlines for magazines and newsletters are similar; however, there are some exceptions. First, some definitional differences exist. A headline, strictly speaking, is for news stories, whereas a title is for features. For example, a news story on a new product might have a headline like this:

New software will "revolutionize education," says APC president

Now, contrast that headline with the following title:

Talking to the past—Learning about the future

The headline tells something about the story, so that even the casual reader can glean some information from reading it alone. The title, by contrast, entices the reader or piques his or her interest. For the following discussion, however, I use the term *headline* to indicate both types. To begin with, a basic rule for writing headlines is to use headlines for news articles and titles for feature articles. And, as with all writing, try to be clear. If your headline or title confuses the readers, they won't read on.

Remember, whether headline or title, it should grab the reader's attention and make him or her want to read the article. It should be informative and brief. Here are some guidelines that should help you in constructing good headlines:

- *Keep them short.* Space is always a problem in any publication. Be aware of column widths and how much space that sentence-long headline that you are proposing will take up. Every column inch that you devote to your headline will have to be subtracted somewhere else. Headlines don't have to be complete sentences, nor do they have to be punctuated unless they are.

- *Avoid vague words or phrases.* Your headline should contribute to the article, not detract from it. Cute or vague headlines that play on words should be left for entertainment publications like *Variety* (famous for its convoluted headlines).

- *Don't use standing heads for recurring articles* such as "President's Message" or "Employee Recognition." It is better to mention something of the article's content in the headline, such as "Packaging Division wins company-wide contest."

- *Use short words.* A long word in a headline often has to be hyphenated or left on a line by itself. You can always come up with a shorter alternative.

Writing Subheads and Crossheads

Subheads are explanatory heads, usually set in a smaller type (or italics), that appear under the headline. For example:

ACME buyout impending
Statewide Telecom makes takeover bid

In most cases, a headline is sufficient; however, there are times when a rather lengthy subhead is necessary, especially if the headline is brief or cryptic:

"A drama of national failure"
A best-selling author talks about reporting on AIDS

Subheads should be used sparingly, if at all, and only for clarity's sake.

Crossheads are the smaller, transitional heads within an article. You shouldn't need them in a typical newsletter article. About the only time they might be useful is in a longer article—perhaps a newsletter devoted to a single subject or a magazine article. Crossheads should be very short and should simply indicate a change in subject or direction. Most writers use crossheads in place of elaborate transitional devices. Space is always a consideration, and using a cross-head instead of a longer transitional device may save you several column inches. However, if you do use crossheads, make sure that more than one is warranted. Like subpoints in an outline, crossheads don't come solo. Either delete a single crosshead or include another one.

Writing Captions

Captions, or **cutlines,** are the informational blurbs that appear below or next to photographs or other illustrations. They are usually set in a smaller point size.

Like headlines, they should contribute to the overall information of an article, not detract from it:

- *Keep captions brief.* Make sure they relate directly to the photograph. (The best captions also add information that may not be included in the article itself.)

- *If your caption is necessarily long, make sure it is clear.* If you are naming a number of people in a photo, for example, establish a recognizable order (clockwise from the top, right to left, from the top, from the left, and so on).

- *Captions, like headlines, should not be vague or cute.* You simply don't have enough space to waste developing that groaner of a pun.

Writing Pull Quotes

Pull quotes are relatively new to newsletters. Traditionally a magazine device, they draw a reader's attention to a point within an article. They almost always appear close to the place in the article from which the quote is taken.

Pull quotes don't have to be actual quotes, but they should at least be an edited version of the article copy. Pull quotes usually suggest themselves. If you have a number of good quotes from an interviewee, you can always find a good one to use as a pull quote. Or, if you simply want to stress an important point in an article, use it as a pull quote.

Pull quotes are useful as both editorial and design elements. Editorially, a pull quote draws attention to your article by highlighting an interesting quote. As a design element, a pull quote can create white space or fill up unused space left over from a short article. If, for instance, you have several inches left over on your page, simply add a pull quote to the middle of the article in the length you need to take up the extra space. A good pull quote can be as long or as short as you want and still make sense. It can span several columns, be constrained to a single column, head the page, appear in the center of a copy-heavy page, or help balance some other graphic element on the page.

Remember, good pull quotes reflect the best your article has to offer. A mundane pull quote is wasted space.

EDITING YOUR ARTICLES

Feature articles probably get and deserve the most editing of the various types of writing discussed in this book. Length has something to do with it, but more than that, it's the freewheeling attitude of some article writers (especially novices) that contributes the most to this need. Because many writers of basic company publications end up dealing with pretty dry topics, an assignment to do an article for the house magazine might be seen as an invitation to creativity. This usually leads, in turn, to a looser style, wordiness, and lack of organization. Whatever the reason, even the best-written article can benefit from intelligent editing.

A quick word here about the term *intelligent editing*. This implies that you are being edited by someone (or yourself, if you're doing the editing) who knows about writing—both grammar and style. Unfortunately, as many of us who have worked on in-house publications for years know, editors are often chosen because of their position within the organizational hierarchy (or the obligatory approval chain) and not for their literary talents. One of the best (if perhaps a little cynical) rules of thumb for dealing with inexpert editing is to ignore about 80 percent of it. You quickly get to recognize what is useful to you and what is not. Basically, editing that deals with content balance and accuracy is usable. Most strictly editorial comment is not. A vice president's penchant for ellipses or a manager's predilection for using *which* instead of *that* are strictly stylistic preferences (and often ungrammatical). In many cases, even if you do ignore these obligatory edits, these same "editors" won't remember what they said when the final piece comes out. A rule of thumb for most experienced writers is to try to avoid being edited by noneditors. If you can't, at least see how much you can safely ignore.

As for editing yourself, there are several methods for cutting a story that is too long, even if you don't think you can possibly do without a single word:

- *Look at your beginning and end to see if they can be shortened.* Often we write more than we need by way of introduction or closing when the real meat is in the body of the article.

- *If you used a lot of quotes, cut the ones that are even remotely fluff.* Keep only those that contribute directly to the understanding of your story.

- *Are there any general descriptions that, given later details, may be redundant?* Cut them.

- *Are there any details that are unnecessary given earlier general descriptions?* Cut them. (Be careful not to cut both the general description and the details.)

- *Are there any people who can be left out?* For instance, will one expert and his or her comments be enough, or do you really need that second opinion?

- *Finally, look for wordiness—instances in which you used more words than you needed.* This type of editing hurts the most because you might have struggled over that wording for an hour.

Your goal is to get the article into the size that you need without losing its best parts or compromising your writing style. Exhibit 8.14 shows how some of these guidelines can be applied.

EVALUATION

Like other forms of writing, newsletters and magazines can and should be evaluated for effectiveness. And, like other forms of writing, the best approach is to test your message and your format on members of your target audience.

Methods of Evaluation

Focus groups have been covered earlier; however, they are useful as both pre- and posttesting measures of evaluation. In addition to focus groups (generally referred to as "informal research"), you'll recall that the most common type of formal research is the survey. And, one of the most common forms of survey for our purposes is the *readership survey*.

Exhibit 8.14

Editing the Article

DGL Wins UL Certification

The sign on the door reads "Grade 'A' UL Central Station." To the people at Dallas General Alarm (DGA) and to the hundreds of businesses and homes they protect, this means the availability of some of the best alarm and intrusion detection systems in the country. In fact, almost every improvement made at DGA over the past few years has had as its goal the attainment of UL certification.

In 1924, Underwriters Laboratories, Inc. began offering a means of identifying burglar alarm systems that met acceptable minimum standards. The installing company can apply for investigation of their services and, if found qualified, may be issued UL certification. To the customer, this certification can mean a large reduction (sometimes up to 70 percent) in insurance premiums, depending on the exact grade and extent of the UL-approved service used.

However, DGA doesn't sell only UL service. "We sell and lease our systems on the merit of the system and the particular need of the customer," says Dave Michaels, director of quality control for DGA. "Of course, those who do have the UL Grade A system installed can usually pay the extra cost entailed with the savings they make on insurance alone."

What makes this Grade A system so effective that insurance companies charging sometimes thousands of dollars a year in coverage are willing to cut 40, 60, or even 70 percent off their premiums?

"The UL people are really tight on their standards," says Michaels. "They conduct a number of 'surprise' inspections of DGA on a regular basis. If we fall down in any of their requirements, we get our certification cancelled."

DGA has its own tight security system consisting of television monitors on all doors and verbal contact with people entering their offices. The central control room is always manned and locked. A thick, glass window allows the operators on duty to check personally all people entering the premises. Other UL requirements are extra fireproofing for the building itself and a buried cable containing the thousands of telephone lines used to monitor the various alarm systems that run out of the building. The cable is unmarked, preventing the adventurous burglar from cutting it and thus disabling the hundreds of systems served by DGA.

The over-a-thousand customers who either lease or buy alarm or detection systems from DGA range from some of the biggest businesses in Dallas to private residences. In addition, all of the schools in the Dallas area are monitored from the DGA central station against break-in and vandalism.

The next four paragraphs, although providing additional information, can be cut without loss to the overall information impact of the story because they deal with details that we can get along without. Given enough space, however, we would opt to leave the story intact.

The monitoring devices, located at the DGA central control, vary from a simple paper tape printout to actual voice communication with the premises being protected. For instance, the card-key system used by Atlantic Richfield Company allows access to certain areas through the use of a magnetic card inserted into a slot in the door. Access is forbidden to those lacking the proper clearance, and the number and time of the attempted access are printed out at the DGA central station.

By far the most impressive system is the Hyper Guard Sound System, which allows the central station operators actually to listen into a building or home once the system is activated. If the building is entered, the sound-sensitive system is activated, causing an alarm to go off at the DGA central station. By the use of microphones installed on the premises, the DGA operators can then determine the presence of an intruder. The owners, of course, sign in and out verbally when they open and close. Most of these customers also carry the special "holdup" feature of this system, which allows them to trigger, unnoticed, an alarm in the event of a robbery.

"We tried out a lot of other sound-activated systems," says Michaels, "but the Hyper Guard made by Associated Products Corporation is the best I've ever seen." Michaels says that the Hyper Guard system is probably 20 times more sensitive than most other brands DGA has tried. "And, in our business, sensitivity is a key component of a successful detection."

Once an alarm is received from any of the hundreds of points serviced by DGA, it is only a matter of seconds before security guards, police, an ambulance, or the fire department are notified and on their way. DGA maintains direct, no-dial lines to all of these agencies.

DGA currently contracts with Smith-Loomis, which dispatches two or three security guards to each of DGA's calls. "Our average response time is under four-and-a-half minutes," says Dave Michaels. "Of course, we often have to wait on the owner to show up to let us in." Michaels says that if DGA keeps a key to the premises, another 10 percent often can be taken off on insurance premiums because it allows a faster response time and a higher apprehension rate. "Recently, we got two apprehensions in three alarms at a local pharmacy," he says. "We roll on every suspicious alarm. UL only allows one opening and one closing time per business unless prearranged," says Michaels. "This way, we know exactly when there should be nobody on the premises."

DGA offers a number of different systems. Some respond to motion and some to sound. There are systems with silent alarms and systems with on-sight alarms fit to frighten the toughest intruder. DGA also handles smoke and heat detection systems. But, the key to a UL Grade A certified system, says Michaels, is the central control. "That's the added factor in a Grade A

Whatever you do, don't edit out the purpose for writing the article in the first place. In this case, it's mention of a product in the next two paragraphs.

(continued)

(continued)

The next two paragraphs are a good example of an extra character who can be deleted without substantial loss to the story. Although this kind of testimony adds credibility to any story, in this case the story is about DGA, and their spokesperson provides the first-person credibility needed for the purpose—which is to get one of the products mentioned.

system," he says. "We know immediately when something has occurred, and we respond."

Frank Collins, president of Southwestern Gemstones, Inc., has had his Grade A system since September. "I was robbed last year of over $400,000 worth of merchandise," he says, "and I was uninsured. That won't happen again." Collins is impressed with his system.

From his office in the Calais Building, Collins can watch everyone who enters his showroom via television monitor. A telephone allows visitors to identify themselves from outside the front door before entry. The showroom has an impressive array of precious gems and gold and a great many antique art objects, frequently handmade turquoise and silver pieces. "I got the complete works," Collins says, "audio sensors, motion sensors, TV monitor, everything," resulting in a good-sized cut in his necessarily high insurance premiums.

For the many high-risk businesses served by Dallas General Alarm, the UL Grade A system seems to be the answer.

"We don't expect more than a couple of hundred customers for the UL system over the next few years," says Dave Michaels, "but that's all right. Our customers know their needs, and they know that they can't get a better system for the price." Michaels smiles. "For the three or four dollars a day this system costs, they couldn't even afford a guard dog."

-30-

Readership surveys are simple questionnaires, usually included with your newsletter or magazine, that seek to find out whether anyone out there is paying attention (see Exhibit 8.15). A few, plainly put questions—about what interests your readers the most, the least, what they would change if they could, what they would include or leave out—will tell you a lot. Most commercial publications run an occasional readership survey just to make sure they're operating on the same wavelength as their readers.

Evaluating Your Production Schedule

In addition to evaluating the success of your publication with its target audiences, you're probably going to want to take a close look at your publication schedule. The first time that you produce your newsletter, you are going to have precious little time to reflect on how it's going during the publication process. However, after the dust has settled, you need to get together with your staff (if you have one) and your supervisor or publisher (unless you're doing it all yourself).

Exhibit 8.15

Developing a Readership Survey

Readership surveys should not be done immediately after your first issue. Instead, you should wait for several issues until your readers have had a chance to absorb your informational approach and develop some reactions to it. A few guidelines will help you develop a readership survey.

1. Keep questions simple, short, and clear. Include only one idea per question. More than one idea will get you more than one answer. For example:

Wrong

Do you read the entire newsletter or only part of it?

Yes   No

Right

Do you read the entire newsletter?

Yes   No

If not, which part(s) do you typically read? (Check all that apply)

Feature story   Editor's column   Personal   Calendar

2. Use words whose meanings will be understandable to your readers. Check to make sure that both the denotative and connotative meanings of your words are clear. Avoid jargon. For example:

Wrong

How do you rate the overall grid of our newsletter?

Good   Fair   Poor

(Are your readers going to know what a grid is?)

Right

Do you think the three-column format of our newsletter is

Easy to read?   Fairly easy to read?   Fairly difficult to read?   Difficult to read?

3. Don't lead your readers' answers by implying a bias. For example:

Wrong

Our newsletter recently won "Outstanding Newsletter Design" from IABC. What do you think about the new design?

Good   Fair   Poor

Right

How would you rate the overall design of our newsletter?

Good   Fair   Poor

(continued)

(continued)

Wrong

Do you like our bright, new banner style?

Yes   No

(Words like *bright* and *new* imply that your readers *should* like your banner.)

Right

Do you like our banner style? If you don't like it, please explain why.

Yes   No

Wrong

Do you think that we should increase the amount of personal news?

Yes   No

(This question implies that the current amount of personal news is the only point of comparison.)

Right

Do you think the amount of personal news should

Be increased?   Be decreased?   Remain the same?

4. In general, if you ask a question that can be answered yes or no, you might need a follow-up question to plumb the reasons why a reader would answer no. This is especially important if you want more than just one-dimensional answers. For example:

Do you read the personals column?

Yes   No

If *no*, why not?

(This will give you a better idea of how to improve the column to enhance readership or let you know whether you should drop it altogether.)

5. Try to get the most precision possible from each response. For example, the question above could have been stated this way.

How often do you read the personals column?

Every time   Sometimes   Not often   Never

6. Decide exactly what information will be most valuable to you and construct your questions and choices of answers to get that information. For example:

On a scale of 1 to 5 (1 being the lowest rating and 5 the highest), how would you rate the overall design of the newsletter?

1   2   3   4   5

(This scaled response allows you to rate your newsletter's design numerically.)

How would you rate the overall design of the newsletter?

Excellent   Good   Fair   Poor

(This scaled response calls for a connotative rating.)

Do you think the overall design of the newsletter

- Is fine the way it is?
- Could use some improvement?
- Could use a lot of improvement?
- Should be totally redesigned?

(This method limits options, but most respondents like something to choose from that is concrete and not abstract.)

7. The following areas are basic topics to cover in readership surveys.

- Reader demographics such as age, gender, income, and occupation. This information will tell you if your readers are really who you think they are according to your original audience analysis.

  Please check the applicable ranges.

Age	Income	Occupation
25–30	$10k–$20k	(include a list appropriate to
31–40	$21k–$30k	your audience analysis, leaving
41–50	$31k–$40k	a space for *other*)
51–60	$41k+	

- Reader reaction to content of articles (usually rated on a scale ranging from *very important* to *not important*).

  How important do you think a personals column is to this newsletter?

  Very important   Important   Not very important   Not important

  Do you find the general topics of the articles

  Very interesting   Interesting   Not very interesting   Not interesting

- Reader reaction to design elements, listed one element at a time for clarity.

  Do you think the number of photographs included in the newsletter is

  Just right?   Not enough?   Too many?

- Reader reaction to appropriateness of language, use of jargon, and so on.

  Do you find the level of technical language used in the articles

  Appropriate   Somewhat appropriate   Inappropriate

- Reader recommendations for improvement (usually open-ended questions and last on your survey).

  Please list, in order of importance, what you would change about the current newsletter.

8. Always thank your readers for their time. If possible, offer them some incentive to respond, such as coupons or free passes. And make it easy for them to send their surveys back to you. *Never* make them pay postage. If possible, use a self-mailer with postage paid.

Regardless of how many people are involved, or even if you're the only one involved, you should look at every aspect of your publication schedule to see where problems occurred and to make recommendations for streamlining the process for the next issue.

Among business management strategies for maximizing efficiency, there is a fairly complex strategic planning method known as PERT analysis. PERT analysis is used to allocate resources based on how much time it takes to accomplish the *most time-consuming activity* in a given project. The assumption is that you can't get a job done any sooner than it takes to do the most time-consuming part of it. The trick, then, is to locate activities that don't take as long to accomplish and see if the people who worked on those jobs can help speed up the slowest activity. A simplified version of PERT analysis can be used to determine ways in which your own newsletter production schedule can be streamlined.

The first step is to develop what is known as a Gantt chart. A Gantt chart is a quick, visual representation of the order in which various parts of a job occur and how long it takes for each part. You will need to take your original schedule and construct a Gantt chart based on various jobs listed on it (see Exhibit 8.16).

Once you've got a Gantt chart made, the rest of the process goes something like this.

1. Look at your schedule. Go over it item by item.

2. Locate the blockages as well as the places where things went faster or smoother than you had expected.

3. Calculate an average time for each item on your schedule. List the times by each of the scheduled items on the Gantt chart.

4. Locate the most time-consuming activity.

5. Locate the least time-consuming activity.

6. Ask yourself if any resources allocated to the least time-consuming activity can be transferred to the most time-consuming activity in order to speed it up.

7. If the answer is no, locate another activity that took less time than the longest activity and ask the same question.

8. Continue this way until you can reallocate some of your resources to help shorten the longest part of your schedule.

You will notice that activities usually break down into two basic categories: those handled in-house (such as interviewing and writing) and those jobbed out (such as photography and illustration). The only way to speed up activities that freelancers have done is to set tighter deadlines or contract faster freelancers. However, at the points at which you become involved (selection and sizing of photos and artwork, for instance), you may find ways to cut down on the time. Otherwise, your best bets for streamlining are in-house activities—those that involve people under your direct control, including you.

Let's say that after looking at your schedule, you discover the job taking the longest in-house time was obtaining critiques of the first and second drafts of

Exhibit 8.16

A Gantt Chart

Activity	Mon.	Tues.	Wed.	Thurs.	Fri.	Mon.	Tues.	Wed.	Thurs.	Fri.
Decide on basic content for current issue.	▓									
Determine number and type and approximate length of stories.		▓								
Make up layout for current issue.		▓								
Gather information and/or interview appropriate sources.			▓							
Write first draft.				▓						
Obtain critiques and edit first draft.					▓					
Create artwork for each story (photos taken, illustrations created or obtained, charts/graphs created, and so on).			▓	▓	▓					
Write final draft.						▓	▓			
Obtain critiques, edit final draft, and copyfit articles.							▓	▓		
Write headlines, captions, and pull quotes and copyfit.							▓	▓	▓	
Fit artwork.									▓	
Finalize and proof layout.										▓
Send to printer.										▓
Check proofs.										▓

your articles. Perhaps you have a long list of supervisors who must sign off on each draft, and the copy tends to spend too much time in transition. You might try setting stricter deadlines, reducing the number of approvals needed, or back timing the deadline for receipt of the first and second drafts to accommodate the delay at the approval's end.

Or, perhaps the most time-consuming activity turns out to be gathering information and writing the stories. You might be able to assign an extra writer to the job, handle the feature story yourself each issue to ease the load on the other writers, or set stricter deadlines.

If there are areas in which others can help, pinpoint these activities and seek in-house support. For instance, your secretary or assistant might be able to help you edit the copy or set it on the computer. If you have writing help (lucky you), they could develop their own headlines, captions, and pull quotes.

The real key is making yourself delegate part of *your* job to others who can help you out. If you're like most newsletter editors, you probably hate to relinquish any part of your control to others. You're afraid that they won't take the same care that you do. Don't worry. Tell them exactly what you want, how to do it, and when you want it. You will still be the editor, and as such, you retain ultimate control over your newsletter. Remember, an editor edits. He or she doesn't have to create everything from scratch.

BROCHURES

Like newsletters, brochures often are written and designed by the same person. This is not universally true, of course, but in many nonprofit agencies or small offices a single person is put in charge of "making" a brochure. The following discussion therefore includes a bit about brochure design as well as writing. It is my belief that this particular medium unites design and copy in a unique and nearly inextricable way.

Most brochures are used to arouse interest, answer questions, and provide sources for further information. Even when used as part of a persuasive campaign, brochures are seldom persuasive in themselves; rather, they are support pieces or part of a larger media mix. Brochures can serve as stand-alone display rack literature, as a component of a media kit, or as part of a direct-mail packet. Brochures vary enormously in length; the amount of information to be imparted is the determining factor. Most brochure copy is abbreviated, however. Longer copy is best suited to other formats such as booklets or pamphlets. Be aware that an odd-sized brochure probably will be more expensive to produce because printers will have to make special adjustments to their equipment to accommodate the brochure.

Brochures usually are formed of a single sheet of paper folded one or more times. The folded brochure often is pocket sized, but it doesn't have to be—part of the fun of designing a brochure is choosing its size and number of folds. Although writing for a brochure implies that you already know what size and shape the finished product will be, you can also write first and then determine the size and shape that fits your copy. As with any in-house publication, you can work it either way, fitting copy to design or design to copy. Take the approach that works best for you, though you may need to cut costs by trimming your copy or accommodate mandatory information by expanding it.

Planning Your Brochure

Before you begin to write, you need to plan your brochure and determine exactly what your message is and how it can best be presented. Who is your intended audience? Are you trying to inform or persuade? Is a brochure the best medium for your message? Your format and your style must match your audience's expectations and tastes.

Know Your Intended Audience

In addition to following the procedures discussed in Chapter 3 for knowing your intended audience, begin by assuming that your audience is seeking or processing an abbreviated amount of information. Most readers understand that brochures aren't intended to provide long, involved explanations.

You should consider three other audience-centered questions before you begin writing for your brochure:

- *Is your audience specialized or general?* If it is specialized and familiar with your subject, you can use the trade language or jargon familiar to readers, no matter how technical it might be. For example, in a brochure on a new chemical product (a copolyester, let's say) you can deal with durometer hardness, temperature-related attributes, resistance to pollutants and weather, and stress characteristics. None of these concepts should be new or surprising to a specialized audience of chemical engineers or designers who use polymers. By contrast, if you are writing a brochure for a lay audience, you will have to deal in lay terms, or generalities.

    Here are two examples of a piece on an imaginary copolyester—one for a technical audience (engineers) and one for a less specialized audience (retailers of a manufactured product made from the raw product):

    Technical
    The results of laboratory testing indicate AXON 11® polyester elastomer is resistant to a wide variety of fuels including leaded and unleaded gasoline, Gasohol, kerosene, and diesel fuel. With a hardness range of 92A to 72D durometer, tests show the most fuel-resistant type of copolyester to be the 72D durometer; the other family types also show an impressive amount of fuel resistance.

    General
    AXON 11® polyester elastomer offers design potential plus for applications in a variety of industries. On the toughest jobs, AXON II ® is proving to be the design material of the future. Its unique properties and flexibility in processing make

it applicable in areas previously dependent on a range of other, more expensive products.

- *Are you persuading or informing?* If you are persuading your audience, you can use the standard persuasive techniques covered in Chapter 4, including emotional language, appeal to logic, and association of your idea with another familiar concept. As with print advertising, the tone of the brochure (whether persuasive or informative) is set in the introductory headline. For example, here are two cover titles or headlines from two brochures on graduate programs in journalism. The first is persuasive, and the second is informative:

  Persuasive
  Is one graduate program in journalism better than all the others? Yes. The University of Northern Idaho.

  Informative
  Graduate studies in journalism at the University of Northern Idaho

- Regardless of your intent, the brochure copy should always be clear on what you expect of your audience. If you are trying to persuade, state what you want the reader to do—buy your product, invest in your stock, vote for your candidate, or support your bond issue. Persuasion works only if people know what it is you want them to be persuaded about.

- *How will your audience be using your brochure?* Is the brochure intended to stimulate requests for information on a topic for which detailed information can be obtained in another form? Will it urge readers to send for more information? Is it meant to be saved as a constant reminder of your topic? Many health-oriented brochures, for example, provide information meant to be saved or even posted for reference, such as calorie charts, vitamin dosages, and nutrition information. If your brochure is designed to be read and discarded, don't waste a lot of money on printing. By contrast, if you want the brochure to be saved, not only should you make the information valuable enough to be saved, but also the look and feel of the brochure should say "don't throw me away." The same is true of any publication. Newspapers, by their inexpensive paper and rub-off ink, say "read me and then throw me away," whereas a magazine like *National Geographic* says "throw me away and you'd be trashing a nice piece of work."

Determine a Format

Format refers to the way you arrange your brochure—its organizational characteristics. As with everything else about brochures, format can go two ways: You can either fit format to your writing or fit your writing to a predetermined format. For instance, if you are told to develop a Q & A (question-and-answer) brochure, you'll have to fit both writing and design to this special format. If you are writing a persuasive piece, you might decide to go with a problem-solution format, spending two panels of a six-panel brochure on setting up the problem and three on describing the solution (the sixth panel is reserved for the cover).

Some organizational formats work well in brochures, and some don't. Space organization (up to down, right to left, east to west), which can work well in book form or in magazine articles, doesn't seem to fit in a brochure. Neither does chronological organization. The reason for this may be the physical nature of the brochure itself. Magazine and book pages are turned, one after the other, and each page contains quite a lot of information. A brochure demands a more concentrated effort, one that is less natural than leafing through pages. Because each panel is limited in space, development has to take place in "chunks." Organizational formats that require continuous, linked development or constant referral to previous information aren't suited to brochures. The sole exception would be brochure points that are numbered, which by definition means the points are sequential if not chronological.

More common formats for brochures include Q & A or FAQs (frequently asked questions), problem–solution, and narrative (storytelling). Pick a format that is suited to your topic and then design your brochure to suit your format. Creative brochure design is part of the fun of working with this type of publication.

Position Your Brochure

Positioning refers to placing your piece in context as either part of some larger whole or as a standout from other pieces. Is your brochure to be used as part of a larger communication package (a media kit, for instance), or is it meant to be a stand-alone piece? If it is part of a larger package, then the information contained in the brochure can be keyed to information elsewhere in the package. If it is a stand-alone piece, it will need to be fairly complete—and probably longer. Knowing how your brochure fits into a larger communication program helps you position it properly.

If your brochure is part of a larger program, you also need to be sure that your writing style mimics the style of the overall package. Obviously, this doesn't mean that the brochure should read like a magazine because it is packaged with a magazine, but it should resemble the companion pieces as closely as possible. If the other pieces are formal, the brochure should be formal; if they are informal, the brochure should be also. The key is consistency.

Decide on Length

Succinctness is an art. Almost all writers are able to write long, but very few can write short without editing down from something originally longer. Your information will probably be edited a number of times to make it as spare and succinct as possible because short copy is the ideal for brochures—for space limitations, to leave enough white space for aesthetic value, type size considerations (for example, a brochure for senior citizens must use a fairly large typeface), or cost considerations. Whatever the reason, you must learn to write short and edit mercilessly.

The brochure in Exhibit 8.17 uses what can be considered the most common style. The two-fold brochure has a cover and five following panels combining graphics and subheads to lead the reader easily through the layout. Exhibit 8.18 shows a two-fold brochure that is laid out horizontally to take advantage of a flyer-style inside spread. This format allows for more copy and greater flexibility of its placement within the layout. Exhibit 8.19 shows a larger-format brochure with not that much copy but a heavy use of large graphics.

Remember, there are few design restrictions on brochures. They simply have to appeal to your target public to be successful.

The key to editing brochure copy is to realize exactly how much your reader would need to know about your subject. If you include too much in a piece designed merely to attract attention, you may lose your readers. By contrast, if you don't provide enough basic information, you may never pique their interest. Although some edited elements may in fact influence the final decision-making process, they may not be important in the awareness stage of the adoption process. Once you have decided on the purpose of your brochure, writing and editing become a much easier job.

Fitting It All Together

Whether you write for a specific size or you fit the size to the amount of information that you have (especially if your boss simply can't live without that detailed explanation of how beneficial your new widget is to Western technology), your copy will have to fit the unique characteristic of the brochure—the number of folds.

Brochures are designated by how many folds they have (see Exhibit 8.20). A **two-fold,** a sheet with two creases, has six panels—three on one side and three on the other. A three-fold has eight panels, and so on. Each fold adds two or more new panels. Although some very interesting folds have been developed, the usual configuration consists of panels of equal size.

Each panel may stand alone—that is, present a complete idea or cover a single subject—or may be part of a larger context revealed as the panels unfold. Either way, in the well-designed brochure, careful attention is paid to the way the panels unfold to ensure that the information is presented in the proper order. Good brochures do not unfold like road maps but present a logical pathway through their panels.

Research indicates that the first thing that a reader looks at in a direct-mail package is the brochure. The last thing is the cover letter. Exactly how you present the brochure may determine whether it gets read or is thrown away.

The Order of Presentation

The first thing you must do is establish where the front panel is and where the final panel is. The first panel or front cover need not contain any information, but it should serve as an eye catcher that draws the reader inside. It should employ a hook—an intriguing question or statement, a beautiful photograph, an

Exhibit 8.17

Standard Two-Fold Brochure in Horizontal Layout

We're national leaders in the recycling industry.

Weyerhaeuser is one of the nation's top-five recycling companies, with more than 20 years of experience. But we're not stopping there.

We continue to expand our capacity and improve our technology. We currently operate 29 recycling facilities in the United States and Canada that we keep efficient and up to date with the latest in recycling technology.

In 1993, we recycled nearly 2 million tons of material, a figure that will grow to 3 million in 1995. We use half the fiber in our own paper mills and make the rest available to other manufacturers. And we collect many non-fiber materials throughout our network of plants.

Here's how it works.

As our customer, you simply call our toll-free number for all your solid-waste and recycling needs. We handle the rest.

We dispatch the services, receive and process all invoices or rebates, handle equipment repairs, answer questions, and solve problems. You get a single monthly report and invoice for all your facility's services.

For more information:

Weyerhaeuser Solid Waste
Service Center
7015 Pueblo
Wichita KS 67209
Telephone: (316) 943-2008
Fax: (316) 943-1972

Stretch Your
Waste Management Dollars
With The

WEYERHAEUSER SOLID WASTE SERVICE CENTER

50% RECYCLED
10% POST CONSUMER

How can you manage your waste more cost-effectively?

You need access to the best markets, the latest technical data, a strong negotiating position within the hauling industry, and a trained and dedicated staff.

The Weyerhaeuser Solid Waste Service Center has it all. We can:

■ Reduce your waste-management costs.

■ Increase your recovery of recyclable goods.

■ Streamline your operations.

All this...plus our commitment to quality service and customer satisfaction.

By merging your waste-management and recycling operation into a larger negotiating group, we're able to secure the lowest costs for hauling and the highest revenues for recyclable commodities.

■ Simplify your operations.

We'll help you select the most efficient equipment, design effective material-recovery strategies, and guarantee that vendors are properly licensed and insured. We can help you identify other materials for recovery, maximize your use of existing equipment, or find ways to change your processes — all geared to reducing your waste.

■ Meet your community's recycling goals.

Good business and good citizenship go hand in hand. We can help you increase your recovery of recyclable materials and reduce your waste stream.

■ Get the data you need — quickly and efficiently.

We'll track your solid waste and recycling activities, audit and consolidate invoices and receipts, and provide information on the best markets for hundreds of different commodities. Use our accurate and timely summaries to report your waste reduction and recycling accomplishments.

■ Tap into our years of experience.

Waste management is becoming increasingly complex. From new legislation to volatile markets, just keeping up to date has become a specialty. Take advantage of our unparalleled expertise in the field.

Exhibit 8.18

Two-Fold Brochure in Vertical, Flyer Layout

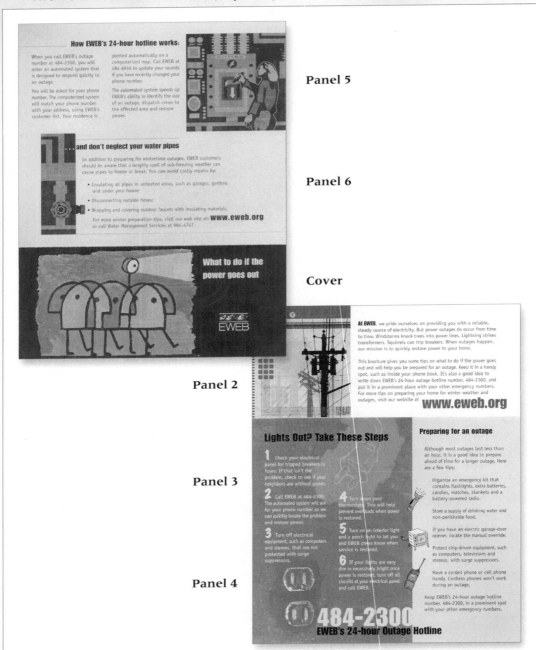

Exhibit 8.19

Large-Format, Two-Fold Brochure

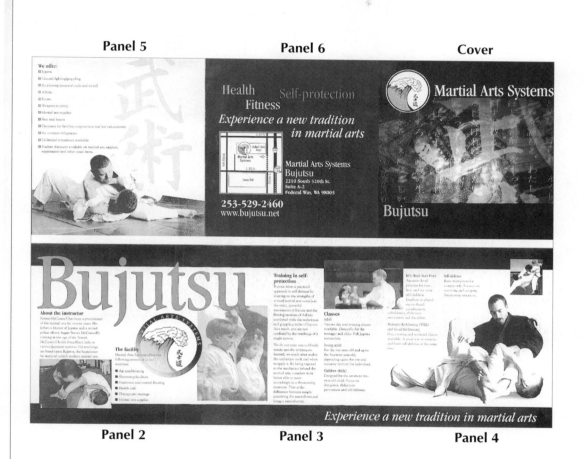

Exhibit 8.20

Standard Brochure Folds

Single Fold

Two-Fold

Three-Fold

Horizontal Two-Fold

Brochure folds are usually dictated by size and number of panels. Whether vertical (the most common orientation) or horizontal, brochure folds usually increase with size and length of copy.

eye-catching graphic, or any other device that will get the casual peruser to pick up and read the complete brochure.

If you begin your printed matter on the front cover, the headline or title becomes important. Most informational brochures use a title simply to tell what's inside. After all, most people looking for information don't want to wade through a lot of creative esoterica. A brochure headline should be to the point. Headlines that tell the reader nothing (called **blind headlines**) are of no use in a brochure. For example:

Reaching for the stars?

Is this headline for a product (maybe telescopes)? A service (astrology)?

In the U.S. Air Force, you can reach for the stars!

Now, both the intent and the sponsor are clear. For the information-seeking reader, a blind headline might work; however, if you really want to be sure—and if you want to pick up the browser as well—avoid using this type of headline.

The second panel, at least in a two-fold brochure, is the first panel of the inside spread. Its job is to build interest. The opening section should explain the purpose of the brochure and refer to the title or headline. This is the **bridge.** It is usually copy heavy and may contain a subhead or crosshead. In fact, panels may be laid out around crossheads. But make sure that the reader knows which panel follows which. Never let your copy run from panel to panel by breaking a sentence or a paragraph or (worst of all) a word in half. Try to treat each panel as a single entity with its own information. This isn't always possible, but it's nice to strive for.

The rest of the inside spread (panels 3 and 4) carries the main load. It may be constructed to present a unified whole with words and graphics bleeding from one panel to the next, or the panels may retain their individuality.

The back panels (panels 5 and 6) serve various purposes. Panel 5 may be used as a teaser or short blurb introducing the inside spread, or it may be incorporated into the design of panel 2 (especially useful because this panel is often folded in and seen as you open the front cover). It may also simply continue the information begun on panels 2, 3, and 4. Panel 6 may be left blank for mailing or contain address information. It doesn't usually contain much else.

Most of us are used to seeing two-folds folded so that the far right panel (inside panel 4 and outside panel 5) is folded in first with the far left panel (outside panel 1 and inside panel 2) folded over it (see Exhibit 8.21). But this approach has always presented problems. For instance, what do you put on panel 5? It is the first panel you see when you open the cover, yet it is technically on the back of the brochure. You can use it as a teaser or simply as the informational panel that follows the inside spread. Or, you can experiment with the fold (see Exhibit 8.22). So much depends on the presentation of your information, and because they are folded, brochures are among the hardest collateral pieces to present properly. If readers are even slightly confused, you've lost them.

Crossheads

Crossheads, or subheads, should be used liberally in a brochure. They help break up copy and give your brochure a less formidable appearance. Studies have shown that copy formed into short paragraphs, broken by informative crossheads, gives the reader a feeling that he or she can read any section independently without

Exhibit 8.21

Traditional Folds

The standard two-fold folder places the cover on the far right panel of the outside spread. Panel 5 (inside panel 4) folds in first.

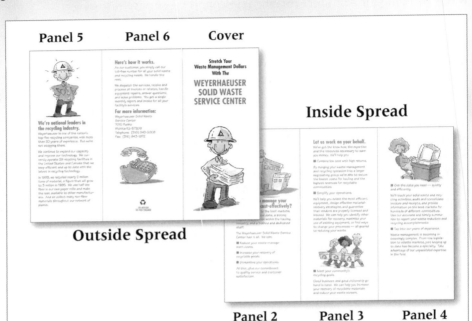

Panel 5 **Panel 6** **Cover**

Outside Spread

Inside Spread

Panel 2 **Panel 3** **Panel 4**

This traditional fold requires two "unfolds" to access the inside spread—the cover and panel 5; however, panel 5 may or may not be intended as part of the inside spread. More often, it follows panels 2 through 4, yet it appears as the first panel seen when the folder is opened.

Panel 2 **Panel 3** **Panel 4**

Exhibit 8.22

Nontraditional Folds

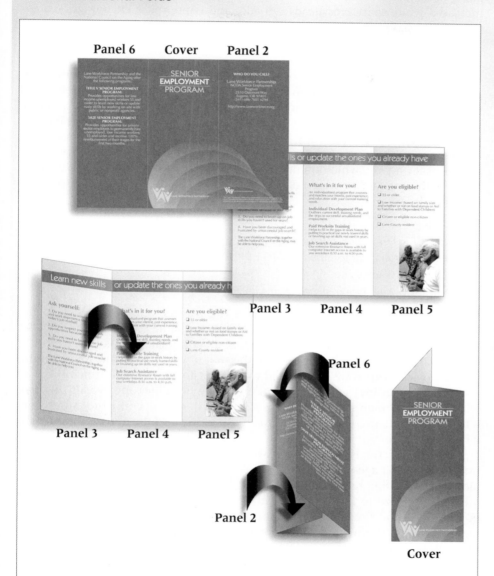

The standard two-fold folder is redesigned here placing the cover in the center of the outside panel. This allows panel 2 to fold inside.

Outside panel 2 (inside panel 3) folds inside, becoming the first copy panel seen when the folder is opened. Panel 6 folds over it to become the back (or mailer). This presents the center outside panel as the cover and sets up two "unfolds" to get to the inside spread; however, there is no doubt that panel 2 (even though it is folded inside) is the first panel to be read. This fold alleviates the "panel 5" problem of the traditional fold.

being obligated to read the entire piece. Although in some instances this may be self-defeating, reading one pertinent paragraph is often better than reading none; and if you run your copy together in one long, unbroken string, you're going to limit readership to a hardy few. Your brochure will look better with the increased white space crossheads can add, and white space encourages readership as well.

Copy Format

As you create your brochure, you may have to present the copy to others for approval. It helps to place it into a format that conveys the look of the finished product. The best way to show anyone how a finished piece will look is to mock it up; however, copy often must be approved prior to any mockup, so indicating headlines, visuals, and copy blocks in the order in which they appear is an important visual aspect of the brochure copy format. This type of format is like the script for a play, which traditionally describes visual action that takes place along with dialogue or monologue. Remember reading those Shakespearean plays in school?

> **ACT I**
>
> SCENE I *Elsinore. A platform before the castle.*
>   [FRANCISCO *at his post. Enter to him* BERNARDO]
> BERNARDO *Who's there?*
> FRANCISCO *Nay, answer me: stand, and unfold yourself.*

This play script sets the scene, introduces the players, and indicates dialogue. Using a brochure "script" accomplishes much the same thing, as Exhibit 8.23 shows. Visuals (the scene) are described, and copy (dialogue) is indicated. If a visual change is indicated, it appears in the spot in which it would appear in the finished piece, with copy interrupted to account for the visual—much the way a scene change is indicated in a script. Indicating headlines and visuals this way will help you formalize your thoughts if you are doing the entire brochure yourself and will enhance continuity between the writer and the designer if they are different people.

Producing a script is as far as most writers go; however, if you work for a small firm or nonprofit agency, you may be solely responsible for producing collateral pieces from writing to layout. Remember, you can write first and then develop a length and size to fit your editorial needs, or you can limit your copy to a preset design and size. Either way, you have to be aware of copyfitting requirements. Once you know how much you must write, stick to your guns. If you find that you have written more than will fit your original design concept, you can increase the number of folds and, thus, the number of available panels, or you can edit your copy to fit the original design.

If your supervisor isn't clamoring for every ounce of information that you can provide in 93½ square inches of space, stick with editing your copy. The best brochures are almost always the short ones.

Exhibit 8.23

Script Format for Brochure Copy

"Phone Fraud"
3-fold folder
Attorney General

PANEL 1

HEADLINE:	WE THOUGHT YOU'D LIKE TO KNOW ABOUT (graphic splits head line here) PHONE FRAUD
VISUAL:	Stylized graphic of telephone
SUBHEAD:	A consumer guide to your rights and obligations when dealing with telephone sales

PANEL 2

SUBHEAD:	WHAT IS PHONE FRAUD?
COPY:	We've all been asked to purchase something or donate to a cause over the phone.

Most of the people who contact us represent legitimate   firms that use the telephone to sell quality goods and services or raise money for worthy causes.

However, there are companies that are involved in telemarketing fraud. According to the Federal Trade Commission, telemarketing fraud is the use of telephone communications to promote goods or services fraudulently. And this can cost you money!

VISUAL:	Cartoon drawing of telephone receiver
SUBHEAD:	WHAT ARE THEY TRYING TO SELL YOU?
COPY:	Fraudulent sales callers try to sell us everything from vacations and time-share condominiums to vitamins and magazine subscriptions. They say they represent film clubs, vacation resorts, charities, magazine and book clearing houses, and even churches. Sometimes they want money sent to them directly, or sometimes they just want your credit card number. (This is especially dangerous because they can charge any amount they want with your number.)
SUBHEAD:	WHAT DO THEY SAY TO YOU?
COPY:	Although fraudulent sales callers may have vastly different products or services to sell, there are frequently similarities in their "pitches." These pitches often sound very professional. Sometimes, you are even transferred from person to person to make it sound more like a business setting. Do the following lines sound familiar?

--"You've been specially selected to hear this offer!" (How was the selection process made?)

--"You'll get a wonderful prize if you buy..." (How much is this prize worth?)

--"You have to make up your mind right away..." (They make it seem like this is a now or never opportunity.)

--"It's free, you just have to pay the shipping and handling!" (If they get only $7.00 shipping and handling per person and con 100 people into paying up front, they

-more-

(continued)

(continued)

Phone Fraud--Page 2

make $700!)

--"But first, I'll have to have your credit card number to verify..." (To verify what and why?)

PANEL 3
SUBHEAD: WHAT HAPPENS THEN?

COPY: If it is a fraudulent sales call, you sometimes actually receive the merchandise--but it is often over priced, of poor quality, or the wonderful prize you won is usually a cheap imitation.

Or, if you've been asked to invest in something, it may turn out to be non-existent.

Or, you find out the worthy cause you donated to only got a tiny part of your actual donation while the caller got the bulk of it.

Or, unauthorized charges start appearing on your credit card bills.

PANEL 4
SUBHEAD: HOW CAN YOU PROTECT YOURSELF?

COPY: 1. First of all, always find out who is calling and who they represent. Ask how they got your name. Ask who is in charge of the company or organization represented. Get specific names and titles. Ask for the address and telephone number of the firm calling you. Be extremely cautious if the caller won't provide that information.

2. Be cautious if the caller says an investment, purchase, or charitable donation must be made immediately. Ask instead that information be sent to you.

3. Be wary of offers for free merchandise or prizes. You may end up paying handling fees greater than the value of the gifts. And, don't ever buy something just to get a free prize.

4. If you're interested in the offer, ask for more information through the mail. Also ask if it's possible to obtain the names and numbers of satisfied customers in your area.

5. If you're not interested in the offer, interrupt the caller and say so. Remember, part of their job is to talk without pause so you can't ask them questions. Don't be afraid to interrupt.

PANEL 5
SUBHEAD: WHAT DO YOU DO IF YOU'RE VICTIMIZED...
Report the facts to :

Financial Fraud Section
Department of Justice
240 Cottage Street S.E.
Salem, Oregon 97210

-more-

```
Phone Fraud--Page 3

    KICKER:         REMEMBER, YOU HAVE RIGHTS. DON'T BE VICTIMIZED BY TELE-
                    PHONE FRAUD!
    PANEL 6
    HEADLINE:       HOW TO RECOGNIZE PHONE FRAUD AND WHAT TO DO ABOUT IT,
                    FROM THE STATE OF OREGON ATTORNEY GENERAL'S OFFICE

                                    -30-
```

OTHER INFORMATION PIECES

In addition to brochures, a wealth of other formats is used to impart information in print. These range from near-magazine-length booklets to single- and double-sided flyers to posters and pamphlets. Each is designed for a slightly different purpose, but they all aim at the same target publics as brochures and all are written roughly in the same manner. The only real difference is length. The longer the piece, the more organized the writing has to be and the more unified the design. (see Chapter 9 for more on unity and design.)

Flyers

Flyers are a quick way to disseminate information, even to large audiences, cheaply. A flyer is typically a single sheet of paper, usually letter sized, printed on one or both sides (see Exhibit 8.24). A flyer is most often photocopied but is sometimes printed if slickness is important.

Flyers can be folded, but this is most often done only for mailing purposes. Usually, they are distributed flat because the most common form of flyer dissemination is still by hand. In fact, the term *flyer* refers to the rapidity with which they can be delivered—historically by children running through the streets handing them out.

Flyers are handed out on street corners, at entrances to events, and practically anywhere that large numbers of people gather. Flyers are distributed in employee mailboxes and door-to-door. They are pinned on bulletin boards and office doors. In short, flyers are one of the most useful—and ubiquitous—forms of information dissemination around.

Unlike brochures, good flyers are often laid out like good print ads or sometimes, depending on the amount of information needed, like a good newsletter page. But, like a brochure, the copy is written and the graphics designed to work together to bring the reader's attention directly to the message being imparted. The same script format is therefore used for flyers and posters as for print ads and brochures.

When writing for flyers, keep in mind how much information that you need to impart versus how much space that you have to work with. In most cases, you have a considerable amount of space—the same space as a standard brochure

Exhibit 8.24

Flyers

Seen here are three flyers. The two smaller flyers are the same dimensions as a standard brochure, printed on both sides. These are quick and inexpensive to produce because of the small size. The larger flyer is 8½ × 11 inches and is printed on one side only.

with none of the restrictions that panels impose. This leaves plenty of room for creativity.

If you have a lot to say, consider using a newsletter- or magazine-style approach to layout. Divide the page into columns and work within those borders with both words and graphics. Use subheads to break up the copy and plenty of bulleted items for clarity.

Choose your graphics carefully and for full impact. Only the most striking graphics should appear on flyers because you usually have only one shot to capture attention. Why? Because you are competing for attention against dozens of other information pieces just like yours.

If you have only a little to say (maybe an announcement of an event), then use full-impact language—as in advertising. Get readers' attention with a big headline and striking graphic. Make them pay attention to your copy, brief though it may be.

The main selling points of a good flyer are its ease of production, the easy way it lends itself to creativity, and its relatively low cost.

Posters

The only real differences between posters and flyers are size and cost. Whereas most flyers are inexpensive to produce, posters are usually more costly for a number of reasons. First, they are larger, anywhere from 11 × 17 inches to several square feet in size. Second, although some are in black and white, most are in color. The most common use for posters is announcements. They have historically heralded plays, movies, gallery openings, rallies, and other special events. They have called us to arms and called us to save the planet. Posters are incredibly useful communication devices; however, their prohibitive costs have usually limited their usefulness to public relations.

A resurgence of sorts began in the late 1980s with corporations realizing that posters could be used in the workplace to keep employee morale up. Since that time, they have proliferated in some corporations and businesses (see Exhibit 8.25). Their usefulness depends on the purpose for which they are created. The most useful employee posters seem to be those designed with information in mind; however, posters can be used for everything from enhancing employee morale to imparting historical company information. Advancements in computer printing techniques have allowed even small-run posters (fewer than what would be cost effective using traditional printing techniques) to be produced. Traditional printing methods such as offset printing (see Chapter 9) simply wouldn't allow for the printing of a single poster—a job that can now be done by most print shops and many copy shops for under $100.

Displays, especially internal company displays, are often posterlike in presentation. A number of organizations have chosen to decorate their premises with displays geared specifically to the employee public. The objective is to enhance morale, in many cases, as well as to provide information about company ethos, history, and mission.

Exhibit 8.25

Posters

The larger poster (top right, 22 × 34 inches) is designed to be seen by both employees and visitors. The smaller one (bottom right, 11 × 17 inches) is a recruitment poster and is designed to be pinned up on bulletin boards. The large, display poster (left) is one of a series of hanging panels outlining characteristics important to the organization.

Booklets and Hybrids

Booklets are produced for nearly every imaginable reason. Usually, the subject is too complex or too lengthy to fit into a brochure, yet a print publication is needed because of its semipermanence. Booklets also run the range of sizes, depending on the use to which they are put (see Exhibit 8.26). A small "facts and figures" booklet might be sized to fit into a pocket, much as the standard brochure is designed to be pocket sized. Or it might replicate a magazine in size and heft and be designed to be kept and referenced frequently.

Writing style varies according to the purpose of the booklet; however, you will rarely see anything resembling feature style in even a lengthy booklet. They are sales pieces and, like brochures, need to stick to the details. Space is still limited,

Exhibit 8.26

Booklets

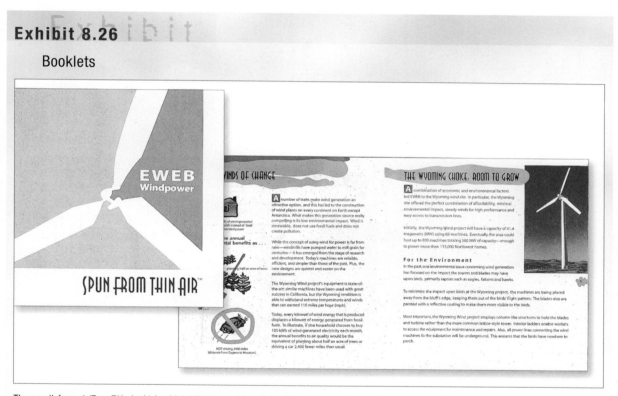

The small-format (7 × 7½ -inch) booklet (above) explains to electric utility customers the uses and savings associated with wind power. It is a three-color job printed on recycled paper. The 12-page booklet (next page) details the services of a group of counselors who deal with substance-abuse problems. The entire booklet is designed using stock photography purchased in CD format; however, it is a full-color job, adding to the expense of producing it.

(continued)

(continued)

and production costs will often dictate size and length. Format is the same as for brochures and includes notation of graphics and copy in the order in which they will appear in the booklet.

Hybrids include basically anything that is neither a brochure nor a booklet. This can be what might otherwise be termed a large-format brochure. It could also be a large-format booklet with covers designed to hold additional information, much like a media kit (see Exhibit 8.27).

The Nonprofit Annual Report

A corporate annual report is required by the Securities and Exchange Commission (SEC) for all publicly traded companies in order to provide their investors with a yearly financial statement. This type of report is highly specialized, with the content strictly dictated by the SEC. As such, corporate annual reports are

Exhibit 8.27

Hybrids

(continued)

(continued)

Although the Weyerhaeuser hybrid piece (on the facing page) folds like a brochure, it is the size of a newsletter and draws from both brochure and newsletter design in its layout. The 14-page Intel booklet (above) has a large format (9 × 12 inches) with an extremely heavy cover stock. The inside back cover is die cut to create a pocket for additional information.

usually farmed out to agencies or writers who specialize in their production and design. Increasingly, however, annual reports are being produced by organizations other than publicly traded corporations.

The overriding reason is that stakeholders always benefit from seeing where their money is being spent or how their efforts are being rewarded. Did their donation go directly to support the charity's constituents? Was part of it diverted to administrative costs? An accounting of expenses and an assessment of how the organization did during the previous year will go a long way toward ensuring continued involvement.

Because the SEC has no control over the **non-profit annual report,** the writing is much less specialized and can be done by any good public relations writer. There really isn't much difference between writing for a social responsibility report and an annual report, except that you can put in pretty much whatever you feel is important. See Exhibit 8.28.

The nonprofit annual report should be targeted to all your stakeholders. Here is a list of potential stakeholders:

- Volunteers and fund-raisers
- Boards of directors, management, or trustees
- Staff
- Service users
- Members
- Clients/beneficiaries
- Potential staff
- Partners
- Local groups
- Voluntary organizations in same field of work
- Local media
- Local community
- Donors—current and potential
- General public

Contents

Nonprofit annual reports usually consist of four sections:

1. *Letter from the board chairperson.* The board chair's letter is much the same as in a corporate report, except that the focus is usually on human capital rather than financial capital. Accomplishments are usually described with broad strokes because the next section provides the details.

2. *Description section.* In this section, the activities of the organization are described: what it has accomplished over the past year and who has supported it.

3. *List of directors and officers.* Many public agencies and nonprofits have boards of directors drawn, usually, from the local community. Listing the board members and agency officers gives an idea of the caliber of the individuals associated with the organization. Most agencies try to cull board members from a cross section of the community. They often are officers in other, for-profit organizations or are simply well-respected community members.

Exhibit 8.28

Non-profit Annual Report

As you can see, a non-profit annual report can be every bit as attractive as a corporate annual report. Large graphics and an interesting layout support the importance of the copy. As with most annual reports, this one was written through a group effort, compiled by a single editor, and laid out by a good designer.

4. *Financial statement.* As with the corporate annual report, the financial statement is one of the most important areas. This statement often includes the following sections:

- *CPA opinion letter.* The CPA opinion letter tells the reader whether something is out of whack with the organization's finances. Qualifications are carefully inserted here and should be an indication of any problems.

If there are no qualifications, the letter will be short and simply state that the organization has followed standard GAAP (generally accepted accounting principles) rules in the United States.

- *Income statement.* The income statement shows what money came in and where it went. The percentage of revenues going to salaries, management services, and fund-raising expenses are important to consider. For example, the National Charities Information Bureau (NCIB) recommends that organizations spend at least 60 percent of annual expenses for program activities.

- *Balance sheet.* The balance sheet shows where funds have been placed over the years. The NCIB recommends that organizations (a) have net assets available for the following fiscal year of not more than twice the current year's expenses or the next year's budget, whichever is higher, and (b) not have a persistent or increasing deficit in unrestricted net assets.

- Footnotes. Footnotes are important to read because they can alert the reader to lawsuits, litigation, IRS problems, loans to directors or officers, loans for other purposes, and "extraordinary charges."

Structure

When structuring your annual report, remember that most of your constituency will read it with an eye to accuracy. Opinion surveys show that this is the only information about a nonprofit that many people trust. It is your opportunity to let people know exactly what you stand for and how you conduct your business. Consider the following general guidelines when structuring your annual report.

- Explain what the organization does and what more needs to be done.

- Communicate why the organization does what it does, how and on what it spends its money, and the rationale behind its actions.

- Address the assumptions that the public makes about the organization.

- Demonstrate accountability and transparency.

- Inspire confidence by showing a spirit of openness about how the organization is managed, its policies, and its performance.

- Demonstrate how the organization's achievements represent good value for donors.

Specifically, the following should be considered, although you may not need to include everything.

General Information

- All contact details—full mailing address, telephone and fax numbers, and e-mail and Website addresses

- Charity number/Company Limited by Guarantee status and Company Registration number if appropriate

- Year of annual report

- List of members of committee or board and their positions

- The full title of the organization if it is usually known by its initials

- Organizational structure

What the Organization Does and How Well

- An explanation of what the organization does, whom it helps, and how it does so—with figures and examples
- The organization's strategy and how it is implemented
- Activities in which the organization has been involved
- An interpretation or measure of effectiveness against some standard or previous achievement (for example, increase in figures from previous year)
- Developments and achievements of the past year
- Future plans, including risks
- Examples of how what the organization has done fits its aims and objectives

The Involvement of Others

- Partnership activity (for example, local authority, health board, joint work with other voluntary organizations)
- Use of volunteers; effect of their contribution
- Thanks to personnel—management, staff, volunteers, clients

Donors

- Acknowledgment of support
- Thanks to donors
- Use of donors' logos where required

Finances

- Accurate balance sheet
- Explanation of unusual items on balance sheet
- Explanation of support services costs (for example, administration)
- Details of fund-raising, its effectiveness, and how much it has cost
- What the money is being spent on
- Projection of future financial position

KEY TERMS

newsletter	referral ending	format
downward communication	response ending	positioning
	profile	two-fold
upward communication	subhead	blind headline
	crosshead	bridge
style sheet	caption	non-profit annual report
feature style	cutline	
summary ending	pull quote	

CHAPTER 9

Design, Printing, and Desktop Publishing

In This Chapter, You Will Learn

- What design is and why it is important in communication.
- The principles of design.
- How to choose the appropriate typeface, ink, paper, and printing process for a publication.

- What desktop publishing is and how it has changed the design and printing process.
- How to work well with a printer.

Design is central to the success of any communication. In fact, most designers would go so far as to suggest that design is just as important an element of a publication as writing. Don't get me wrong: If your writing stinks, graphic cartwheels and high-design acrobatics won't cover up the smell. But the point must be made that good design attracts and holds readership, whereas bad design repels and discourages it. If you don't get them in the tent, they won't see the show.

Like it or not, we read externally first and internally second. That is, we judge publications not only by their covers but also by their overall visual appearance. Design provides an outward structure upon which we further communicate our messages, sell our soap, project our images, inform our publics, and otherwise hang our corporate hats. Although most companies pay plenty of attention to the design of their ads, packaging, logos, and other images, they often lose sight of the importance of design when it comes to their publications.

But make no mistake, whether the publication is internal (a newsletter, benefits folder, or employee recruitment kit) or external (a brochure, annual report, or company magazine), its design requires careful planning. Without structure, visual thought, and order, a publication will not get the attention it deserves. No matter how well written and carefully edited your message may be, readers will pass over poorly designed print materials. It's as simple as that.

For these reasons, then, I want to spend some time talking about design. First, as a public relations writer, you must understand and be able to use basic design principles. Second, you need to develop a design vocabulary so that you can communicate clearly with designers, printers, and other publication professionals. Third, you must know how the eye moves through a page (so that you can direct and redirect visual traffic) as well as understand how to attract and hold readers. Finally, you need to comprehend the "parts of sight" as clearly as you know the parts of speech.

DESIGN: WHAT IT IS AND WHY IT MIGHT BE GREEK TO YOU

Before venturing further, I need to define what I mean by design. Essentially, *design* is the act of bringing order to whatever surrounds us. It is planning and organizing physical materials and shaping and reshaping our environment to accommodate specific needs. There's nothing particularly mysterious about design, but many of us are intimidated by it.

For one thing, few of us have had much visual education. That fact is especially ironic when you consider how much our learning and survival depend on sight. Think about it: With few exceptions, our verbal literacy is learned, broadened, and specialized through vision—that is, through reading and writing skills. We study letters, words, spelling, vocabulary, grammar, syntax, style, writing, and literature. Grammar is apt to be central to our language studies from third grade through our first year of college. Writing begins before we start our formal education and continues throughout. Visual studies, however, tend to end somewhere between the second and third grades when crayons are either thrown or taken away.

Another reason why we underestimate the impact of design is the effortless nature of sight itself. Our eyes are designed to receive and process lines, shapes, textures, colors, intricate spatial relationships, and other complex visual information almost instantly. As long as we keep our eyes open, we don't run red lights, fall down stairs, open the wrong end of a soda can, or trample people. That sight works so easily is both good and bad: Good in that our visual sense operates automatically, is well greased, and complete beyond our wildest dreams. Bad in that we take it for granted and often assume that to have sight is to have visual literacy. Of course, this is no more the case than to assume that to be able to speak a language is the same as to read and write that language.

It should come as no surprise, then, that design seems foreign to most of us. It enjoys its own vocabulary, grammar, syntax, composition, and meaning. Additionally, it possesses a unique literature, history, and heritage—one that, in fact, precedes written language. But, happily, acquiring this new visual language is considerably less painful than the average root canal procedure. Let's get started.

DESIGNING PUBLIC RELATIONS MATERIALS

Do different print formats require different design approaches, principles, and strategies? Or, more simply stated, do you design differently for different formats? Well, yes and no. Or, as Winnie the Pooh might say, it all depends.

A set of design principles applies to whatever we create, regardless of format, medium, intent, or audience. In each instance, we plot a visual course that becomes the blueprint for our publication's architecture. And although publication formats vary, just as buildings differ, they possess similar structural principles—just as skyscrapers, shopping malls, museums, and homes have some characteristics in common. Publications, like buildings, use a structural plan that mixes serious pragmatic and aesthetic concerns while providing a sound framework and foundation.

But every publication deserves a good design that takes into account its format, medium, intent, and audience (see Exhibit 9.1).

- *Format.* The exaggerated vertical format of a brochure presents a set of spatial concerns much different from those of a poster. The brochure's long, relatively small and narrow area is arranged in a series of panels—of equal or unequal size—that can be folded two, three, or more times vertically or horizontally. These properties make the brochure's continuity and sequence especially important. A poster, by contrast, presents a single face to its reader and is therefore designed much more like a print ad with a point of emphasis for entry and a series of guides leading the reader through the integrated communication.

- *Medium.* The medium also brings its own eccentricities and needs to the design. Although an annual report may bear a strong resemblance to a magazine—and the best ones seem to—special care is required to design a report that communicates with its many audiences while conforming to

Exhibit 9.1

Connection Newsletter

The Weyerhaeuser newsletter *Connection* is a 12-page tabloid, printed in two colors (a different second color each issue) and full of large graphic photos and images.

Inside:

New fiber line, a look at Wilton Connor, our retail strategy, ethics training and more…

Weyerhaeuser Company
Containerboard Packaging and Recycling
EC2-2D7
P.O. Box 9777
Federal Way WA 98063-9777

PRESORTED
Standard Rate
U.S. Postage
PAID
Seattle WA
Permit No. 3597

CONNECTION

The newsletter of   Weyerhaeuser Containerboard Packaging and Recycling   May/June 2003

Not a moment to spare

At a glance: Getting in there JIT

As companies react to the strict requirements of mega-retailers, many are going to a just in time (JIT) concept — reducing their inventories and asking for product only when they need it. For box plants, that means coming up with quick and creative packaging solutions.

Quick service

"Customers are being more and more driven by their customers — like Wal-Mart. If Wal-Mart's needs change, so do our customers', and they come to somebody like us to meet their needs," says Andy Fescoe, general manager at the Rochester,

N.Y., box plant. "We try to think of ourselves as a service company with a product. We provide a product, but we have to be able to react very quickly to an ever-shortening time frame."

Speedy solutions

Two of Rochester's customers, Kodak and Sentry, continually put the team to the test.

For Kodak, Rochester services multiple divisions and runs hundreds of SKUs. "Over time, the delivery requirements have become shorter and shorter," says Andy. "They have reduced inventory but still need the product available quickly and at a reasonable cost."

Three methods are used to meet Kodak's needs:

▪ Delivering made-to-ship orders, which are called in five days in advance.

▪ Maintaining inventory at the plant of 15 popular items. Orders are faxed in at night, and the boxes are delivered each morning — meeting a four-hour turnaround requirement.

▪ Delivering orders as small as 25 boxes to Kodak's internal warehouse, called the Kodak Hub. Those orders require a four-hour turnaround.

Changing the system

Although the Kodak Hub solves Kodak's JIT needs, the requirements are hard for the Rochester team to meet, and it's costly.

"Presently, we're working at a way to exit the Kodak Hub situation and begin 'self-hubbing.' We're working with Kodak now on establishing the logistics necessary here to be able to accommodate the four-hour turnaround requirement," says Andy. "We have our IT people as well as Kodak's IT people working diligently to come up with a method of

Continued on page 2

Weyerhaeuser

Not a moment... Continued from page 1

communication that still allow the four-hour turnaround."

Different looks, one box

Another way Rochester helps speed up its response time is through label application. Its customer Sentry, a metal-safe manufacturer, needs similar-sized boxes but requires quick deliveries of many different models going to different retailers. Boxes are generic until the product-specific labels are applied.

> "But whether you are bringing in a day's worth or an hour's worth of material, inventory is required someplace. And at some point, the lines of economy and space cross."

"In this case, we can inventory for them but not in the finished-goods form," says John McCormick, sales manager at Rochester. "We can bring the boxes off the corrugator, and even diecut them in some cases, prior to having the labels applied. And we can react rapidly when Sentry calls — even if it's within a 48-hour time frame."

Who's holding the box?

Although inventory creates flexibility and often allows a plant to meet the time-sensitive specs, it is expensive.

"In my opinion, there's a paradox with the JIT delivery concept," says John. "Everyone is trying to eliminate inventory. But whether you are bringing in a day's worth or an hour's worth of material, inventory is required someplace. And at some point, the lines of economy and space cross."

Maximizing the machine

There are other hidden costs associated with JIT delivery besides just inventory.

"In our business, you have to set up your finishing equipment for each specific order," says Andy. "It doesn't make sense to run a machine five minutes if it has a setup time of 45. We want to spread that setup over a much larger quantity of boxes so it is more effective — and that is part of the JIT trade-off."

Open lines of communication

But despite the costs, the trend is set. Customers continue to want less quantity, larger varieties and quicker turnarounds. To achieve that requires fine-tuned logistics.

"Communication is the cornerstone of it all," says Mike Rougeux, plant superintendent at the Elmira Heights, N.Y., box plant, which serves customers such as Corning Glass and Leprino Foods.

"We've really had to hone the "can-do" attitude," says Mike. "Our customers' needs are complicated, and we have to understand them. And it's the open communication between ourselves and our customers that gives us the flexibility to work through obstacles."

Some steps the team takes to ensure JIT deliveries include:

■ A design review process for all new items. A cross-functional team studies expectations and obstacles.

■ Limiting work behind each machine to remain as flexible as possible.

■ Scheduling by customer service of the lineup behind converting machines for maximum efficiency.

■ Strong partnering with quality vendors for tooling and quality raw materials.

"We have a 98 percent on-time delivery since we started tracking," says Mike. "We have strong processes in place, but we also have strong relationships, whether it's between our customers and ourselves or internally between sales and manufacturing. You have to all work together to meet the customers' needs. When you start acting independently, you lose."

Andy agrees, "You have to continually work together to come up with a workable solution, because it's an ever-changing climate."

MAKING THE RIGHT DECISION

Steve Rogel leads SMT in discussion on ethical business practices

At a glance: Ethics training coming this spring

A new employee who has not been fully trained dumps solvent down a storm drain. What should you do? As it turns out, this very situation may be one of the topics you will be discussing in the upcoming 2003 ethics training.

The code

Every three years, Weyerhaeuser revises its code of ethics. This year's 6th edition, entitled *Our Reputation: A Shared Responsibility*, includes:

■ A new section on privacy.

■ Reformatting to make it more reader-friendly.

■ A rewritten section on electronic resources for easier understanding.

■ Revised language to reinforce compliance with new laws and regulations.

Every employee will be receiving a copy of the updated document.

Training

Following distribution, training will be conducted companywide. The objective is to ensure that all employees are aware of the company's current guidelines for conducting business in an ethical manner. It also provides information on how to raise any concerns or report potential unethical or illegal activity.

Weyerhaeuser has a well-earned reputation for conducting business ethically. Nurturing this ethical culture is important because it:

■ Provides a competitive advantage in the marketplace.

■ Enables us to attract and retain good people who share our values.

■ Provides us with credibility in the marketplace.

■ Gains support from the communities where we do business.

Adding excitement

Neil Moir, manager, ethics and business conduct, admits that some may find the code a little dry. "That's why we've tried to put a little life into the training," he says. "The first segment will be familiarizing people with the program. The second part is much

more interactive. There is a video where different scenarios are presented to open up dialogue on a range of issues. It's set up to get people thinking and talking about the code in daily practice.

"In the video, employees can see how ethical dilemmas affect them, which gets the ethical juices flowing," says Neil. This year, the SMT will be featured throughout the video, giving guidance in certain situations.

Top to bottom

On March 17, Steve Rogel led a training session for his direct reports. The training will start "cascading" through the businesses June 1, 2003. The SMT will give the course to the leaders under them, who will take it the supervisors under them, and so on, until everyone has received the training.

"Our business will continue the cascading approach until every employee has received the training from their manager. We expect that that bulk of that training will be completed by the end of 2003. This training is refreshed every two years," said Jim Keller, senior vice president, CBPR.

Sonja Narcisse, CBPR HR director, will be communicating the deployment and tracking process to managers in mid May.

"We want to remind folks that this training is not a change in the company's ethics," says Jim Keller, senior vice president of CBPR and the CBPR BMT. "Our employees are ethical and know this information. Integrity is a part of everything we do. This is a refresher course — one with the support of Mr. Rogel, the Board of Directors and the SMT."

Contact:
Weyerhaeuser Business Conduct office: Neil Moir, 253-924-4955
CBPR & process questions: Sonja Narcisse, 253-924-2821

exacting Securities and Exchange Commission requirements that prescribe everything from logistics to point size. Designing a poster that will be read from across a room by a moving audience—or that may itself be moving—presents a different challenge.

- *Intent.* Intent also figures squarely into the design formula. Let's assume that a company has had a financially disastrous year. Although it can easily afford a full-blown, four-color report with portraits of smiling CEOs in three-piece suits, perceptive company planners might decide that a more austere approach is warranted. Or, perhaps due to a corporate takeover or a major image overhaul, a company decides to completely reposition itself and court a changed or new audience. To do so, it redesigns everything from its newsletter to its logotype. Simply put, your purposes affect the look and structure of what you publish.

- *Audience.* All publications should be designed with their audience in mind. Too often we forget the audience by neglecting to notice that it has changed dramatically or is in the process of a major change. Or, we're so insulated that we don't measure what we publish by the most important touchstone—our consumers. There's nothing like a sudden decline in readership for the company newsletter to alert an editor to potential problems.

PRINCIPLES OF DESIGN

Most of us don't pay much attention to a design when everything is correctly ordered. In fact, the average person seldom sees design in anything at all. We read newspapers daily without noticing the skeletal framework that orders the headlines, photography, graphics, text, and other style elements of a page. Similarly, we raise our wineglasses to toast without realizing that stems are designed to keep our hands from warming the wine. The best design is like that: It exists but doesn't call attention to itself. As a friend once remarked, "A good designer doesn't design for design's sake. The best design serves its purpose, period—without calling attention to itself."

Although a number of basic **design principles** exist, most public relations writers can get by well enough if they understand only an indispensable few. These principles are balance, proportion, sequence and emphasis, and unity. Other design choices facing the public relations writer involve grids, alignment, and type and typefaces. I'll discuss these issues, too.

Balance

Most of us intuitively understand balance—at least to the extent that we notice immediately if something is out of balance. As children, we seemed to just know that if the person on the other end of the teeter-totter was bigger than us, we had to sit closer to the end to counterbalance his or her weight. In a way, we might say that balance is natural to human beings. We seek it in our lives, our budgets, and in the way we view the world. The very fact that we walk upright (at least most of the time) suggests that we understand balance somewhere deep in our genetic programming.

In its simplest form, *balance* as it relates to design means that what is put on one side of a page should "weigh" as much as what is on the other side. All the elements you place on the page have weight, even the white space you leave by not placing elements. Size, color, and degree of darkness all play a part in balance.

There are two ways to achieve balance (see Exhibit 9.2). The easiest is the *symmetric approach*. To balance symmetrically means to place exactly the same amount of weight in exactly the same positions on either side of the page (or spread). Symmetrically balanced pages tend to appear more formal and can be used to impart a nonverbal conservatism to your layout. The *asymmetric approach* is generally more interesting. The technique involves shifting weight on one side of a page or spread to balance the opposite side (much like in the teeter-totter example). For example, if a two-page spread has a big photo near the gutter (center line of a two-page spread) on one side of the layout, you can achieve balance by placing a smaller picture closer to the outside edge of the opposite page. Remember, this arrangement works with all elements of varying weight, including white space. An asymmetric layout appears less formal than its symmetric counterpart.

When you increase the number of elements on a page or spread, you increase the difficulty of working with symmetric balance. It is difficult, for instance, to ensure that all your photos will be the same size, all your illustrations roughly the same shape, or all your headlines the same length (especially if you want to emphasize a story over others on the page). In fact, you are almost forced into asymmetry on most layouts unless you plan carefully for the opposite effect.

For the beginner, you can check whether your layout is balanced in a number of ways, all based on looking at it from an altered perspective: For example, you can squint at your layout. The blurring attained through narrowing your eyes tends to block out the light areas and bring the darker areas of your layout to the forefront. Or you can turn your layout upside down or look at it in a mirror. Both of these methods provide you with an opposite view and thus a new look at your layout. Balance, or lack of it, will jump out at you almost immediately.

Proportion

We tend to think of proportion in terms of comparison. For instance, a picture on a page is bigger or smaller than another picture on the page, or it is the largest element on the page in comparison to the other elements. Thus, *proportion* is a measure of relationship in size. It helps show one object's relationship to other objects in your layout. For example, articles and their accompanying pictures, cutlines, and pull quotes typically will form a proportional whole in relationship to the rest of the page. Or the space that separates articles from one another may be greater than that which separates the elements within an article. We use proportion to tell us what belongs with what on a page.

Our sense of proportion has, or should have, a parallel in nature. Pythagoras, the Greek mathematician and philosopher, noticed this over 2,000 years ago when he suggested that the most pleasing proportion is based on a roughly

Exhibit 9.2

Balance

The easiest way to achieve balance is through pure symmetry (top). Place identically weighted elements on either side of the center axis of the page. Symmetry can also be affected by centering objects. Asymmetry, by contrast, requires more practice to achieve (bottom). The fundamental rule in asymmetric balance requires visualizing your layout as a teeter-totter. Balance the objects on either side of your vertical axis according to weight and distance from the fulcrum. In this case, the large image is counterbalanced by the white space and headline on the left.

2:3 ratio. In Pythagorean terms, the lesser dimension in a plane figure is to the greater as the greater is to the sum of both. Using the 2:3 ratio, 2 is to 3 what 3 is to 5. Get it?

Fortunately, there is a simpler method of explaining the concept. Think of a page of typing paper. It is 8½ × 11 inches—roughly, a 2:3 ratio. In other words, it has an asymmetric proportion rather than a 1:1 symmetric proportion. For designers, this means avoiding dividing a page into halves, or any increment of a 1:1 ratio, such as 4:2 or 6:3. Not that this rule has to be followed religiously, but it does add visual interest to your layout. A layout based on halving the page is more formal, more constrained.

A more practical—and easier—method of working with a page layout is the **rule of ground thirds.** This method requires that you divide a page into thirds and that you balance the page using a two-thirds to one-third ratio (see Exhibit 9.3). You've probably already noticed that two-thirds is roughly equivalent to three-fifths, the Greeks' favorite aspect ratio. This two-thirds to one-third ratio is commonly used in newsletter layout, but it is most often apparent in print advertisements in which a large graphic image takes up two-thirds of the page while the copy takes up the other third.

Don't get the idea that you have to group two-thirds of your elements into two-thirds of every page. This ratio can be achieved in a number of ways. For instance, you can have a page two-thirds full and one-third empty. Or you can have a page that is two-thirds empty and one-third full (although your boss might think this a little wasteful).

Sequence and Emphasis

When we look at a page, we tend to move from big elements to smaller elements, dark areas to lighter areas, colored elements to black-and-white elements, bright colors to muted colors, and unusual shapes to usual shapes. A proper *sequence,* or order, of the elements on your layout will literally lead your readers through your page (see Exhibit 9.4).

Emphasis has to do with focusing your readers' attention on a single element on a page (see Exhibit 9.5). This is what you want them to see first and is usually where you want them to start interpreting your page. We emphasize elements by assigning them more optical weight than other items on the page. These emphasized elements are larger, darker, more colorful, oddly shaped. They draw the readers' attention first among all the other items on the page.

A number of simple techniques exist that, if used properly, will show your readers exactly where to look first and where to go from there. Although these guidelines are meant specifically for newsletter layout, they can be adapted to many other types of layout as well:

- *All elements.* Elements placed high on the page will gain emphasis; elements placed at or near the bottom will have less emphasis. Placement near or at the center of the page will also gain emphasis, especially if used in conjunction with another form of emphasis such as color or size. The left side of a page or the left page of a two-page spread has priority over the right. The

Exhibit 9.3

Proportion

Proportion is achieved by using the Greek principle of ground thirds. In this example, the headline and copy take up approximately two-thirds of the page and the picture occupies the other third.

Exhibit 9.4

Sequence

Retractable leashes, odor coverups, and pooper-scoopers:

The paraphernalia of dog walking

by John Garry

It's not uncommon for the accoutrements of walking to cost more than the dog being walked.

A Quickie Price List

Leashes	$45–$300
Clothing	$60–$500
Footwear	$80–$300
Deoderizers	$2–$12
Pooper-Scooper	$25–$150
Training	$500–$1500
Dog Walker	$50 per

In this example, the headline bleeding into the white space in the upper left corner draws your eye naturally to the starting point (helped by our natural inclination to look there anyway). The natural column flow, the pull quote, and the final graphic (moving off the page to the right) all lead you to the exit point at the lower right of the layout.

outside margins of a two-page spread (the left margin of the left page and the right margin of the right page) are focal points as well.

- *Headlines.* For heavier emphasis, place headlines at the top or near the center of the page. The eye naturally falls in these areas. Additional emphasis can be gained by using a larger point size or stretching the headline over more than one-column width. Typical options are one-column heads in a smaller point size, more than one-column heads in a smaller point size, one-column heads in a larger point size, and more than one-column heads in a larger point size.

Exhibit 9.5

Emphasis

The graying of hi-tech

As the hi-tech industry ages, so do its movers and shakers.

Lorem ipsum,Dolor sit amet, consectetuer adipiscing elit, sed diam nonummy nibh euismod tincidunt ut laoreet dolore magna aliquam erat volutpat. Ut wisi enim ad minim veniam, quis nostrud exerci tation ullamcorper suscipit lobortis nisl ut aliquip ex ea commodo consequat. Duis autem vel eum iriure dolor in hendrerit in vulputate velit esse molestie consequat, vel illum dolore eu feugiat nulla facilisis at vero eros et accumsan et iusto odio dignissim qui blandit praesent luptatum zzril delenit augue duis dolore te feugait nulla facilisi.

Lorem ipsum dolor sit amet, consectetuer adipiscing elit, sed diam nonummy nibh euismod tincidunt ut laoreet dolore magna aliquam erat volutpat.

Lorem ipsum dolor sit amet, consectetuer adipiscing elit, sed diam nonummy nibh euismod tincidunt ut laoreet dolore magna aliquam erat volutpat. Duis autem vel eum iriure dolor in hendrerit in vulputate velit esse molestie consequat, vel illum dolore eu feugiat nulla facilisis at vero eros et accumsan et iusto odio dignissim qui blandit praesent luptatum zzril delenit augue duis dolore te feugait nulla facilisi.

Lorem ipsum dolor sit amet, consectetuer adipiscing elit, sed diam nonummy nibh euismod tincidunt ut laoreet dolore magna aliquam erat volutpat. Ut wisi enim ad minim veniam, quis nostrud exerci tation ullamcorper suscipit

lobortis nisl ut aliquip ex ea commodo consequat.

Lorem ipsum dolor sit amet, consectetuer adipiscing elit, sed diam nonummy nibh euismod tincidunt ut laoreet dolore magna aliquam erat volutpat. Duis autem vel eum iriure dolor in hendrerit in vulputate velit esse molestie consequat, vel illum dolore eu feugiat nulla facilisis at vero eros et accumsan et iusto odio dignissim qui blandit praesent luptatum zzril delenit augue duis dolore te feugait nulla facilisi.

Lorem ipsum dolor sit amet, consectetuer adipiscing elit, sed diam nonummy nibh euismod tincidunt ut laoreet dolore magna aliquam erat volutpat. Ut wisi enim ad minim veniam, quis nostrud exerci tation ullamcorper suscipit lobortis nisl ut aliquip ex ea commodo consequat. Duis autem vel eum iriure dolor in hendrerit in vulputate velit esse molestie consequat, vel illum dolore eu feugiat nulla facilisis at vero eros et accumsan et iusto odio dignissim qui blandit praesent luptatum zzril delenit augue duis dolore te feugait nulla facilisi. Lorem ipsum do- lor sit amet, consectetuer adipiscing elit, sed diam

nonummy nibh euismod tincidunt ut laoreet dolore magna aliquam erat volutpat. Ut wisi enim ad minim veniam, quis nostrud exerci tation ullamcorper suscipit lobor- tis nisl ut aliquip ex ea commodo consequat.Lorem ipsum dolor sit amet, consectetuer adipiscing elit, sed diam nonummy nibh euismod tincidunt ut laoreet dolore magna aliquam erat volutpat.

Duis autem vel eum iri- ure dolor in hendrerit   in

Lorem ipsum,Dolor sit amet, consectetuer adipiscing elit, sed diam nonummy nibh euismod tincidunt ut laoreet dolore magna aliquam erat volutpat. Ut wisi enim ad minim veniam, quis nostrud exerci tation ullamcorper suscipit lobortis nisl ut aliquip ex ea commodo consequat. Duis autem vel eum iriure dolor in vulputate velit esse molestie con- sequat, vel illum dolore eu feugiat nulla facilisis at vero eros et ac- cumsan et iusto odio dignissim qui blandit praesent luptatum zzril delenit augue duis dolore te feugait nulla facilisi.

Lorem ipsum dolor sit amet, consectetuer adipiscing elit, sed diam nonummy nibh euismod tincidunt ut laoreet dolore magna aliquam erat volutpat.

Lor.

'Our CEO is 55, so is our COO, while the average age of our new hires is 25.'

facilisis at vero eros et accumsan et iusto odio dignissim qui blan- dit praesent luptatum zzril delenit augue duis dolore te feugait nulla facilisi.

Lorem ipsum dolor sit amet, consectetuer adipiscing elit, sed diam nonummy nibh euismod tincidunt ut laoreet dolore magna aliquam erat volutpat. Ut wisi enim ad minim veniam, quis nostrud exerci tation ullamcorper suscipit lobortis nisl ut aliquip ex ea commodo conse- quat.

Lorem ipsum dolor sit amet, con- sectetuer adipiscing elit, sed diam nonummy nibh euismod tincidunt ut laoreet dolore magna aliquam erat volutpat. Duis autem vel eum iriure dolor in hendrerit in vulputate velit esse moles- tie consequat, vel illum do- lore eu feugiat nulla facili-is at vero eros et accumsan et iusto odio dignissim qui blandit praesent luptatum zz- ril delenit augue duis dolore te feugait nulla f.

Lorem ipsum dolor sit amet, consectetuer adipi-

em ipsum dolor sit amet, con- sectetuer adipiscing elit, sed diam nonummy nibh euismod tincidunt ut laoreet dolore magna aliquam erat volutpat. Duis autem vel eum iriure dolor in hendrerit in vulpu- tate velit esse molestie consequat, vel illum dolore eu feugiat nulla

scing elit, sed diam nonummy nibh euismod tincidunt ut laoreet dolore magna aliquam erat volutpat. Ut wisi enim ad minim veniam, quis nostrud exerci tation ullamcorper suscipit lobortis nisl ut aliquip ex ea commodo consequat. Duis autem vel eum iriure dolor in hen-

drerit in vulputate velit esse moles- tie consequat, vel illum dolore eu feugiat nulla facilisis at vero eros et accumsan et iusto odio dignissim qui blandit praesent luptatum zzril delenit augue duis dolore te feugait nulla facilisi.

Lorem ipsum dolor sit amet, consectetuer adipiscing elit, sed diam nonummy nibh euismod aliquam erat volutpat. Ut wisi enim ad minim veniam, quis nostrud exerci tation ullamcorper suscipit lobortis nisl ut aliquip ex ea com- modo consequat.

Lorem ipsum dolor sit amet, consectetuer adipiscing elit, sed diam nonummy nibh euismod tincidunt ut laoreet dolore magna aliquam erat volutpat. Duis autem vel eum iriure dolor in hendrerit in vulputate velit esse molestie con- sequat, vel illum dolore eu feugiat nulla facilisis at vero eros et ac- cumsan et iusto odio dignissim qui blandit praesent luptatum zzril delenit augue duis dolore te feugait nulla facilisi.

Lorem ipsum dolor sit amet, consectetuer adipiscing elit, sed diam nonummy nibh euismod tincidunt ut laoreet dolore magna aliquam erat volutpat. Duis autem vel eum iriure dolor in hendrerit in

Use of strong graphics, color, unusual shapes, or large type will indicate to your readers where you want them to look first; however, this may not mean you want them to start reading there. Although emphasis can be used to establish sequence, it can also be used simply to draw attention to something, with the understanding that the reader should then know where to look to begin reading. In this example, that entry point is established by the headline.

Depending on the number of columns that you are working with and the range of point sizes that you choose, the degrees of emphasis are many. Keep in mind, however, that you should vary headline size by no more than a few basic increments. For example, if minor heads are set at 18 points, major heads should not be larger than 24 or 30 points. This closeness in point size adds to the unity of your design. The rare exception might be the major headline on the front page of your newsletter. You might go all the way to 36 points, but be sure that your headline doesn't then conflict with and lessen the impact of your banner or nameplate.

- *Articles.* Place lead articles at or near the top of the page. Also place continued articles at or near the top. Because continuation lines (for example, "continued from page 1") are usually small, you can still emphasize another article on the same page as a jumped article by working with the headline. By using boxes and tint blocks (see Exhibit 9.6), you can emphasize an article by setting it off from other elements on the page. Also, dividing your page into ground thirds and placing an emphasized article in either portion by itself will get it attention.

- *Graphics.* Larger photographs and other graphic devices impart greater emphasis, no matter where they are placed. Smaller elements placed at the top or bottom of the page can also gain emphasis. A small photo, for example, placed at or near the bottom of a page might help balance a large headline placed at the top of the page.

  Again, graphic elements should follow the general restrictions of your grid (the number of columns that you are using; see discussion below). Thus, a three-column grid will allow photos of one, two, or three columns in width. Remember, too, that the darker the graphic element, the more emphasis it will have. This applies to boxed articles and tint blocks as well.

- *White space.* White space is not usually thought of as an element of emphasis. Rather, it is usually an element of contrast—that is, it is used to emphasize something else, not to draw attention to itself. The one rule to remember when using white space is, Don't surround it with other elements. White space should be pushed to the outside of your pages, not the inside. On a two-page spread, the only white space between the two pages should be the gutter. Wide side margins, heavy **drops** (the amount of white space at the top of a page), or uneven bottoms all add contrast. The creative use of white space will add an air of affluence to your publication, making it look more sophisticated. Too much white space, by contrast, will make a newsletter look like its editor ran out of stories. Remember, white space is weighted just like any other design element. Using it effectively requires a lot of practice.

Unity

Unity is one way of providing readers with a whole by drawing relationships among its various parts. This means that body type and headline type should be compatible. Photos should be either all black and white or all color. The layout should be all formal or all informal. In other words, unity is the creation of a recognizable pattern (see Exhibit 9.7).

Perhaps the best way to gain unity of design has more to do with an overall look, a unifying design. Following are some basic guidelines for gaining unity in your publication:

- Stick with one or two typefaces (described in detail below). You can gain a lot of variety by simply changing size and weight and working with the various forms that any one particular typeface offers. For example, some faces come in light, text, regular, bold, black, and ultra, not to mention the italic versions of these variations. Two typefaces should be plenty.

Exhibit 9.6

Tint Boxes

Boxes and tint blocks can be used as effective design elements, if they are used correctly. For example, never allow your text to "bump up against" the lines of you boxes or the edges of your tint blocks. This makes the text and the layout look crowded. Also be very careful not to indicate too dark a screen or your copy will be unreadable. The best way to check on screen darkness is to print it out on the ultimate output printer you are planning to use, or seek the advice of your printer.

20%

Boxes and tint blocks can be used as effective design elements, if they are used correctly. For example, never allow your text to "bump up against" the lines of you boxes or the edges of your tint blocks. This makes the text and the layout look crowded. Also be very careful not to indicate too dark a screen or your copy will be unreadable. The best way to check on screen darkness is to print it out on the ultimate output printer you are planning to use, or seek the advice of your printer.

30%

Boxes and tint blocks can be used as effective design elements, if they are used correctly. For example, never allow your text to "bump up against" the lines of you boxes or the edges of your tint blocks. This makes the text and the layout look crowded. Also be very careful not to indicate too dark a screen or your copy will be unreadable. The best way to check on screen darkness is to print it out on the ultimate output printer you are planning to use, or seek the advice of your printer.

50%

Boxes and tint blocks can be used as effective design elements, if they are used correctly. For example, never allow your text to "bump up against" the lines of you boxes or the edges of your tint blocks. This makes the text and the layout look crowded. Also be very careful not to indicate too dark a

60%

When using tint blocks, ensure that your type reads well over the percentage screen you've chosen. Top to bottom are 20, 30, 50, and 60 percent screens.

Exhibit 9.7

Unity

Unity means using compatible elements in your layout (type, artwork, photos, design, and so on). The best way to lose unity is to combine too many disparate elements in a single layout. In this simple brochure layout, only three typefaces (headline, subhead, and body copy) and a single illustration style are used.

- Use justified type for a formal look, unjustified type for an informal air (see discussion of alignment below). To increase the formality of unjustified type, just increase the hyphenation. This will make your lines less ragged on the right and, thus, more formal.

- Use rules (lines), tint blocks, and boxes for more formality; eliminate them for informality.

- Use top and bottom **anchors** (lines or strips of color) for more formal layouts.

- Make sure that all illustrations are of the same type. If you are using cartoons, stick with cartoons throughout. If you're using pen-and-ink illustrations, stick with those. Too much variation in artwork will lend an air of confusion to your publication.

- Increase white space for a more informal look. The same goes for the use of larger graphics, especially those that are unboxed.

Grids

As already noted, a **grid** is another term for the columns used in a layout (see Exhibit 9.8). Although the use of grids is most common to newsletter, annual report, and magazine layout, they also can be valuable for complex brochures and flyers as well as ad layouts.

For publications such as newsletters, the most common formats are three- and four-column layouts. Both formats are quite flexible. Three-column layouts are more appropriate for smaller formats and four-column layouts for larger. Remember, the more columns you have, the narrower they will have to be and the smaller your type needs to be to accommodate the column width.

If you're just beginning, try a basic three-column grid for all your pages. The column width is enough to give you a readable type and to use graphics in legible sizes. The basic rule of laying out a newsletter is to use the columns as your grid and lay out all your elements (in our three-column grid) in one-, two-, and three-column widths.

Alignment

Alignment refers to the way your copy is arranged in relation to column margins (see Exhibit 9.9). The two most typical alignments are *flush left* (sometimes called *ragged right*) and *justified*. Flush left, ragged right copy is getting to be common for newsletters, some in-house magazines, and other types of publications. It imparts a less formal look, involves less hyphenation, and takes up more space.

Justified copy looks more formal, is more hyphenated, and takes up less space. However, when using justified copy, keep in mind that the width of your columns severely affects word spread. The narrower your columns, the more your words will separate from one another to maintain justification. Computers allow for minute adjustments to word and letter spacing to help correct this spread, but the best way to avoid it is to keep your columns at the average or maximum width for your type size.

Other alignment possibilities exist, such as *flush right* and *centered*. Flush right copy should be avoided because it is difficult to read. However, it is sometimes useful for very brief text blocks such as pull quotes that appear in outside left margins. Centered body text should always be avoided. Centered headlines are not in fashion these days, although centered pull quotes are still found quite a bit.

The best idea is to pick either flush left or justified for your body copy and not to deviate. Stick with flush left for headlines. Use either flush left or justified for pull quotes and captions.

Exhibit 9.8

Grids

Clockwise from upper-right: A three-column grid laid out "newspaper style" with two-thirds of the layout at the top; a four-column grid with an illustrated table of contents in the bottom third; a two-column grid, also in newspaper style, with two stories on the front page; and a two-column grid with a large feature story column to the left and a boxed sidebar as the second column.

Exhibit 9.9

Text Alignment

What's the difference between a therapist, psychologist, psycho-therapist, psychiatrist, and counselor? If you don't know, you're among the millions of people who are confused about the multi-tiered mental health counseling field.

In an effort to clear up some of the confusion, the American Mental Health Counselors Association (AMHCA) has "hired" a university student group to produce a public information campaign for them.

The Public Relations Student Society of America (PRSSA) at the University of Oregon has been retained by the Association to develop a program of information that will better define the various roles contained under the umbrella term "mental health counselor." Jane Weiskoff, regional director of AMHCA says that the confusion seems to stem from a mis-

What's the difference between a therapist, psychologist, psycho-therapist, psychiatrist, and counselor? If you don't know, you're among the millions of people who are confused about the multi-tiered mental health counseling field.

In an effort to clear up some of the confusion, the American Mental Health Counselors Association (AMHCA) has "hired" a university student group to produce a public information campaign for them.

The Public Relations Student Society of America (PRSSA) at the University of Oregon has been retained by the Association to develop a program of information that will better define the various roles contained under the umbrella term "mental health counselor." Jane Weiskoff, regional director of AMHCA says that the

What's the difference between a therapist, psychologist, psycho-therapist, psychiatrist, and counselor? If you don't know, you're among the millions of people who are confused about the multi-tiered mental health counseling field.

In an effort to clear up some of the confusion, the American Mental Health Counselors Association (AMHCA) has "hired" a university student group to produce a public information campaign for them.

The Public Relations Student Society of America (PRSSA) at the University of Oregon has been retained by the Association to develop a program of information that will better define the various roles contained under the umbrella term "mental health counselor." Jane Weiskoff, regional director of AMHCA says that the

Notice that the justified text (left) takes up less space than the flush left text (center). The flush right text (right) is nearly impossible to track (move from end of one line to the beginning of the next).

Type and Typefaces

Type is the generic term for the lettering used in printing, whereas **typeface** refers to the nearly limitless alphabets and ornaments available as type. **Font** is the classification within a given typeface, such as bold or italics. The array of type and typefaces that you can choose from is truly bewildering. But if you learn a few basics now, that array can be narrowed down to just a few choices for you and your public relations material.

The first thing to know is how to classify type. Let's start with the most general and useful classification for publication purposes. First, type is measured in *points* (in type, this is a vertical measurement). There are 72 points in 1 inch. Imagine trying to designate 11-point type in inches, and you know why printers have traditionally used a different scale. Small type, up to 14 points, is called **body type.** Type that is 14 points and above is called **display type** (normally headlines). Most typefaces come in both body and display sizes; however, there

Exhibit 9.10

Type Samples

Serif Type

Times

Serifs are the small lines that cross
the end strokes of the letters in serif
type. Roman serifs have the
traditional thick and thin strokes.

Lubalin

Square or slab serifs have fairly uniform
thicknesses of both the letter strokes and
their serifs.

San Serif Type

Helvetica

In this example of sans serif type (Helvetica),
notice the uniformity of stroke width. This is
characteristic of most, but not all, sans serif
type.

Optima

Optima is one of several sans serif
typefaces with some interesting variation
in strike width. This variation (along with
a hint of serifs) tends to make the face
more readable.

Italic/Oblique Type

Type *Type*

There is quite a bit of difference between a
true italic face (Palatino italic) left, and a
slanted version of the upright face, right. Type
designers would just as soon you didn't distort
their original typeface designs.

Type *Type*

Sans serif typefaces don't have italic
versions per se. Instead, they have obliques.
Like italics, obliques are specifically
designed to be set at a slant. They are not
simply slanted versions of the upright face.

are subtle differences between the sizes. The best way to choose type is to look at a complete alphabet in all the sizes and weights that you are going to be using and check out the differences for yourself. Look for straight or curved serifs, for example, or whether the loops close or are left open on certain letters. Most of these distinctions boil down to a matter of taste. Only you know which is best for your job.

Next, type can be broken down into five other, fairly broad categories: black-letter, script, serif, sans serif, and italics. We'll look at just the last three (see Exhibit 9.10):

- *Serif.* Most **serif typefaces** are distinguished by a variation in thick and thin strokes, and by *serifs*—the lines that cross the end strokes of the letters. Serif type can be further broken down into Roman and slab or square serif faces. Roman typefaces have the traditional thick and thin strokes, whereas slab serif faces have relatively uniform strokes and serifs. Serif faces are usually considered easier to read, especially in body type sizes.

- *Sans serif.* **Sans serif typefaces** are without serifs (*sans,* from the French, meaning "without"). They are usually, but not always, distinguished by uniformity of strokes. They typically impart a more modern look to a publication, especially if used as display type. Setting body type in sans serif is unwise because the uniformity of the strokes tends to darken your page and makes for difficult reading. There are some exceptions. Optima, for example, has some variation in stroke and reads fairly well in smaller sizes. Additionally, Stone Sans, a new face designed by Sumner Stone of Adobe Systems, makes excellent use of thin and thick strokes.

- *Italics.* Some typographers don't consider italics a separate category of type because most typefaces today come with an italic version. However, true Roman italic versions of many typefaces are completely different from their upright versions. Since the advent of desktop publishing, editors have had the option of italicizing a typeface with a simple keystroke. This method typically slants only the existing face; it does not always create a true italic version of that typeface. Only by selecting a typeface that has been designed specifically as an italic do we get true italics. Because they are slanted, italics tend to impart an informality and speed to your message. However, because of the slant, they are more difficult to read and should be used for accent only.

As a point of interest, italics refers only to a version of a serif face. A slanted version of a sans serif typeface is called *oblique.* Like italics, true obliques are designed as separate fonts (a complete alphabet, number series, and set of punctuation points and miscellaneous marks) and are not simply the original face at a slant.

If you are typesetting or desktop publishing your publication, then you will have to select typefaces. Following are some of the most common questions regarding that selection:

- *May I use just one typeface?* Yes. The safest route to take is to stick with one typeface. Using a single face lends your written material unity and consistency. Pick one that comes in as many variations as possible—style, weight, size, and width.

  Most typefaces come in regular and/or light versions. These are sometimes called *book* or *text.* They also come in *upright* (Roman) and italics (or oblique, if the typeface is sans serif). In addition, they may have *demibold* and *bold* versions in both upright and italics or oblique (these versions may be called *heavy* or *black;* or heavy and black versions may be in addition to bold). And the demibold and bold versions may come as *extended* or *condensed* (referring to the width of the letters).

  The greater the variety available, the more flexibility you will have in a single typeface. For example, you could use the regular version for body type, the bold version for headlines, and the regular italic version for captions, pull quotes, and subheads (in different point sizes).

- *May I use more than one typeface?* Although you may have access to a type library of 400 or more faces, try to limit yourself to no more than two different typefaces in a publication and make sure that they don't conflict with each other. This is the most difficult part of using more than one face. Here are a few guidelines to remember:

  - If your body type is serif, try a sans serif for headlines. Two different serif faces will probably conflict with one another.

  - If you are using a light body type (as opposed to its regular version), use a regular or demibold headline type. You don't want your headline weight to overpower your text weight.

  - Above all, don't pick your type just by looking at a type chart. Have a page set, complete with body copy and headlines, to see for yourself whether your two faces are going to harmonize.

- *Where do I go to select type?* If you are working on a computer, you probably have 20 or so typefaces that come with either your system software or your layout software or both. In addition, you can easily add anywhere up to 500 choices, depending on the sophistication of your desktop publishing system. Stick with a small array of type. It's easier and saves a lot of frustration in the long run. If all you have is Times Roman, use it. If you have Times Roman and Helvetica, use Times for the body copy and Helvetica for the headlines. If you have access to a larger type library on your computer, explore your options by experimenting with several combinations, printing out a page with each one.

Don't forget to try several different point sizes for body copy also. Readability can vary a great deal between 12-point Times and 12-point Palatino, as well as between 12-point Palatino and 10-point Palatino, for example.

Be aware that your type will also look different when printed on different printers. Decide which printer that you're going to use to print your final camera-ready copy and check its print quality against your type choice. Typefaces with thin serifs may not print as well on a laser printer as on an imagesetter. Bold or heavy faces (especially if condensed) will tend to clog and fill on laser printers but will print cleanly on an imagesetter. If you don't have access to different typefaces on your computer, ask your printer for samples of type set in copy blocks and as display type. Most printers can provide you with more than just a type chart.

WORKING WITH PROFESSIONAL PRINTERS

The relationship between the writer-designer and professional printer should be a symbiotic one; however, both of you will probably have to work at it for a while until you get comfortable with the relationship. The trick to working successfully with printers is to know what you are talking about—there's no substitute for knowledge. You have to know a bit about the printing process to get along with your printer. Every writer can tell you horror stories about printers who, after seemingly understanding exactly what you want, proceed to print exactly what they want. This is not to say that it is hard to get along with printers. It simply means that you have to know what you want and be able to explain it in printer's terms. I recommend that you try out several printers and work with those who not only give you the best deal but also are willing to give you guidance. This is not an easy process, but it does pay off in a lower frustration factor in the long run.

It used to be that printers took over as soon as you handed them your copy. These days, however, it's just as likely that you've not only written the copy but also designed the piece and laid it out before you ever talk with a printer. You no longer have to go through a typesetter, for instance. However, most printers can still desktop publish your piece for you if you don't know how. And although you can often even upload your work directly to a printer's file server, it is still wise to speak with them in person first in order to avoid the almost inevitable hardware and software incompatibilities.

For example, does the printer carry the typefaces you use in your publication? If not, can you legally supply them or do you have to "print" your publication to a PostScript file, thus embedding all the fonts in the publication itself? Do you even know how to print to a PostScript file? Do you know what a PostScript file is? You're probably beginning to get the picture. No matter how sophisticated we may get, for the foreseeable future we will still be relying on printers for much of what we need in the way of finished product.

In addition, printers can be an invaluable aid in selecting printing methods, papers, inks, bindings, and so on. Even the seemingly simple process of picking a paper can be mind numbing. Literally thousands of papers are available for printing, and you can size, fold, and otherwise decorate your printed product in an unlimited number of ways. Just remember, you can get what you want if you know how to ask for it.

Printing Processes

Many writers simply entrust the choice of printing method to the printer. Although a number of printing processes are available to you, the two that you will likely have the most contact with are offset lithography and quick printing or quick copying. Most collateral pieces and many newsletters are simply offset printed, which is one of the fastest and cheapest methods to get good-quality printing today. Quick-print and quick-copy methods will usually result in a loss of quality. Other, more detailed printing jobs, such as embossing or special paper shapes, may require specialty printing. Be advised that specialty printing is costly. Make sure that you are willing to bear the extra cost before you decide on that gold-foil stamp on the cover of your new brochure.

Offset Lithography

The most common printing process used today is offset lithography. The process is based on the principle that oil and water don't mix. During the printing process, both water and ink are applied to the printing plate as it revolves.

The nonprinting area of the plate accepts water but not ink, while the image, or printing, area accepts ink but not water. It is named offset printing because the plate isn't a reverse image as in most printing processes (see Exhibit 9.11). Instead, the plate transfers its right-reading image to an offset cylinder made of rubber (which reverses the image), and from there to the paper. Because the plate never comes in contact with the paper, it can be saved and used again and again, saving cost on projects that have to be reprinted periodically—unless, of course, you make changes.

Most public relations documents are printed using offset lithography. It is relatively inexpensive, compared to other processes, and it results in a high-quality image. Although small press runs of 1,000 or less can be made using offset lithography, it is especially cost effective for larger runs because presses are capable of cranking out hundreds of copies a minute.

Exhibit 9.11

Offset Printing

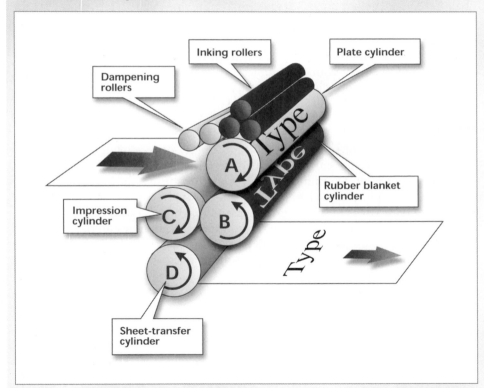

Offset gets its name from the indirect printing process in which the printing plate's image is offset to a rubber blanket that puts the ink on the paper. Notice how the type and image go from right reading to reversed to right reading again.

Quick Print and Quick Copy

The quick-print and quick-copy processes involve two methods of reproduction. *Quick print* involves a small cylinder press using paper-printing plates. The plates are created using a photoelectrostatic process that results in a raised image created with toner (much like the toner used in photocopy machines). This raised image takes the ink and is imprinted directly onto the paper.

Quick copy used to mean exclusively xerography; however, many of the newer quick-copy setups, such as Xerox's Docu-Tech, don't use this now familiar process at all. Instead, these machines (literally computers) use laser technology to print.

The result is a rapid-print method that is not limited to black and white, like xerography, but can present a wide range of grays. This is a great boon to newsletter editors who use a lot of photographs, for example. Anyone who has ever photocopied a photograph knows how bad the quality can be. The larger-model photocopiers used in this process can rapidly produce multiple copies in sizes up to 11 × 17 inches.

Neither of these processes is useful for two-color work, but both are inexpensive and fast. If you are going to use quick copy, reserve it for rush projects or those that won't suffer from single-color xerography. Also, there can be major differences between photocopiers and even between copies run on the same machine. A copier that ran your last job beautifully may not repeat the same quality the next time if the toner hasn't been changed recently. Don't be afraid to ask for a test print of your most difficult page to make sure that the blacks are really black and no fade-out occurs on any part of the page.

Paper Choice

Paper choice is one of the most important aspects of producing effective public relations documents, particularly a collateral piece such as a brochure. Your choice of paper may determine whether your brochure is picked up and read, whether it lasts more than 1 or 2 days before it falls apart, or whether it even works well with your chosen type style, graphics, and ink color.

When choosing a paper, you need to consider three major criteria. First, does the paper suit the use to which it will be put? In other words, does it have the right look, feel, color, durability, and so on? Second, how much does it cost? Third, are you using a laser printer?

Suitability

In judging the suitability of your paper choice to your job, you must first determine the nature of your information. Some pieces, such as flyers or announcements, are printed on relatively cheap and lightweight stock and are meant to be thrown away soon after reading. Others need to be more permanent. A brochure outlining company benefits to employees, for example, probably will be kept and used over and over again. It will need to be on a heavier and more durable stock. A company magazine printed in four colors will need a durable paper that will take constant opening, closing, and general handling without tearing because the publication will probably be passed on to other readers.

Aside from durability, three other factors need to be considered in judging the suitability of your paper: weight, texture, and color.

- *Weight.* Papers come in various weights. Weight is determined by taking 500 sheets of the paper and weighing it. Although a heavier weight usually indicates a thicker stock, it doesn't have to. One 25-pound bond paper may be thicker than another. Likewise, one 60-pound book paper may be lighter and less durable than another. The best way to judge weight versus thickness is to handle the paper for each type of stock personally. Most printers have hundreds of samples of paper stock and can help you select the weight and thickness that you want for your job. As a general rule, stick with text weights for newsletters and magazines and heavier, or cover, stocks for magazine covers and brochures.

- *Texture.* Texture is also an important consideration when choosing a paper. Heavily textured paper may impart a feeling of quality or a feeling of roughness, depending on the paper stock and the method of manufacture. Basically, papers break down into two broad categories for texture: matte finish and coated stock. *Matte finish paper* ranges from a paper with a rather smooth but nonglossy surface to heavily textured paper. *Coated stock paper* refers to any paper that is slick or glossy. Again, the range is considerable. Photographs often reproduce better on coated stock, which is what most magazines use. Using a matte stock will soften the color and give a photograph an entirely different feeling. Some heavily textured stocks may not take ink well but may be perfect for foil stamping or embossing. The best way to tell if your idea will work on a certain texture stock is to ask the printer, look at some samples, and come to an informed decision.

- *Color.* Paper color has to complement all the other graphic elements of your collateral piece: typeface, ink color, photographs, and artwork. It will also set the mood of your piece. Color preference is a very personal matter. Remember, however, that you are producing pieces to be read by certain target publics who may or may not like your color choice. Thus, to an extent, color choice is a matter of gauging your intended audience's reaction to a particular color. Research has shown, for instance, that businesspeople will not respond to questionnaires printed on hot-pink paper (not much of a surprise). They will respond well to beige and various shades of white, but respond very little to pale blue and green. All colors carry connotations for most people. You need to stay away from outrageous combinations and any color that you think might not get the desired response to your information piece.

Cost

The determining factor in your paper choice may well be cost. Don't despair, though, just because your budget may be limited. Paper comes in thousands of weights, colors, and textures, and one of them will fit your cost restrictions. Remember that a few extra dollars on a good grade paper may well pay off in the long run by impressing your readership.

Paper for Laser Printing

Some papers are made specifically for laser printers, and some papers definitely should be avoided. Ask yourself three questions when you pick laser printer paper:

1. Will the laser copy be used as a finished piece or for reproduction?
2. Does the paper say what you want it to say? In other words, what is its look and feel?
3. Does the paper run well in your printer?

Keeping in mind the paper specifications presented earlier, consider the following guidelines when you select the paper for your needs and your printer:

- Brighter paper reproduces well on laser printers. (This doesn't mean whiter paper; there are varying degrees of brightness even among white papers.) Brighter papers are also good for reproduction masters. In fact, several manufacturers make papers specifically for laser printer output that will be used for reproduction. Also, because it's hard to predict the degree of darkness of your printer, the brighter the paper, the more contrast you are likely to have between the print and the paper. In general, avoid colored paper; however, some interesting effects can be obtained with lighter colors such as gray and beige.

- Stay away from heavily textured paper. The heavier the texture, the more broken your type will look because it will be harder for the toner to adhere to the paper's surface. Texture also affects any large, dark areas such as screens and display type. Some texture, like that found in bond paper and linen stock, is fine. The trick is to experiment.

- Avoid heavy papers weighing 90 pounds or more (like cover stock), unless you enjoy removing jammed paper from your printer. Similarly, extremely light papers, such as onion skin, may stick to the rollers or jam as they feed into the printer. Don't experiment much here. Just settle for a text-weight paper (generally around 60 pounds) and consign the choice of cover paper to your commercial printer.

- Use a fairly opaque paper, especially if the laser-printed copy is to be your final version. If you use a paper with high opacity, be sure it isn't also heavily textured.

- Don't expect heavily textured papers to retain their texture. Unlike offset presses, laser printers flatten the paper as it moves through the printer. In most cases, any texture will be lost.

- By the same token, don't use embossed or engraved papers in your laser printer because they might jam the mechanism and will flatten out anyway.

- Make sure that your paper is heat resistant. Because laser printers work at temperatures of around 4,000 degrees Fahrenheit, certain letterhead inks may melt or stick and any metal or plastic will certainly ruin your printer. Above all, don't use acetate in your laser printer unless it has been specifically designed for your particular printer.

Ink Choice

Choosing an ink can be a nightmare for the novice. Even the most experienced designers often have a short list of their favorite inks. Inks come in virtually limitless color combinations, and each color will be affected by the paper on which it is printed. For example, coated paper will result in brighter colors whereas matte finish paper will soften the color. The texture of the paper also affects ink color, as does the use of colored paper.

There are no easy ways to learn what inks to use. The best way for a beginner to choose an ink is to look at other work done using the same ink-and-paper combination. Also, obtain a copy of the Pantone Color Matching System. It's really just a color sample book, like the ones you see when you pick out house paint, but it is the most commonly used system among printers and designers. You'll be amazed at the variety of colors available to you. Don't be embarrassed, however, to stick to the basic colors to begin with. They are usually the safest to work with. Your printer will usually have a Pantone book that you can use while there. Pantone's address is on the sample book. Just write them and ask about obtaining your own copy.

If you don't want any surprises, ask to see samples of work that your printer has done using different papers and inks. Most printers take great pride in their work and will be more than happy to share it with you.

Color brings an added dimension to any publication, whether it's as simple as a second color to help accent, unify, or dress up a publication or as complete as full color. To use color effectively, you should have a rudimentary understanding of how the different color processes operate.

Spot Color Printing

Spot color printing (also known as *two-color printing*) is the placement of a second color (black—or whatever the primary inking color—being the first) in a publication. (Note that in printing, black is counted as a color.) Unless you're using a multicolor press, applying the second color means an additional press run. That translates into more ink, materials, handling, press time, and money.

In two-color printing, two sets of printing plates are made, one for each color run. Often, a designer will use the black (or other first color) for the type and use the second color for the art and graphic highlights—such as dropped-initial letters. This also means that you have to create two originals, one for the black plate and one for the second color. This is not an easy process for most people and is usually left to a designer or printer. Check with your printer first to determine their requirements for two-color printing.

Process Color Printing

Process color printing (also known as *four-color printing*) is used for reproducing full-color artwork or photography. This illusion of full color is accomplished by optically mixing the three primary colors—yellow, red (actually magenta), and blue (called cyan)—along with black. Four-color plates are shot through a screen to reduce solid areas to printable, graduated dot patterns. Because each color is shot through a slightly different angle screen, the screened halftone of each blends through the overlaid dot patterns.

During printing, each color is applied separately, one plate at a time and one color atop the others. The quality of this four-color overprinting method largely depends on the quality of the original work; the quality of the cameras, plates, and printing press used; and the skills and professionalism of those who operate the equipment. Process color is best left to your printer to handle for you. As always, ask the printer in advance about their requirements.

Binding

With binding, as with everything else, if you want to know what to expect, ask your printer and seek out samples on your own. Basically, there are two types of binding: that used for relatively thin publications such as magazines and pamphlets and that used for thicker publications such as books. I discuss only those most applicable to public relations output here.

Regardless of what you are binding, it will probably be organized either into signatures or single pages. **Signatures** are groupings of pages printed on both sides, usually 16 to a signature, but sometimes less, as long as they're in multiples of 4 (pages printed for binding are usually printed 4 to a two-sided sheet of paper).

After signatures or single pages have been collated, they may be bound. Among the most common bindings that public relations people are likely to use are *saddle stitching* (stapled signatures), *perfect binding* (glued, single sheets), or *spiral binding* (hole-punched single sheets bound in plastic or wire). Most quick printers can do saddle stitching and spiral binding; however, only larger printers will be able to do perfect binding. More traditional forms of binding, such as *case binding* (for hardcover books), are reserved for publications that you want to last longer than you will.

Swipe Files

One of the best ways to tell your printer what you want is to show them an example. A **swipe file** is a collection of your favorite pieces done by other people or companies. They will help you a great deal with design, layout ideas, and writing style, as well as with communicating your ideas to printers. You may find a particular brochure, for instance, that is exactly the right size and design for the information piece that you want to produce. You may decide to use similar paper, ink color, or even design. Most graphic artists, designers, and printers use ideas generated from a variety of sources. Don't plagiarize your source, however, and don't steal the artwork right off the source brochure. Be careful to differentiate between emulation and plagiarism. If you do decide that you must borrow directly from another piece, obtain permission from its originator in advance of the publication of your piece.

Keep a swipe file of samples to show your printer. If you find a piece that you would like to emulate, show it to the printer to get an idea how much it will cost to produce. The printer can tell you what the type is and whether your copy will fit in that size, as well as the paper stock and weight, ink color, and mechanical specifications—all of which will affect the price. For the beginner, a sample is worth a 10,000-word explanation.

Submitting your Layout for Printing

The final stage of the preparation prior to printing is your finished layout. With today's technology, it's become a lot easier. For example, if you're working in a layout program such as Adobe InDesign, your final layout can be saved to a PDF format for transport to the printer. Many printers will accept these as uploads to their file servers, or you can copy your layout to a disc and hand-carry it to the printer. Be sure to check with your chosen printer first to see what parameters they need for the PDF to print properly. For example, most printers want your layout in CMYK format because of the four-color process they will be using. There is also the resolution issue. Most printers prefer at least 300 dpi to print properly. Most layout programs have options for saving to PDF format. Learn how to use those options for best results in the final print job. When in doubt, ask your printer for help.

The most important interface between the desktop publisher and the printer is when the print order is submitted. Following are several sets of suggestions for getting your publication out of your computer and onto paper:

In General

Always call your chosen printer in advance to see how he or she can meet your publishing needs. Find out the following:

- If the printer supports your computer platform (Macintosh or Windows)
- If the printer can use your fonts, has his or her own versions of the fonts you used, or accepts only PostScript files
- If you can upload directly to the printer or if you have to bring your work in on disk

When you submit your material, include the following:

- The name and version (3.0, 5.4, and so on) of the software application that you used to create your publication

- File names under which your publication is stored
- Hard copy of the publication (if you've laid it out already)
- Type of output desired (laser printer, offset lithography)

Regarding Photos and Artwork

If you do not include your artwork and photos directly in your file and require that the printer either mechanically or digitally work with your graphics, observe the following guidelines:

- Photos and artwork should be cropped and marked with the finished size, either a percentage of the original or the final image dimensions.
- Place crop marks in margins of photos and artwork. If there are no margins, then tape the piece to a larger sheet and indicate crop marks.
- Use a felt-tip pen to put instructions on the backs of photos. Marks made by graphite pencil or ballpoint pen can leave impressions on the face of the photo that reproduce. Avoid putting paper clips or staples on photos.
- Keep photos and artwork free of dirt, glue, wax, and other foreign material.
- If you mark instructions near artwork or copy, it is best to use light-blue pencil or pen.
- Avoid rolling maps, charts, or artwork into tubes. Keep these items flat if possible.
- Find out in advance the maximum sizes that can be handled by your printer's reproduction equipment.
- Find out the maximum sizes that your printer's digital scanners can accommodate.

Proofs

- Read proofs carefully and mark corrections plainly so that they can be seen easily; a red pencil or pen is best. Use standard proofreader's marks.
- Avoid changes on **bluelines** (the final printer's proof) unless they are essential. Changes at this stage are costly because the plate (if it is to be offset printed) has already been made.

A WORD ON DESKTOP PUBLISHING

Although a desktop publishing system won't make you an instant designer, it does provide the writer, editor, and designer with more tools to better accomplish their respective jobs. Without the knowledge and experience gained through a study of the basics of writing, editing, and design, however, even the best hardware and software won't help you.

The greatest benefit of desktop publishing to the public relations writer is that it allows you to control your own output, right down to the printing. Its greatest drawback is that it allows you to control your own output, right down to the printing. In other words, its greatest asset is its greatest deficit, and you are the deciding factor. Unless you become skilled at not only writing and editing but also layout and design, the complete benefits of desktop publishing may never be realized for you. But that's OK. You need to realize exactly what you can do, what you are willing to learn to do, and how much you can afford to spend to get it all done. Remember, everybody has to begin somewhere, and, fortunately for us, there is a wealth of programming to fit every need.

Ultimately, your final, printed publication is going to determine how successful your desktop publishing system is—and a lot of that success depends not on your hardware and software, but on you. You are the final ingredient in this system. Your energy, talent, interest, and organizational abilities will be the final determinant in the success or failure of your publications. Truthfully, you can get by on a lot less than you think you can if you possess the right attitude and the requisite abilities. Fancy hardware and expensive software only enhance and streamline a process that you should already have down to a fine art. Computers have made and are continuing to make a tremendous difference in publishing. But always remember that the multithousand-dollar system that you sit down in front of every day is only a tool. The system doesn't make you an artist, just as sitting in front of a computer keyboard doesn't make you a writer. Dedication, hard work, and talent do. Keep in mind the following points:

- Don't expect desktop publishing to give you something that you don't already possess.

- If you're looking for an answer to your design problems, check out your own abilities first. However, if you're expecting the technology to streamline the process and save you some money, it probably will.

- Are you willing to take the time needed to make yourself an expert on your system? If you aren't willing to become an expert, you're wasting your money. Anyone can learn the basics (or just enough to cause trouble), but if you're serious about desktop publishing, you'd best dedicate yourself for the long haul. Be prepared to immerse yourself in the process, the programs, and the machinery. The more you know, the more streamlined the process becomes.

Above all, don't set yourself up for frustration. Realize the limitations of your system and of desktop publishing in general. Understand how it works and why it does what it does. You don't have to become a computer expert to gain a fairly complete understanding of your hardware and software. The more you know, the less frustrated you'll be when something does go wrong. Most of the frustration of working with computers comes from not knowing what's happening in software or hardware problem situations. Keep those technical support hotline numbers close at hand and use them. Don't be afraid to ask questions, but read the manuals first so that you'll know what to ask.

Finally, take it all with a grain of salt. A computer is just a tool of the trade. Misuse it, and your shortcomings will become apparent to everyone who looks at your work. Use it wisely, and it will show off for you.

PRINT SCHEDULING AND BUDGETING

Scheduling

To create a budget for your print materials, you should create a rough schedule so that you know what your staff timeline is and think about distribution (that is, quantity).

The first rule in scheduling is to work backward from your anticipated distribution date. Starting there, here are some scheduling rules of thumb:

- *Delivery date.* This is the end date of your schedule. You want your pieces to reach their target public in enough time so that they can absorb the message or respond to it, if that's your goal.

- *Distribution.* If you're mailing your piece nonprofit bulk, allow 4 to 6 weeks for delivery. Also, if you have a very big mailing, ask your distributor how fast those pieces can get out the door. Some distributors can label about 20,000 pieces a day (so a 100,000-piece mailing could take 5 days). Check with your printer. Printers can often give you the best estimates on delivery costs from various vendors, including the post office. Sometimes, printers can handle distribution as well.

- *Printing.* Printing depends on quantity and complexity. If you're doing 20,000 four-color brochures, expect printing to take 3 weeks; if it's two-color, expect 2 weeks. Ten thousand postcards require even less time. Check with your designer as early as possible. You can always ask for a rush job, but it will cost you more.

- *Design.* The length of the design stage depends on whether you're working with a freelancer, an in-house design department, or an independent design firm. In all cases, your project is probably not the only thing the designer is working on. It may take 20 hours to do your job, but he or she may not be able to start the project immediately. The more notice you can give your designer, the better off you will be. If you're doing a multiunit piece, you can save time by having the designer create a pilot unit with rough copy before your final copy is complete. In a busy office, you should allow at least 2 weeks for a brochure or poster and 3 to 4 weeks for a complicated piece such as a company magazine. Don't forget to factor in time for your own review and proofing of the designed piece.

- *Copyediting.* Don't forget to schedule time for copyediting and fact checking. Include a week for a magazine-length piece. Remember to schedule a day or two to enter the changes and proof the manuscript.

- *Entering changes after review.* Leave yourself time to incorporate changes from anyone who will be reviewing your final manuscript—clients, supervisors, other writers, designers, and the legal department. How many days this will take depends on how busy you are. You could incorporate changes in a day if nothing else is going on. You might want to plan for 2 or 3 days in case significant changes need to be made.

- *Final review.* Think about who needs to review the final piece: your supervisor (if you work in-house), the legal department (always a good idea), your client (if you work for yourself or a public relations firm), and your designer. Give them a week if possible, especially if this isn't their only job, and make sure to tell them well in advance when they can expect the piece.

- *Editing the piece.* Generally leave 2 to 5 days to edit the final manuscript that you receive from the various reviewers.

So now you've developed your schedule and discovered that you should have started 4 months ago. What to do? Tweak and pinch and squeeze. The sooner you let people know what's coming when, the better. You will be much more certain of success if your designer tells you she can do a job in 3 days than if you bring it to her and tell her that's all the time she has. You also don't want to be surprised by an unexpected vacation in the middle of your production schedule. The key is to set a schedule, keep to it as tightly as possible, and if it starts going off, immediately look for ways to shave time in other places.

Budgeting

After you've created a schedule, it's time to add budget items. A budget can be done separately or as part of the overall schedule (timeline). Budgets will vary widely, depending on what your piece is, your distribution needs, and who is creating it. Common elements you need to consider include the following:

- Editor and editorial assistant, if appropriate
- Other staff, such as financial and administrative personnel
- Administrative costs and supplies
- Fees for vendors—designers, researchers, and so on.
- Production costs, including design, photo rights, illustration, printing (see sample printing estimate in Exhibit 9.12).
- Any collating costs (for putting together press kits, etc.)
- Packaging costs (Is this a self-mailer, or do you need to purchase envelopes, jiffy bags, or boxes? Do you need to create any mailing labels?)
- Distribution costs, including mailing list rental, postage (the post office can help you calculate based on the weight of your piece), and handling (check with a mail house if it's being labeled, stuck in an envelope, or stuck in a box with a bunch of stuff)

Exhibit 9.12

Printing Estimate

Name of Printer _____

Name of Job _____

	Item	Description	Cost
Quantity	_____		_____
No. of pages	_____		_____
Size	_____		_____
Folded to	_____		_____
Paper	_____		_____
Ink color	_____		_____
2nd color	_____		_____
3rd color	_____		_____
4th color	_____		_____
Color separations	_____		_____
Artwork	_____		_____
Reverses	_____		_____
Bleeds	_____		_____
No. of photos	_____		_____
Type of binding	_____		_____
Mailing	_____		_____
Misc.	_____		_____
	_____		_____

KEY TERMS

design principles	type	sans serif typeface
rule of ground thirds	typeface	signatures
drop	font	swipe file
unity	body type	blueline
anchor	display type	
grid	serif typeface	

CHAPTER 10

Television and Radio

In This Chapter, You Will Learn

- The methods for reaching broadcast audiences.
- The basic concepts of television production.
- How to write scripts for television production.

- How to produce an effective television public service announcement.
- How to write public relations material for radio.
- How to get your radio public service announcements on the air.

Broadcasting is pervasive. Since the advent of radio, people have become more and more dependent on the broadcast media for their information and entertainment. Despite the advent of the internet, the public still views the world largely through the window of the television. The average U.S. family spends more than 6 hours a day watching television, and according to recent research, they find it the most credible news source by a wide margin. Radio reaches more people each day than any other medium, with more than 500 million radios in U.S. homes and cars.

For the public relations practitioner, use of these two powerful and influential media is often restricted. Whereas approximately 90 percent of the nonadvertising content of print media is informational, 90 percent of the nonadvertising content of broadcast media is entertainment. There is simply very little time available for news-related items. Radio usually airs news but often in an abbreviated format. Each of the 30-minute network television news shows has only 22 minutes of actual news, which would fill about one-quarter of the front page of a daily newspaper. And although cable news has expanded greatly since the early 1990s, it is devoted almost exclusively to national and international news, leaving very little opportunity for the local public relations practitioner.

There are some obvious advantages to using the broadcast media, however. Most obviously, they reach millions of people each day. Moreover, television and radio involve their audiences more than print does, and the media can be highly memorable. People tend to react more personally to broadcast than they do to other media. Think of the influence that television celebrities have on the youth of today. Consider the power of national newscasters such as Brian Williams or Anderson Cooper in influencing opinion. Even local newscasters display a certain amount of charisma. Why would local events such as fund-raisers try so hard to get them as hosts otherwise? Think of all the times that you've seen local radio announcers as "talent" on TV commercials. All of this speaks to the power of broadcast celebrity status and the power of broadcasting to influence.

REACHING BROADCAST AUDIENCES

Although getting public relations material aired on network radio and television is difficult, local broadcast media offer some avenues for the experienced practitioner. There are five basic methods for the public relations writer to reach broadcast audiences: news releases (covered in Chapter 7), video news releases, radio and television tapes and actualities, interviews and talk shows, and corporate advertising and public service announcements.

Video News Releases

Video news releases (VNRs) were originally simply prepackaged publicity features meant to be aired on local, regional, or national television. Now they have become staples of many local news shows searching for time-filling informational pieces.

The entertainment industry was among the first to recognize the potential in producing its own videos for publicity purposes. For example, the publicity department for a new motion picture might produce a tape including collages of footage from the film in varying lengths, special behind-the-scenes looks at production, and interviews with key stars. Each of these segments has both an "A" and a "B" sound track. The A sound track contains both music and voice-over, whereas the B sound track contains music only. The varying lengths allow a television station to air a segment suited to its particular time requirements. The choice of sound tracks allows the station to drop in its own announcers' voices to give the piece a local feel.

VNRs are most successful in local television. Filling an hour with local news is sometimes difficult for programmers, and program managers are constantly seeking out fillers to plug 30-, 60-, or 90-second holes in newscasts. In fact, some polls show more than 75 percent of all television stations regularly use VNRs.

Organizations and their public relations agencies and departments have been quick to capitalize on this opportunity. The key is to produce fillers in various lengths that have certain news value yet are not time bound. This way, stories can be produced, packaged, and distributed to stations around the country with no fear that the news will be old before it is received. A good distribution network allows organizations to get even the most time-sensitive news on the air soon enough to be effective. For example, a company can stage an important news conference, tape interviews and visuals from the event, combine this with preproduced or stock footage of the company, and send it out via satellite all over the country in a matter of hours.

This publicity vehicle has some problems, however. A major criticism in the news industry is that much of what is packaged as video "news" releases is really advertising in disguise. This may be true, in part—VNRs are an excellent means of plugging a product by wrapping it in a soft news format. The same thing has been done for years in product-oriented articles for trade publications; however, the difference is that VNRs are being sent to mainstream media outlets that deal in hard news, not product publicity. The old advertising adage "Buyer Beware" should hold here. Alert journalists should always be aware of the publicity angle inherent in any sort of release—print, video, or otherwise. On the public relations side, practitioners won't gain any media support by deliberately disguising product plugs as hard or soft news. The best approach is to tag clearly any VNR as to its sponsor and content and let the media do the gatekeeping.

How you write for a VNR depends on the format of the release. Recorded press conferences and the like should follow a straight news format, as should straight news print releases. Features should follow feature style. Most of the following techniques discussed also apply to writing for VNRs. Simply be aware of the format and target media and conform to their accepted styles. Remember, as with all media, the broadcast media will accept only that which fits their needs and format.

Radio and Television Actualities

Radio and television rely heavily on taped actualities in covering the news. An **actuality** is simply a firsthand, recorded account of a news event. Actualities lend credibility to any newscast. They may feature news people describing the event or interviews with those involved in the event, or they may simply provide ambiance or background for a voice-over.

Rarely will the public relations writer be in the position to provide a finished actuality to a radio or television news program. Most of the time, he or she will act as the intermediary or spokesperson for the organization. Or the public relations practitioner may arrange a taped interview with another company spokesperson, typically outside the public relations department. In some cases, the medium may be interested enough to send out a reporter or news team to cover an event firsthand. In that case, the public relations practitioner usually acts as liaison, arranging the schedule and making sure that everything is in order for the taping.

Interviews and Talk Shows

Local radio and television stations often have talk shows or other vehicles for which information about your organization is suitable. These shows are usually listed in media directories (see Chapter 5) or can be gleaned by contacting the station personally and asking. The public relations practitioner, here again, usually acts as liaison, arranging the interview for a spokesperson, getting preparatory materials together, and making sure that the spokesperson gets to the interview or talk show on time. As the media specialist, you may also be called on to coach the spokesperson or even write his or her responses (see Chapter 5 for media interview tips).

Corporate Advertising and Public Service Announcements

The object of corporate advertising is not usually to sell a product but rather to promote an idea or image. Realizing that profit-making organizations don't usually need free air time, the Federal Communications Commission requires them to purchase time for their ads, even if the messages presented are in the public interest.

Like corporate public interest advertising, the **public service announcement (PSA)** is aimed at providing an important message to its target audience. However, unlike corporate advertising, even that done in the public interest, the PSA is reserved strictly for nonprofit organizations—those that qualify as not-for-profit under federal tax laws. Such organizations may air their public service announcements for free.

Remember that PSAs and image advertising, though different under the law, are identical in format and style. They are an attempt to sell something, whether it's a product, an idea, or an image. The discussion that follows is applicable to both.

WRITING FOR TELEVISION

Broadcast messages, whether paid-for advertising or PSAs, are called **spots.** Producing a complete television spot is usually beyond the expertise of the public relations writer and is best left to professional film and video production houses. Many practitioners, however, prefer to write their own scripts, so knowledge of the proper form is essential. A good script tells the director, talent, or anyone else reading it exactly what the spot is about, what its message is, and the image it should convey. In a well-written script, virtually nothing is left to the imagination. A good working knowledge of recording techniques is necessary so that you can visualize your finished product and transmit that vision to someone else. Before beginning a script, you therefore need to become familiar with some basics of television production and the language of script writing.

Basic Concepts

Television spots are produced on either film, videotape or increasingly, in a digital format. Because these formats involve similar aesthetics, a discussion of one will cover both. Television spots, and all commercials and programs for that matter, are composed of a series of scenes or camera shots joined together by transitions. A scene usually indicates a single locale, so a 30-second commercial might be composed of a single scene composed of several camera shots. Or a 30-minute program might be composed of many scenes composed of many camera shots. These scenes and shots are joined by transitional devices, usually created by switching from one camera to another (a form of on-the-spot editing) or, in the case of a single-camera production that is edited later, by switching from one kind of shot to another. The script tells the director, camera operators, and talent what sort of composition is required in each shot.

Camera shot directions are scripted in a form of shorthand. The most common designations are described below. We will assume that the shots are of a person:

- *CU,* or *close-up.* A shot that takes in the neck and head but doesn't extend below the neck.
- *ECU,* or *extreme close-up.* A much tighter version of the CU, usually involving a selected portion of the object, such as the eyes.
- *MS,* or *medium shot.* A shot that takes in the person from about the waist up.
- *Bust shot.* A shot of a person from the bust (chest) up.
- *LS,* or *long shot.* A shot of the entire person with little or no room at the top or bottom of the screen.
- *ELS,* or *extreme long shot.* A shot with the person in the distance.

There are variations on these basic shots, such as MCU (medium close-up), MLS (medium long shot), 2-shot (a shot of two people), and 3-shot (a shot of three people). When designating shots in scripts, you just need to be in the ballpark—you don't have to have it down to the millimeter. Whatever you write in your script may ultimately be changed by the artistic collaboration between the director and the camera operators.

Camera shots are accomplished in one of two ways: by movement of the optical apparatus (or lens) or by movement of the camera itself. The most common designations for lens movement are *zoom in* and *zoom out*. Physical movements generally are scripted for studio productions in which cameras can be moved about to accommodate certain shots. However, the following terms also are applied to scripts in general to indicate certain camera effects that can be accomplished by cameras either handheld or mounted in other ways, such as on rails or booms:

- *Dolly in/out.* Move the camera in a straight line toward or away from the object.
- *Truck right/left.* Move the camera right or left, parallel to the object.
- *Pan right/left.* Move the camera head to the right or left.
- *Tilt up/down.* Move the camera head up or down.

Each of these movements creates a different optical effect, and each will impart a different impression to the viewer. Dollies and trucks, for instance, impart a sense of viewer movement rather than movement of the object being filmed or taped. In other words, the camera becomes the viewer. This type of shot is frequently called *point of view,* or *POV.* Pans and tilts appear as normal eye movement, much as if the viewer were moving his or her eyes from side to side or up and down. Remember that the camera represents the eyes of the viewer limited by the size of the screen.

Transitions are the sole domain of the director and editor. In the case of a studio production, such as a live talk show, the director and technical director work together—the director giving transitional directions, and the technical director following those directions by electronically switching between the cameras. Transitions in field productions and single-camera productions are taken care of in postproduction editing through a cooperative effort between the director and the editor. The following are the most-used transitions:

- *Cut.* An instantaneous switch from one shot to another.
- *Dissolve.* A gradual replacement of one image with another.
- *Wipe.* A special effect in which one image is "wiped" from the screen and replaced by another. This was used extensively in silent movie days and in adventure films of the 1930s and 1940s.
- *Fade.* A gradual change, usually to or from black, designating either the beginning or end of a scene.

Other shorthand notations are specific to audio directions. The most common are as follows:

- *SFX,* or *sound effects.* Anything from crashing cars to falling rain.
- *SOF,* or *sound on film.* The sound source is the audio track from a film.
- *SOT,* or *sound on tape.* The sound source is the audio track from a videotape or audiotape.

- *SIL,* or *silent film.* No sound has been added or occurred naturally (ambient).
- *Music up.* Signifying that the volume of the music bed is raised.
- *Music under.* Signifying that the volume of the music bed is lowered, usually to allow for narration.
- *Music up and out.* Usually designating the end of a production.
- *VO,* or *voice-over/voice only.* Indicating that the speaker is not on camera.
- *OC,* or *on camera.* Indicating that the speaker or narrator can be seen. This is usually used when the speaker has been VO prior to being OC. In other words, it indicates that he or she is now on camera.

Writing for the Eye

When you write for television, you write for the eye as well as the ear, which means that you have to visualize what you want your audience to see and then put that vision on paper. Your image must be crystallized into words that will tell others how to re-create it on tape or film.

To end up with the best possible script, you must begin with an idea. Try to think in visuals. Take a basic concept and try to visualize the best method for presenting it to others. Should you use a studio or film outdoors? Will you use ambient sound or a music background? Will you have a number of transitions or a single scene throughout? Answering these questions and others will help you conceptualize the television spot.

Television Scripts

Once you have a basic idea of what you would like to say, the next step is to write a **script treatment.** This is a narrative account of a television spot. It is not written in a script format but may include ideas for shots and transitions. The key is to keep it informal at this point—there will be plenty of time to clean it up in later drafts. Exhibit 10.1 is a treatment for a promotional ad for a documentary to be shown on television.

Shooting Scripts

The next step is to sharpen your images in a **shooting script,** which will ultimately be used by the director to produce your spot (see Exhibit 10.2). As you work through what will inevitably be several drafts, you should include all the information necessary for a complete understanding of your idea. Your goal is to get to a final product that is finished enough to be used by your director. You should begin to flesh out camera shots, transitions, audio (including music and sound effects), narrative, acting directions, and approximate times. Here are some guidelines that will help you as you move through your shooting script:

1. Open with an attention-getting device—an interesting piece of audio, an unusual camera shot, or a celebrity. The first few seconds are crucial. If your viewers are not hooked by then, you've lost them.

Exhibit 10.1

Script Treatment

"IDITAROD"

30 second promo

Treatment

Opening shot of dog team against setting sun across long stretch of tundra. Cut to flashes of finish line hysteria, dogs running, racers' faces frozen or exhausted, stretches of open ground, trees, checkpoints, etc., perhaps terminating at starting gun. Images continue under narration.

Voice over: WHAT MAKES SOME PEOPLE SPEND LITERALLY AN ENTIRE YEAR TRAINING BOTH THEMSELVES AND THEIR DOGS, OFTEN WITH HEARTBREAKING RESULTS? WHAT DRAWS A PERSON TO DOG SLED RACING? IS IT A MYSTIQUE UNIQUE ONLY TO ALASKA, OR IS IT SOMETHING COMMON TO ALL PEOPLE AT ALL TIMES?

Cut to closeup of winner of last year's Iditarod race … exhaustion … joy … satisfaction. Zoom in to freeze-frame of face.

Voice over: JOIN US FOR A TWELVE-HUNDRED MILE RACE ACROSS ALASKA WHEN NATIONAL GEOGRAPHIC PRESENTS "IDITAROD: THE RACE ON THE EDGE OF THE WORLD."

NGS logo… super day and time.

#####

Exhibit 10.2

Shooting Script

PRODUCTION: A.P.P.L.E.   9/17 Revised   Page 1 of 33

PRODUCER: University of Alaska Media Services

VIDEO	AUDIO
ELS moutain range, AERIAL	(ambient sounds of birds)
Camera PANS range, descends through wooded area, zeroing in on the edge of a grassy clearing.	(sound of wind)
DISSOLVE to LS grassy clearing	
Colorful objects can be made out scattered within the clearing.	
DISSOLVE to MLS grassy clearing	NARRATOR: ALASKA'S LAND IS PRETTY
At ground level, camera slowly PANS across objects and stops on box labeled "non-renewable resources."	COMPLEX AND UNDERSTANDING IT CAN BE COMPLICATED. THERE ARE A FEW BASIC THINGS, HOWEVER, THAT YOU
DISSOLVE to MS mime	SHOULD KNOW SO THAT WHEN THE TIME
Camera PANS as mime enters scene and approaches box.	COMES FOR YOU TO MAKE DECISIONS ABOUT LAND, YOU CAN MAKE GOOD
DISSOLVE to CU mime and box	ONES.
FREEZE FRAME as mime starts to open box.	YOU SHOULD KNOW ABOUT RESOURCES, RENEWABLE AND NON-RENEWABLE.

2. Open with an establishing shot if possible—something that says where you are and intimates where you are going. If you open in a classroom, for instance, chances are you are going to stay there. If you jump too much, you confuse viewers.

3. If you open with a long shot, you should then cut to a closer shot and, soon after, introduce the subject of the spot. This is especially applicable if you are featuring a product or a celebrity spokesperson.

4. Vary shot composition from MS to CU throughout, and somewhere past the midpoint of the spot return to an MS, then to a final CU and a *superimposition (super)* of a logo or address. A super involves placing one image over another.

5. Don't call for a new shot unless it adds something to the spot. Make your shots seem like part of an integrated whole. Be single-minded and try to tell only one important story per spot.

Although a director will feel free to adapt your script to his or her particular style and to the requirements of the production, you should leave as little as possible to the imagination.

Accompanying Scripts

The **accompanying script** is the version sent with the taped spot to the stations that will run it (see Exhibit 10.3). It is written on the assumption that the shooting script has been produced as it was originally described. The accompanying script is stripped of all but its most essential directions. It is intended to provide the reader a general idea of what the taped spot is about and is to be used only as a reference for broadcasters who accept the spot for use.

It is customary to send out taped spots in packages that include a cover letter explaining what the package is, a form requesting the receiver to designate when and how often the spot is used, and an accompanying script for each spot. Sometimes a *storyboard* also is sent with an abbreviated frame-by-frame summary of the major points, both audio and video, of the spot.

Choosing a Style

The two styles most common to television spots are talking heads and slice-of-life. In a **talking heads spot,** the primary image appearing on the television screen is the human head—talking, of course. This style is often chosen for reasons of cost—a talking heads spot is relatively cheap to produce—but it can be very effective. Exhibit 10.4 is an example of a script for a talking heads spot.

Talking heads spots often are criticized for being boring or unexciting, but this does not need to be the case. The key is to make what is said forceful and memorable while introducing enough camera movement and varied shot composition to make the video image visually interesting. By incorporating the simplest of camera movements into your scripts, you can hold the attention of the audience long enough to impart your verbal message. With this in mind, read through Exhibit 10.4 again and notice how closely the subtle camera movements are tied to the verbal message.

Exhibit 10.3

Accompanying Script

PRODUCTION: Iditarod DATE: 9/17/94   Page 1 of 1

PRODUCER: Northstar Associates

VIDEO	AUDIO
Open on LS dog sled racing into setting sun.	(National Geographic music up)
Series of quick CUTS of finish line excitement, checkpoints, racing, and scenery.	
Narration begins as series of shots of winning team flash by.	NARRATOR: WHAT MAKES SOME PEOPLE SPEND LITERALLY AN ENTIRE YEAR TRAINING BOTH THEMSELVES AND THEIR DOGS, OFTEN WITH HEART-BREAKING
Quick series of CUs and MSs of racer.	RESULTS? WHAT DRAWS A PERSON TO DOG SLED RACING? IS IT A MYSTIQUE
PAN of faces in crowd at finish line.	UNIQUE ONLY TO ALASKA, OR IS IT SOMETHING COMMON TO ALL PEOPLE AT ALL
CUT to CU of winner's face showing joy and exhaustion.	TIMES?
FREEZE FRAME of face MATTED on magazine cover.	JOIN US FOR A TWELVE-HUNDRED MILE RACE ACROSS ALASKA WHEN NATIONAL
SFX logo.	GEOGRAPHIC PRESENTS "IDITAROD: THE RACE ON THE EDGE OF THE WORLD."
SUPER station air date.	(music up and out)
	# # # # #

Exhibit 10.4

Talking Heads Spot

The American Tuberculosis Foundation
1212 Street of the Americas
New York, NY 00912

"Your Good Health"
30-Second TV Spot   Page 1 of 1

VIDEO	AUDIO
Open on CU of young woman's face against a neutral background. She is smoking.	NARRATOR:(VO) YOU KNOW THE DANGERS OF CIGARETTE SMOKING.
Woman looks unconcerned. She takes another puff as narrator talks.	SMOKING CAUSES HEART DISEASE, EMPHYSEMA, AND CANCER. BUT DON'T STOP SMOKING JUST BECAUSE YOU
Pull back to MS to reveal child of about 4 yrs. looking up at her.	MIGHT DIE FROM IT.
Child covers his mouth and coughs.	STOP SMOKING BECAUSE SOMEONE YOU LOVE MIGHT DIE FROM IT. WHEN YOU
	SMOKE AT HOME, YOUR CHILDREN
Slow zoom to CU woman, still holding cigarette. Looks concerned.	BREATH THE SAME CANCER-CAUSING
	SMOKE YOU DO… AND THEY DON'T HAVE
	ANY CHOICE. THEY CAN'T DECIDE TO
	QUIT SMOKING. BUT YOU CAN. IF YOU
	WANT TO STOP SMOKING, WRITE US.
	WE'LL SEND YOU A FREE PROGRAM THAT
	WILL HELP YOU STOP IN 30 DAYS.
	REMEMBER, SOMEONE YOU LOVE CARES
Fade to black, super address.	ABOUT YOUR GOOD HEALTH.
	# # # # #

As its name implies, the **slice-of-life spot** sets up a dramatic situation complete with a beginning, middle, and end (see Exhibit 10.5). In the slice-of-life spot, the focus is on the story, not the characters. The message is imparted through an interesting sequence of events incorporating but not relying on interesting characters. Slice-of-life spots usually use a wide variety of camera movements and postproduction techniques such as dissolves and special effects. Although this type of spot is often shot with one camera, the effect is one of multiple cameras due to the postproduction process. Slice-of-life spots may be more difficult to produce than talking heads spots, but they are just as easy to script.

Timing Your Script

How do you know when you have written a script that will end up running 30 or 60 seconds on the television screen? Timing a script isn't easy and requires a certain amount of "gut feeling." The best way to time a script is to read through what you have written as if it were already produced. Always exaggerate your delivery—people usually talk faster than you think they do. Pause for the music, sound effects, and talent reactions. You also need to simulate movements as if they were occurring on screen. If your script calls for the talent to walk up a classroom aisle, for instance, walk the equivalent distance while you read the narrative. This type of live-action walk-through will give you a ballpark idea of how long your script will be when finally shot.

Remember, the director will ultimately make the adjustments necessary to fit your script into the required time slot; but it's always in your best interest (as far as your reputation as a writer is concerned) to be as close as possible.

Cutting Your Script

Cutting a script means understanding the message you want to impart and then making sure that it is still intact after editing. Remember, a 30-second spot is half the length of a 60-second spot. That may sound obvious, but 30 seconds lost out of a 60-second spot can result in the deletion of a lot of valuable set-up and development time. That 10 seconds you took to pan slowly around the classroom scene now has to go. What do you do instead? Here are some guidelines for cutting your script:

1. Always begin with the longer script. It is easier to cut down than to write more.

2. Look first at the opening and closing sections to see if you can eliminate long musical or visual transitions or fades.

3. Check for long dissolves or other lengthy transitions within the body of the script to see whether these can be replaced with shorter transitional techniques such as cuts or whether they can be eliminated altogether.

4. See if you can eliminate minor characters. Cutting a character with only one or two lines will save you a lot of time.

5. See if you can eliminate any narrative assigned to your major spokesperson. Leave only the key message, slogan, any necessary contact information, and enough narrative transition to allow for coherent development.

Exhibit 10.5

Slice-of-Life Spot

Institute for Higher Education
Box 1873. Washington, D.C. 19806

"Payoff"
60-Second TV Spot   Page 1 of 3

VIDEO	AUDIO
Open on MLS large crowd shot, city street, people walking. We see a young man in front of crowd as it stops at crosswalk.	(Music up: "You've Earned Your Chance")
Continue MLS as light changes and crowd crosses.	"THE CITY'S HOT, THE DAY'S BEEN LONG,
ARC LEFT and AROUND as young man crosses street and FOLLOW shot behind him as he reaches other side.	BUT YOU'VE BEEN OUT THERE HANGING ON.
CUT TO MLS as young man stops in front of building, checks address on slip of paper in his hand. and enters.	THE FACES START TO LOOK THE SAME, YOU WONDER IF THEY KNOW YOUR NAME.
CUT TO MS young man as he rushes to squeeze into elevator.	THERE'S ONE MORE SHOT BEFORE YOU'RE THROUGH.
CUT TO MCU young man looking uncomfortable in crowded elevator. He looks to right and left as others ignore him.	YOU KNOW YOU'RE TIME IS COMING DUE. IT'S YOUR TURN NOW, YOUR DUES ARE PAID.
CUT TO MS of elevator doors opening as young man exits, looks both ways and turns screen left.	YOU'VE EARNED YOUR CHANCE, YOU'VE MADE THE GRADE."
CUT TO MS of young man pausing before door, checking number, and entering.	(Lyrics end, music under)
	-more-

(continued)

(continued)

VIDEO	AUDIO
CUT TO MLS young man entering front office. Secretary is seated at desk and glances up as he enters room.	
CUT TO CU secretary's face	SECRETARY: MAY I HELP YOU?
CUT TO CU young man's face	MAN: YES. I'M HERE FOR AN APPOINT-MENT WITH MR. ALDRICH.
CUT TO 2-SHOT secretary and young man.	SECRETARY: YOU MUST BE MR. ROBINSON. MR. ALDRICH IS EXPECTING YOU. I'LL LET HIM KNOW YOU'RE HERE. WHY DON'T YOU HAVE A SEAT. I'M SURE HE'LL BE RIGHT WITH YOU.
Follow MS young man as he seats himself. He picks up a magazine and begins to read.	
CUT TO MCU young man as he glances at office door.	ANNOUNCER: YOU'VE PREPARED FOR THIS MOMENT FOR FOUR YEARS. NOW IT'S PAYOFF TIME. YOU'RE CONFIDENT AND POLISHED. YOU'VE GOT A COLLEGE EDUCATION AND THE TRAINING YOU NEED TO GO WHERE YOU WANT TO GO, AND DO WHAT YOU WANT TO DO IN LIFE. YOU HAD THE INSIGHT AND THE DRIVE TO BETTER YOURSELF THROUGH HIGHER EDUCATION, AND NOW IS THE MOMENT YOU'VE WAITED FOR.
CUT TO CU young man's face exuding confidence.	

-more-

"Payoff"
60-Second TV Spot   Page 3 of 3

VIDEO	AUDIO
CUT TO MLS as office door opens and interviewer steps out to shake young man's hand. CUT TO CU interviewer's face.	INTERVIEWER: MR. ROBINSON? I'VE BEEN LOOKING FORWARD TO MEETING YOU. I'VE GOT TO TELL YOU--YOU'RE JUST THE KIND OF PERSON WE'RE LOOKING FOR. WE'VE GOT A LOT TO TALK ABOUT.
CUT TO CU young man's face, smiling.	
CUT TO MEDIUM 2-SHOT as two men chat. LOSE focus and SUPER address.	ANNOUNCER: MAKE YOUR DREAMS A REALITY. GO TO COLLEGE. EDUCATION PAYS OFF. FOR MORE INFORMATION, WRITE: INSTITUTE FOR HIGHER EDUCATION BOX 1873 WASHINGTON, D.C. 19806
FOCUS on MEDIUM 2-SHOT as two men enter office and close door behind them.	(Music and lyrics up) "YES, YOU'VE EARNED YOUR CHANCE, NOW GIVE IT ALL YOU'VE GOT." #####

6. Finally, try out the cut-down version on someone who hasn't seen the longer version to make sure it flows and makes sense.

Read Exhibit 10.6, the 30-second version of the slice-of-life spot in Exhibit 10.5. Notice what was left out and what remains. Is the message still clear? Did the story lose anything in the cutting?

Effective Television PSA Production

The following production tips may enhance your chances of getting your PSA on the air:

- Keep your PSAs simple. Covering one or maybe two points in 30 seconds is the best you should shoot for; any more will simply dilute your message. It's usually best to stick to one point and repeat it in several different ways.

- This also means fewer scenes. Although a soft-drink commercial may have the money and energy to jump through 30 scenes in 30 seconds, such a frenetic pace doesn't suit most PSAs. Don't take the chance of confusing your audience.

- Work from the general to the specific. A problem–solution format is usually best. Tell or show your audience the problem and then how it can be solved; however, don't dwell on the problem. It'll turn off your audience.

- Demonstrations work well in the visual media. Show how your service works or what you want people to do.

- Always start with something interesting. Remember, you have only a few seconds to hook your audience. After that, they'll simply tune you out.

- Use testimonials when appropriate. People who are directly involved in your work, especially those being helped by it, can be very effective spokespersons. Don't avoid ordinary people. If they know what they're talking about, they can be much more effective than a celebrity who doesn't.

- In fact, avoid celebrities unless they are or can be made to appear to be involved in your cause. Using celebrities simply because of their celebrity status can be self-defeating. Your audience may remember them but not your message.

- By contrast, if you are lucky enough to attract someone who is well known and who believes in what you are doing, you can create a memorable spot.

- Unless you have attracted a practiced professional, avoid stand-ups if possible. A *stand-up* is basically one person delivering your message. Unless you have a superb speaker—one who can really engage an audience with just a voice and a direct gaze—stay away from this approach. Also, make sure that whoever you pick can deliver your message sincerely, from a sound understanding of what you do and represent. Your audience will know if the message rings false.

- If you've got something interesting to show, however, use voice-over. It's ultimately better to show something other than just a face. In many cases,

Exhibit 10.6

Edited Slice-of-Life Spot

Institute for Higher Education
Box 1873, Washington, D.C. 19806

"Payoff"
30-Second TV Spot

Page 1 of 2

VIDEO	AUDIO
Open on LS young man entering front office. Secretary is seated at desk and glances up as he enters room..	
CUT TO CU secretary's face.	SECRETARY: MAY I HELP YOU?
CUT TO CU young man's face.	MAN: YES. I'M HERE FOR AN APPOINTMENT WITH MR. ALDRICH.
CUT TO 2-SHOT secretary and young man.	SECRETARY: YOU MUST BE MR. ROBINSON. MR. ALDRICH IS EXPECTING YOU. I'LL LET HIM KNOW YOU'RE HERE. WHY DON'T YOU HAVE A SEAT. I'M SURE HE'LL BE RIGHT WITH YOU.
Follow MS young man as he seats himself He picks up a magazine and begins to read.	ANNOUNCER: YOU'VE PREPARED FOR THIS MOMENT FOR FOUR YEARS. NOW
CUT TO MCU young man as he glances at office door.	IT'S PAYOFF TIME. YOU'RE CONFIDENT AND POLISHED. YOU'VE GOT A COLLEGE EDUCATION AND THE TRAINING YOU NEED TO GO WHERE YOU WANT TO GO,
CUT TO CU young man's face exuding confidence.	AND DO WHAT YOU WANT TO DO IN LIFE.
	-more-

(continued)

(continued)

"Payoff"
30-Second TV Spot   Page 2 of 2

VIDEO	AUDIO
CUT TO MLS as office door opens and interviewer steps out to shake young man's hand.	ANNOUNCER (CONT.): YOU HAD THE INSIGHT AND THE DRIVE TO BETTER YOURSELF THROUGH HIGHER EDUCATION, AND NOW IS THE MOMENT YOU'VE WAITED FOR.
CUT TO CU interviewer's face	INTERVIEWER: MR. ROBINSON? I'VE BEEN LOOKING FORWARD TO MEETING YOU. I'VE GOT TO TELL YOU—YOU'RE JUST THE KIND OF PERSON WE'RE LOOKING FOR. COME IN. WE'VE GOT A LOT TO TALK ABOUT.
CUT TO 2-SHOT as both enter office and shut door behind them.	ANNOUNCER: MAKE YOUR DREAMS A REALITY. GO TO COLLEGE. EDUCATION PAYS OFF. FOR MORE INFORMATION, WRITE:
SUPER address on door.	INSTITUTE FOR HIGHER EDUCATION BOX 1873 WASHINGTON, D.C. 19806
	-30-

celebrities are easily identifiable by their voices or can identify themselves at the end of the spot. In fact, some celebrities would rather do just a voice-over because it saves them time and they don't have to go through all the preparation it takes to be seen on television.

- If you decide to show your phone number, address, or Web address on the screen, keep it up long enough for viewers to write it down—usually at least 8 seconds. Remember all those handy gadget commercials—"But wait, there's more"? They read their phone numbers so many times you can recite them by heart. That's what you have to do, too.

- However, if it's not really important to have people call or write you—for instance, if your goal is to motivate people—you may not need a phone number or address at all. Determine the purpose of your spot and leave out anything that doesn't contribute directly to that purpose, even if it's your phone number.

- In the same vein, if you do superimpose information on the screen, make sure that what is being seen by your viewers is also being talked about. If it's a written message or an address, your audio should be reading it at the same time.

- Viewers won't listen if they are watching something that doesn't match what's being said. For example, a number of years ago, a famous national news anchor produced a piece on a presidential candidate that showed him stumping the country, smiling and delivering his message of hope and good cheer. However, the news anchor's voice-over lambasted the candidate for avoiding the issues and merely wrapping himself in the flag. She received a phone call the next day from the candidate's press secretary thanking her for the excellent coverage. "But, didn't you get it?" she said. "I spent nearly 3 minutes berating your candidate for avoiding the issues." "Do you think anyone was listening to you?" he replied. "All they were seeing were the great images of my candidate you put up for them to watch." In other words, if what you're saying doesn't match what you're showing, most people will go with what you're showing.

- If you must use music, use good music, either written and performed specifically for your spot or paid for from a commercial source. Be sure to match the feel of your music to your message.

WRITING FOR RADIO

The radio spot, like the television spot, must be absolutely clear to be understood—both by the listener and by the broadcaster who will be airing it. Remember, radio scripts are written for the ear. You must be clear and simple, reducing ideas to their essence.

Radio may be the most flexible of media because it can rely on the imagination of the listener to fill in visuals. In radio, it is possible to create virtually any scenario that can be imagined by the audience. With the appropriate sound effects, you can have elephants perform on stage or lions in your living room; you can position yourself in the middle of the Amazon jungle or on the highest mountain peak. Radio spots are also much cheaper to produce than television spots and can be changed on much shorter notice. Lengths of radio spots vary. Whereas television spots are typically either 30 or 60 seconds in length, radio spots can run anywhere from 10 seconds to 60 seconds and any length in between. The standard lengths for radio spots are as follows:

- 10 seconds, or about 25 words
- 20 seconds, or about 45 words
- 30 seconds, or about 65 words
- 60 seconds, or about 125 words (not as common as the other lengths)

Types of Radio Announcements

Radio announcements are typically of two types: spot announcements and as-recorded spots. The simplest type of radio spot is the **spot announcement** involving no sound effects or music bed and meant to be read by station personnel. This type of spot is usually sent in a package of two, three, or four spots and can be general in nature, geared to a specific program, or tied to some specific time of the year or holiday.

Like television scripts, radio scripts must be uniformly formatted. Although most stations will transfer the information from a spot announcement to a 3 × 5-inch card for ease of handling, you should always send your spots on standard bond paper. Some other rules include the following:

- Head up your spot with the name of the originating agency and its address and telephone and fax numbers. Include a contact.
- Title your spot and give the length at the beginning, not the end.
- Because spot announcements are never more than one page in length, you may be able to get more than one per page. The standard is usually five or six 10-second spots per page, two 30-second spots per page, and one 60-second spot per page. As with news releases, end all spots with #####.
- For ease of reading, type all radio spots in uppercase, double-spaced. Talent directions, if there are any, should be upper- and lowercase in parentheses.

Because spots are typically written as a series, it is necessary to develop a theme that will carry over from spot to spot. This is best accomplished by the use of key ideas and phrases, repeated in each spot. The concepts and ideas should be such that they can be developed more fully as the spots increase in length and time.

The spots in Exhibit 10.7 use some standard methods for creating a cohesive series. Whenever you produce a series of spots, they should reflect a continuity of theme and message. Ask yourself these questions about the spots:

- What is the underlying theme or concept throughout the spots?
- How is this theme carried out from spot to spot?
- What are the key ideas and phrases that are repeated in all the spots?

Exhibit 10.7

Ten-Second Spots

The American Tuberculosis Foundation
1212 Street of the Americas
New York, NY 00912

"YOUR GOOD HEALTH" :10 SEC. LIVE RADIO SPOTS
THE AMERICAN TUBERCULOSIS FOUNDATION AND THIS STATION CARE ABOUT YOUR
GOOD HEALTH. DON'T SMOKE... SOMEONE WHO LOVES YOU WANTS YOU TO QUIT.

# # # # #

(station call letters) AND THE AMERICAN TUBERCULOSIS FOUNDATION CARE ABOUT YOUR
GOOD HEALTH. IF YOU SMOKE, TRY TO STOP. IF YOU'RE THINKING OF STARTING,
THINK TWICE.

# # # # #

SMOKING NOT ONLY HARMS YOUR LUNGS, IT HARMS THE LUNGS OF THOSE AROUND
YOU. SOMEONE YOU LOVE WANTS YOU TO QUIT. THE AMERICAN TUBERCULOSIS
FOUNDATION CARES ABOUT YOUR GOOD HEALTH.

# # # # #

IF YOU'RE THINKING OF STARTING TO SMOKE... THINK TWICE. SMOKING HARMS YOU
AND THOSE YOU LOVE. THE AMERICAN TUBERCULOSIS FOUNDATION AND THIS STA-
TION CARE ABOUT YOUR GOOD HEALTH.

# # # # #

GOOD HEALTH MEANS TAKING CARE OF YOURSELF. DON'T START SMOKING. AND IF
YOU ALREADY SMOKE... TRY TO STOP. SOMEONE YOU LOVE CARES ABOUT YOUR
GOOD HEALTH. A MESSAGE FROM (station call letters) AND THE AMERICAN TUBERCULOSIS
FOUNDATION.

# # # # #

Notice that the longer spots in Exhibits 10.8 and 10.9 elaborate on the theme in some way. The shorter spots, especially the 10-second spots, are the basic message—often only the phrase or idea that will be repeated in the longer spots. The longer spots, particularly the 60-second spot, can take time for development and enumeration of points barely mentioned in the shorter versions.

Unlike the television spot, radio spots come in not only different lengths but also different formats. Television spots are rarely written to be read by a television announcer as a drop-in or time filler. The radio spot, by contrast, can be prerecorded, using many of the same techniques as television—sound effects, music beds, multiple talent, sound fades and dissolves, and changes in scenes. Of course, these effects are more difficult to pull off when you are restricted to audio only, but the challenge is in the trying.

As-recorded spots are produced by the originating agency and are ready to be played by the stations receiving them (see Exhibit 10.10). They are usually sent in the format used by the particular stations. That format may vary widely from station to station. Although a number of stations still use tape, increasingly the format is moving to digital. Be prepared in advance by querying each station as to the format they prefer. As with television spots, an accompanying script is sent along with the standard cover letter and response card.

As-recorded radio spots differ in format from television scripts but contain much of the same information. However, if you are basing your radio spots on already produced or written television spots, you will need to transfer the video cues to audio cues. For instance, if you are using a celebrity spokeswoman who is easily recognizable on your video spots, she will have to identify herself on radio. Scene setting, which can be accomplished easily enough on video, will have to be taken care of verbally or through sound effects for radio. Consider the example in Exhibit 10.8 to see how a radio spot sets the scene.

How to Get Your Public Service Announcements on the Air

The best way to ensure that your spots get on the air is to follow to the letter each media outlet's guidelines for PSAs. Ask each media outlet for its guidelines. If an outlet doesn't have them in writing, ask for a verbal explanation. Some of the things that you should look for in these guidelines are as follows:

- The media are deadline oriented. If you don't work within their deadlines, they won't run your PSAs. Find out what their deadlines are and plan as far ahead as you can.

- Most stations typically run shorter spots, usually 30 seconds. Find out what lengths they will run and produce your PSAs in that length.

- Submit rough versions of your scripts or ideas to the stations if time permits. Ask for their advice to make sure that your needs meet theirs.

- Send your PSAs in the format the station will use. For TV, formats include 3/4-inch, 1-inch, BETA, and BETA SP tape. Most radio stations will accept PSAs that are on CD, DAT, or converted to an MP3 or MP4 format.

Exhibit 10.8

Thirty-Second Spots

The American Tuberculosis Foundation
1212 Street of the Americas
New York, NY 00912

"YOUR GOOD HEALTH" :30 SEC. LIVE RADIO SPOTS

DO YOU SMOKE? IF YOU DO, DO YOU REMEMBER WHEN YOU STARTED? MAYBE YOU WERE A TEENAGER AND YOUR FRIENDS THOUGHT IT MADE THEM LOOK "ADULT." WHATEVER THE REASON, SMOKING ISN'T GROWN UP ANY MORE... IT'S JUST PLAIN STUPID. THE AMERICAN TUBERCULOSIS FOUNDATION AND THIS STATION WANT YOU TO KNOW THAT SOMEONE YOU LOVE CARES ABOUT YOUR GOOD HEALTH. WE WANT YOU TO HAVE THE CHANCE TO ACT LIKE A GROWN UP. IF YOU'D LIKE TO STOP SMOKING, WRITE US. OUR ADDRESS IS:

THE AMERICAN TUBERCULOSIS FOUNDATION
BOX 1892
NEW YORK, NEW YORK 00911

# # # # #

WHEN YOU SMOKE, YOU'RE NOT JUST HURTING YOURSELF, YOU'RE HURTING THOSE AROUND YOU... AND MAYBE EVEN SOMEONE YOU LOVE. THE AMERICAN TUBERCULOSIS FOUNDATION WANTS YOU TO KNOW THAT YOU CAN QUIT. WE'VE DEVELOPED A PROGRAM THAT WILL HELP YOU STOP SMOKING IN 30 DAYS, AND WE'LL SEND YOU THAT PROGRAM FREE. ALL YOU HAVE TO DO IS WRITE US AT:

THE AMERICAN TUBERCULOSIS FOUNDATION
BOX 1892
NEW YORK, NEW YORK 00911

WE CARE ABOUT YOUR GOOD HEALTH.

# # # # #

Exhibit 10.9

Sixty-Second Spots

The American Tuberculosis Foundation
1212 Street of the Americas
New York, NY 00912

"YOUR GOOD HEALTH" ;60 SEC. LIVE RADIO SPOT

SMOKING CAUSES HEART DISEASE, EMPHYSEMA, AND CANCER. BUT DON'T STOP
SMOKING JUST BECAUSE YOU MIGHT DIE FROM IT. STOP SMOKING BECAUSE SOMEONE
YOU LOVE MIGHT DIE FROM IT. THAT'S RIGHT... SECOND-HAND SMOKE IS A PROVEN
CONTRIBUTOR TO HEALTH PROBLEMS IN NON-SMOKERS. WHEN YOU SMOKE AT
HOME, YOUR CHILDREN BREATHE THE SAME CANCER-CAUSING SMOKE YOU DO...
AND THEY DON'T HAVE ANY CHOICE. THEY CAN'T DECIDE TO QUIT SMOKING. BUT
YOU CAN. IF YOU WANT TO STOP SMOKING, WRITE US. WE'LL SEND YOU A FREE PRO-
GRAM THAT WILL HELP YOU STOP IN 30 DAYS. WRITE:

THE AMERICAN TUBERCULOSIS FOUNDATION
BOX 1892
NEW YORK, NEW YORK 00911

(repeat address)

REMEMBER, SOMEONE YOU LOVE CARES ABOUT YOUR GOOD HEALTH.

# # # # #

- Find out whether any of the stations will produce your spots for you. Some will if you provide the script and it suits their needs. Look especially for cosponsorship opportunities through which the station can publicize its involvement with you.
- Be careful, though. Competing stations may not want to run spots produced by a rival station, especially if you use that station's "personalities." However, if a station merely produces your spots for you, find out if you can run them on other stations.

Exhibit 10.10

As-Recorded Radio Spots

Northwest Library Association
1342 Placer Ave.
Seattle, WA 98901

"Werewolf" 30 Sec. PSA—As Recorded

(sfx: sounds of wind, howling, and footsteps running)

WOMAN: DID YOU HEAR THAT? IT SOUNDED LIKE A WEREWOLF!

MAN: DON'T WORRY. WE'RE SAFE.

(sfx: loud sound of bushes rattling and sudden snarling)

WOMAN: (very frightened) IT IS A WEREWOLF! WHAT ARE WE   GOING TO   DO?

MAN: (reassuringly) I TOLD YOU NOT TO WORRY. I HAD PLENTY OF GARLIC ON MY
            PIZZA TONIGHT, REMEMBER?

WOMAN: (sarcastically) I CERTAINLY DO.

WEREWOLF:(in terror) GARLIC! (screams)

(sfx: sounds of rapidly retreating footsteps and howling fading into distance)

WOMAN: (relieved) HOW ON EARTH DID YOU KNOW THAT GARLIC WOULD FRIGHTEN A
            WEREWOLF AWAY?

MAN: I READ IT IN A BOOK AT THE PUBLIC LIBRARY.

WOMAN: (sarcastically again) AND DID THIS BOOK EXPLAIN THE EFFECTS OF GARLIC ON
            YOUR DATE?

MAN: WHOOPS...

ANNCR: YOU'D BE SURPRISED WHAT YOU CAN LEARN AT YOUR PUBLIC LIBRARY.
            GIVE READING A TRY... IT MAKES GOOD SENSE.

MAN: (voices fading as couple walks away) OH, COME ON CAROL, IT SAVED OUR LIVES
            DIDN'T IT... I'LL CHEW SOME GUM... I'LL BRUSH MY TEETH...

# # # # #

- Find out when each station is most likely to run PSAs. Although it might be best for you to get your message out during the Christmas season, the stations will probably be inundated with similar requests. You'll find that most stations have more available air time following major holidays.

Remember, broadcasting (and cable) still reach more people than any other media. The proliferation of cable channels has multiplied your opportunity for placement while further segmenting your audience for you. Don't automatically discount broadcast and cable because of costs. As this chapter has shown, there are ways to cut costs and still use the medium to its fullest advantage. Explore those avenues. It can only help your chances of being heard and seen.

KEY TERMS

video news release (VNR)	spot	talking heads spot
actuality	script treatment	slice-of-life spot
public service announcement (PSA)	shooting script	spot announcement
	accompanying script	as-recorded spot

CHAPTER

11

Speeches and Presentations

In This Chapter, You Will Learn

- The types of speeches and their uses.
- The modes of delivery for speeches and how they differ.
- How to prepare, write, and deliver a speech.

- How to handle a Q & A session.
- How to use presentation materials to accompany a speech and why.

Speech writing is putting words into someone else's mouth—and that's not an easy task. It requires that you know intimately the person for whom you are writing. You need to know his or her style of speaking, body language, tone of voice, speech patterns, and, most important, personality. When you write a speech, you become the person whom you are writing for, and to an extent that person will become you at the moment when he or she begins to speak your words.

Thus, speech writing is a truly collaborative effort. It requires the absolute cooperation of all parties involved. Think of famous speeches that you have heard or read: Patrick Henry's "Give me liberty or give me death," Winston Churchill's "Blood, sweat and tears," John F. Kennedy's "Ask not what your country can do for you," and Martin Luther King's "I have a dream" are a few examples. Often, famous speeches such as these were written by the speakers themselves, but just as often, they were collaborative efforts by the speakers, professional speech writers, and others with valuable input into the process. As in all forms of public relations writing, everybody has something to say about what you write.

Whether you are preparing speeches for others or for yourself, this chapter serves as a good introduction. First, we focus on how to prepare and write an effective speech or presentation and how to handle question-and-answer (Q & A) sessions. In the second half, we discuss using audiovisual materials as support.

TYPES OF SPEECHES

The public relations **speech** is as varied as the purposes to which the speech will be put. In fact, speeches are usually classified by purpose:

- A speech to *inform* seeks to clarify, instruct, or demonstrate.
- A speech to *persuade* is designed to convince or influence and often carries a call to action.
- A speech to *entertain* covers almost everything else including celebrations, eulogies, and dinner speeches.

The type of speech that you use will be determined largely by the topic and the audience. The method of delivery and the degree to which the speech relies on audiovisual aids will also depend on these factors.

MODES OF DELIVERY

There are four basic modes of speech delivery: **extemporaneous, impromptu, scripted,** and **memorized.** For extemporaneous and impromptu speeches, the public relations writer is responsible primarily for the research and compilation of information, usually in outline form. The speaker then studies the notes carefully and is (theoretically) prepared to speak knowledgeably and fluently on the topic. Speeches delivered from script or from memory can be written entirely by the public relations writer.

For all modes of speaking, once the speech is prepared, the primary responsibility of the public relations practitioner is to coach the speaker. This means, of course, that you must know how to give a good speech yourself. If you don't— and many public relations people don't—find someone who can and have that person coach the speaker. This often means hiring outside professionals to do the job, which may be costly, but in the long run may be well worth the effort and expense.

PREPARATION AND WRITING

Preparation is the most important element in any type of speech or presentation. Although some of us are able to speak off the cuff, it is a dangerous habit to get into. Think of the politicians who have lost elections because of candid off-the-record remarks or unwise ad libs. It is extremely important that you prepare in advance everything that you will say and do during a presentation. Don't leave anything to chance.

The nuts and bolts of an effective presentation include the following:

- Specific purpose
- Clear understanding of your audience
- Well-organized ideas
- Adequate support
- Effective delivery

Specifying Your Purpose

Keep two important principles in mind here. First, the speech should be results oriented. Think of the effect that you want it to have on the audience. Decide whether you want the audience to be persuaded, informed, or feel entertained by your presentation.

Second, the purpose of your presentation should be the basis for all the other decisions that you make. This means that the way you organize your ideas, the kind of audiovisual support materials you use, even the way you deliver the presentation, will hinge on why you are giving it in the first place.

Analyzing Your Audience

Your presentation is given for your listeners. Even if you think it is the best presentation that you have ever given, if it doesn't affect them, it will have failed.

- *Analyze the occasion:* What is the reason this group is together at this time, and what do the listeners expect to hear from you?
- *Analyze the people:* What experience and knowledge about the subject do they bring to your presentation? What is their attitude toward the subject? Toward you?

Organizing Your Speech

Good organization lets your audience know that you know what you're talking about. A seemingly confused speaker loses credibility and wastes valuable time. Remember, no one will sit still for long—especially if you're not making sense. And the only way to make sense is to be organized.

It is worth repeating that the best way to organize a speech is to think of its purpose. Use that purpose as the basis for deciding what goes in your speech, how you structure it, what data you present, and even how you choose your style or wording.

Here is a typical speech format:

Introduction

- *Attention getter.* Tell people why they should listen.
- *Establish rapport.* Create a bond with your audience members. Show them what you have in common.
- *Preview.* Tell people what they are going to hear.

Body/Discussion

- *Main points, arranged logically* (usually in order of importance).
- *Data supporting each main point.*

Conclusion

- *Review.* Summarize the key points the audience has heard.
- *Memorable statement.* Create a desired frame of mind that will stay with the audience.
- *Call for action* (if applicable).

Building a speech is like building anything else: You've got to have a solid foundation. It helps if what you build has a look of continuity, coherence, and completion. No one likes a structure that looks haphazard or loosely constructed. For speechmakers, a solid structure implies a solid idea.

You can see from this outline that in speeches it pays to be repetitious. Tell people what you are going to do, do it, and then tell them what you have done.

Most writers find it easier to work on the body of the presentation first, before thinking up a snappy introduction and conclusion.

The body of a speech may be developed in a number of ways:

- *Chronological.* Organized by time. For example, cover first this year's events, then next year's.
- *Spatial.* Organized by direction. For instance, talk about your company's development as it moved from the East Coast to the West Coast.
- *Topical.* Organized by topic. Cover one set of ideas that are related to each other and then move on to the next set of related ideas.

- *Cause and effect.* Organized by need and fulfillment. Describe "what we need" and then "how to get it."

- *Problem and solution.* Organized by question and answer. Describe the problem and then the solution, or vice versa.

Pay attention to how you word the main points that you want to make. Work for parallelism, balance, and good transitions between main points. (Notice how the five types of organization described here begin with parallel openings. Notice, too, that they are balanced in both length and sentence structure.)

With the body of the presentation in hand, attack the introduction. A good introduction is relevant to the audience and occasion, involves the audience personally, positively disposes them toward your presentation, and stimulates them.

A good introduction does not begin with the phrase "Today I want to talk to you about . . . ," nor does it necessarily include a joke. Good introductions can be questions, unusual facts, good examples, stories, illustrations, metaphors, analogies, or any one of a number of other devices.

Once you have an attention-getting introduction, you can work on the conclusion of your speech or presentation. The conclusion should summarize or reiterate the main points of your presentation (tell them what you have done). Finish with a memorable statement that makes the purpose of the speech clear and positions the audience firmly on your side. If your speech is intended to persuade, you will also call the audience to action—for example, to join the group you are pitching or to call their local congressional representative about the issue you have just raised.

One of the best ways to organize a speech is to develop a summary sheet. Include at least the following information:

- *The audience.* What are the ages, educational backgrounds, and demographic characteristics of the audience members? How big is the audience?

- *The purpose.* Are you trying to inform, persuade, reinforce attitudes, or entertain? Complete the phrase "After listening to my speech, audience members will . . ."

- *Organization of the speech.* Is it chronological, spatial, topical, cause and effect, or problem and solution?

- *Supporting materials.* What statistics, quotations, case histories, analogies, hypothetical illustrations, or anecdotes do you have to support your claim?

- *Purpose of introduction and conclusion.* How will you gain interest, create a need for listening, summarize, and call to action?

- *List of visual aids.* Which media will you use (slides, computer presentation, flip charts)? What content (words, charts and graphs)? How will visuals be integrated into the speech (during, following, support only, or stand-alone).

For a complete sample summary sheet, see Exhibit 11.1.

Exhibit 11.1

Summary Worksheet

Preliminary Questions

 I. What are the expectations of this audience?
Toward me?
Toward my topic?
Toward this specific situation? (Are there any extenuating circumstances that should be considered?)

 II. How do I expect my audience to be affected by my presentation? The general purpose of my presentation will be to inform, persuade, reinforce certain ideas, entertain?
The specific thesis: After listening to my speech, the audience will . . .

The Body of the Speech

 III. What is the best structure to follow given I and II above?
Should my presentation be arranged chronologically? Spatially? Topically? By cause and effect? By problem and solution?
The structure that I have chosen is the best in this particular situation because . . .

 IV. What are the three or four main points suggested by the specific structure?
A.
B.
C.
D.

 V. How will I support the main points?
Will I use statistics, examples, analogies, case studies, direct quotations?
A will be supported by:
B will be supported by:
C will be supported by:
D will be supported by:

 VI. How should I adapt my language and word choice to suit audience expectations?
To what extent should I use jargon and buzzwords?
To what extent should I be conscious of defining certain words?

 VII. Should I use any visual aids?
What should be visualized?
How should it be visualized?
Why should it be visualized?

VIII. How should I introduce the speech?
Why should my audience listen to this message? How will my audience benefit by listening to me? How can I make my audience want to listen? You should listen to me because . . .

IX. How should I conclude the speech?
How do I relate the conclusion to the main points I have covered? In conclusion . . .

Supporting Your Ideas

The detail or support that you use to fill out your presentation must be sufficient to ensure that your listeners know precisely what you mean but should not be so overwhelming that you lose your audience in minutia.

Your support must be relevant to your listeners. If it makes no sense to them, you will fail to get their attention, gain their goodwill, or persuade them to your view. For example, if you are writing a speech that intends to persuade the audience to give money to your nonprofit organization, you would want to include some concrete examples about how the money will be used (for example, a pledge of $5 per month will deliver 100 hot lunches to people who are home bound, but you don't need to detail the exact costs of each meal).

Use any kind of support that is appropriate to your purpose and ideas. Facts and statistics are almost mandatory for many business presentations, and examples and illustrations can often make those hard numbers come alive. Quotations from a source that your listeners respect can add proof that what you are saying is true. Analogies and metaphors can often be used to make concrete that which is abstract by putting the abstraction in human terms. Preachers use these two devices all the time. Remember, use enough support and detail to do the job but no more.

DELIVERY

Finally, you are standing in front of your listeners (assuming you are the speech or presentation giver). Now it is your job to make your ideas come alive. The secrets of effective delivery are thorough preparation and lots of practice. You cannot deliver a presentation effectively if you don't know what you want to say. That requires preparation. The only way you can become a fluent speaker is to practice. There is no shortcut!

OK. You are thoroughly prepared and well practiced. Now you must stand up and do two things. First, stick to what you have practiced. Don't get distracted. Don't throw away your prepared presentation for an impromptu effort. Second, keep your eyes on the audience members. Look at them. Watch their reactions to what you say. Don't get engrossed in your script. In fact, try not to use a script at all; use an outline or brief notes instead.

Also, don't get engrossed in your audiovisual material. Watch the audience members, not the screen. Even if you are using 35-mm slides in a dark room, look out at your audience. You won't be able to see them well, but it is important that they get the feeling you can.

Another piece of advice: Look relaxed, even if you aren't. Smile, frown, move your arms, look around the room at everyone. Try to feel as though you are in the middle of a lively conversation with a group of friends. It will do wonders for your delivery.

THE QUESTION-AND-ANSWER SESSION

Anticipation is the key to successful Q & A sessions. If you're the type of speaker who has to have everything written out in advance, then Q & A is not for you. You need to know whether you can handle thinking, analyzing, and speaking off the cuff before you throw yourself to the lions. The best hedge against blowing a Q & A session is practice. It's advisable to have someone who is familiar with the topic of your presentation work with you on possible questions in advance. That way, you have at least some idea of what to expect when you face the real thing. The following advice will help you when you do:

- Repeat the question or paraphrase it in your own words.
- Make sure you understand the question before answering it. Seek clarification if necessary.
- Don't lie, fabricate, or distort information. If you don't know the answer, say so—but don't appear flustered. Offer to find the answer and get back to the questioner. Confidence breeds credibility.
- Refer to any visual aids that will help you answer the question.
- Be concise—don't give another speech.
- Don't allow a questioner to take you on a tangent. Stick to the main points of your speech.
- Don't allow an individual questioner to monopolize the Q & A session.

PRESENTATION MATERIALS

We live in a visual society. Even though most people still watch television, the Internet is fast becoming the medium through which we view the world. We socialize with others, listen to music, and stream videos and movies. The Internet is full of visuals and is a fast-moving canvas that shortens our attention spans while grabbing our attention. Because of this, it's increasingly hard with all this focus on visual appeal, it's hard for a speech or presentation audience to maintain attention, even with the most persuasive of speakers, without something to look at. Used as integrated components of a speech, audiovisual materials can help keep the audience's attention and add valuable information.

Audiovisual support should be for impact—to develop audience interest and hold attention. Use it for effectiveness, to help your listeners remember more, longer. Don't use it simply because it is there. Use it only if it enhances your presentation. If you do use audiovisual support, consider the following points:

- Be sure it adds to your presentation.
- Do not let the support control the presentation. Your ideas must come first.
- Rehearse the presentation with the audiovisual materials. Learn how to use them.
- Do not talk to the visuals; talk to the audience.
- Talk louder. You are competing with the visuals for audience attention.
- Stand clear. Remember, visuals must be seen to be useful.

Preparing Audiovisual Materials

The most common, or traditional, support materials used with speeches have been visual-only support materials such as graphs, diagrams, photographs, and handouts; and audiovisual support materials such as videos and slides. The advent of software programs such as Microsoft PowerPoint and Apple Keynote has ushered in a new age of audiovisual presentation. These programs, and others like them, combine the traditional support of slides with an entirely new element—motion. Now, instead of using charts and graphs on poster board, a videotape, and a slide show, you can prepare all of these support materials in one place.

In the past, it took a lot of work and a pretty hefty investment in equipment just to add dissolves to your slide show (two projectors and a dissolve unit, at least). Today, you can add to your slide show not only dissolves but also fades, wipes, and myriad other effects just by pressing a few computer keys. You can also add music, moving images (captured video, for instance), and voices—all digitized and embedded in your slide show. And now, with the latest projection technology, these shows aren't even limited to your computer screen. They can be projected onto screens rivaling your local theater (they also cost about as much as your local theater's).

Even though the technology has changed drastically, the rules for developing a good slide presentation have not. A good slide show should add zip and clarity to information that may be otherwise dull. It requires that you be well organized, know your audience, and follow a few simple rules:

1. *Define your objective.* Be sure that you know what you want to accomplish, what changes you want to take place in your listeners, and what behavior you want to affect.

2. *Analyze your audience.* Are they laypeople or experts? Do you aim for the lowest common denominator? The middle? The top? The more you know about your audience, the easier it is to make that decision.

3. *Work from an outline when creating your visual presentation.* Don't replicate everything that you are going to say. Keep it to a concise summary of the major points and supporting materials needed to reach your objective with this audience.

4. *Decide what mood or treatment you want.* A light, humorous treatment may mean cartoons and a comic narration. Are you going to threaten? Cajole? Be low key? Mood makes a difference in how you use color and pacing.

5. *Write a script, if you plan to use one.* This will include all of the details not reflected in your visual presentation.

6. *Plan your slides.*

- Convert material originally designed for publication to slide format. *Hint:* You can scan this material and insert it into your slides as needed. In my experience, most of the presentation software accepts JPEG format the best, and images saved in JPEG format typically take up less memory. Also, if you're projecting directly from a computer, or showing your slide presentation on your computer, you don't need the highest resolution. Scan your images at no greater than 100 dots per inch (dpi).

- Use a series of slides or charts, disclosed progressively, to build up complex ideas. *Hint:* If you have a long list of subpoints spread among several slides, be sure to use the same header on each slide so that your audience remembers your major point.

- Keep all copy and symbols simple and legible. Projected letters should be at least 2 inches high and ½ inch wide. What this means to you is that your type size shouldn't go any lower than 18 points, or it won't be legible. *Hint:* Use a sans serif typeface and keep it mostly bold. Serif type tends to be harder to read when projected.

- Make all copy on slides short and to the point. Include no more than 15 or 20 words or 25 or 30 pieces of data per slide. Again, remember to keep the type size legible.

- Keep slides simple and bold. Limit each slide or chart to one main idea.

- Use charts and graphs rather than tables. Tables almost always look complicated and confusing.

- Use variety in layout, color, charting, and graphics for change of pace. *Hint:* Don't use more than one slide background per slide show. The presentation software includes a dizzying selection of background templates. Pick one and stick to it for your entire presentation. *Second hint:* Pick uncluttered backgrounds and dark colors for use with light-colored lettering. Uncluttered backgrounds allow you more space to work, whereas light letters against dark backgrounds are easier to read.

- Avoid mathematical formulas or equations on slides.

- Keep photographs uncluttered.

- Keep moving. Leave slides up only long enough for the audience to read. Remember, the slides are there to supplement and support your words and ideas, not to take your place. *Hint:* Most presentation software allows for manual or automatic mode. In most cases, you'll want to control the speed yourself by using the manual mode. Use the automatic mode only if your slide show is designed to run unaccompanied as a stand-alone display.

- Enlist the aid of a competent audiovisual specialist. Although the new programs aren't all that difficult to learn, your presentations can still benefit from someone trained in visual design.

7. *Edit your slide presentation.* Ask yourself the following questions:
   - Are all major points covered?
   - Does the content of each slide fit the narration?
   - Are all slides legible?
   - Are colors and visuals bold and effective?
   - Does each slide depict one idea only?
   - Is there good continuity from slide to slide?
   - Does the program add up to form a visually coherent and pleasing presentation?

8. *Rehearse, rehearse, rehearse.*

9. *Visit the room where you will be making the presentation* prior to your presentation time to make sure that the projector is there and in working order. Run through your program to make sure all is as you want it. *Hint:* Computer compatibility is still a problem, especially between electronic projectors and notebook computers. Ideally, you would have your own portable set-up. If you don't, meet with the computer technician in charge of the facility where you will be presenting and make sure that everything works before the curtain goes up.

10. Slide programs are almost always given in darkened rooms. The only other light may be the one on the lectern that you use. Even the new computer projection units aren't any brighter than the old slide projectors. That means you must make a special effort to force yourself to look out into a darkened room at people whom you may be unable to see. Don't lose eye contact with them because they can see you just fine. Remember, a slide show is an accompaniment. *You're* the real show.

Scripting for Audiovisuals

Scripts using visual accompaniment are formatted similarly to television scripts, with visuals on the left and narration on the right. No matter whether you are writing for a live presentation accompanied by visuals or a self-contained presentation that will run automatically with narration already added, the technique of scripting is the same. Remember, a script includes everything that you are going to say, not just an outline of your visuals. Unless you (or your presenter) have done this particular presentation a number of times or are very good at *prompted extemporaneous speaking* (using visuals as reminders), you'll probably need a script.

The audiovisual script should be easy to follow. Visuals appear exactly opposite their audio counterparts, often with numbers corresponding to the slide placed within the script narration to indicate the exact point at which the slide will be changed.

Exhibit 11.2

Slide Script

Slide Script
"Building the Future" Page 1 of 5

1. Graphic—"BUILDING THE FUTURE ON THE PAST" over University coat-of-arms	1. BUILDING THE FUTURE ON THE PAST. THESE WORDS REFLECT BUTLER UNIVERSITY'S COMMITMENT TO INNOVATIVE RESEARCH AND EDUCATIONAL PROGRAMS.
2. Aerial shot of campus	2. A COMMITMENT TO DEVELOP THE PROMISE OF IDEAS INTO THE FOUNDATION OF HUMAN PROGRESS.
3. Same, with "RESEARCH" and "TEACHING" supered	3. THIS COMMITMENT TAKES MANY AND VARIOUS FORMS REFLECTING THE INTELLECTUAL DIVERSITY OF THE CAMPUS COMMUNITY.
4. Psychology researcher with experimental subject	4. IMPORTANTLY, THE BOLD AND UNCOMPROMISING INQUIRY SO TYPICAL OF RESEARCH AT THE UNIVERSITY MORE OFTEN THAN NOT PROVIDES THE BASIS FOR THE BEST IN TEACHING AND PUBLIC SERVICE.
5. IEC researcher testing solar cell	5. IT HAS BEEN SAID THAT THE FUTURE IS PURCHASED BY THE PRESENT.

-more-

The major difference between audiovisual scripts and television spots is length. Slide presentations are usually longer with fewer visual changes. To keep them lively, count on changing slides every 5 to 10 seconds. Much depends on the type of presentation. For instance, if you are presenting the annual budget report, you might be severely limited as to the type and number of slides shown. If the slide contains written information, gauge the amount of time it will take to read it by reading it aloud. If you are dealing strictly with visual images, then the 5- to 10-second time allotment should be just about right. The new technology allows for a number of special effects that can alleviate some of the boredom of static slides (for example, points popping on the screen one at a time or graphics moving in and out). Just don't overdo the movement.

Exhibit 11.2 is a simple slide presentation script, but you'll notice it follows the same format as a television script (see Chapter 10).

An additional benefit to slideshow development is that with many software programs you can add your finished slide presentation as a self-running, stand-alone at a booth at trade shows or a kiosk at other locations. And, most websites now allow you to upload your slideshow for on-demand viewing by visitors to your site. You can even add narration, music, and embedded videos for extra interest.

KEY TERMS

speech	impromptu speech
extemporaneous speech	scripted speech
	memorized speech

Glossary

The page numbers on which a term is highlighted are indicated in parentheses at the end of the definition. Boldface terms within a definition are also included in this glossary.

A

Accompanying script. The version of a television script sent with the taped spot to the stations that will run it. The accompanying script is stripped of all but its most essential directions. It is intended to provide the reader with a general idea of what the taped spot is about and is to be used only as a reference for broadcasters who accept the spot for use. (271)

Actuality. An audio- or videotape that features newspeople describing an event, interviews with those involved in the event, or ambiance or background of the event itself for a voice-over. (267)

Anchor. A line or strip of color used at the top or bottom of the page to gain unity in a publication. (243)

Angle. The hook in a news release that attracts media attention. (106)

Non-profit annual report. One of the most-produced organizational publications, annual reports not only provide information on the organization's financial situation but also act as a vehicle for enhancing a corporation's image among its various internal publics. (225)

Appeal strategy. A type of compliance strategy that persuades the audience by calling upon it to help or come to the aid of the communicator or some third party represented by the communicator. (54)

Argument strategy. A persuasive strategy designed to oppose another point of view and to persuade. There are two types: reasoned argument and emotional appeal. Both attempt to persuade by arguing one point of view against another. (54)

As-recorded spot. A radio spot produced by the originating agency and ready to be played by the stations receiving it. Spots are usually sent in the format used by the particular station. (286)

Attribution. A stylistic device whereby quotes are credited to their sources. *Said* is the most common form for journalistic style; however, *says* is commonly used by public relations writers to add immediacy. (108)

B

Backgrounder. Basic information pieces providing background as an aid to reporters, editors, executives, employees, and spokespersons. This is the information used by other writers and reporters to "flesh out" their stories. (146)

Blind headline. A headline that imparts no information useful to the reader's understanding of the story it accompanies. (211)

Blogging. *Blog* is short for *weblog*, a frequent and chronological publication of comments and thoughts on the Web. Users post informal journals of their thoughts, comments, and philosophies, updated frequently and normally reflecting the views of the blog's creator. Typically, some mechanism is used to allow responses to entries by site visitors. (96)

Blueline. A printer's proof that should be checked for accuracy before a print job is started. (258)

Body type. Type set smaller than 14 points and used for body copy. Distinguished from display type, which is 14 points and larger. (246)

Bridge. The part of a brochure that explains the purpose of the piece and refers to the title or headline. (211)

C

Caption. The informational description that appears below or next to a photograph or other illustration. Also known as a **cutline.** (191)

Central route. One of the two methods by which receivers of messages process information according to the elaboration likelihood model. The central route is used by people who think about messages extensively before becoming persuaded. In other words, they "elaborate" on a message and will be persuaded only if the message is cognitively convincing. (51)

Command strategy. A type of **compliance strategy** that persuades through three forms: (54)

- Direct requests with no rationale or motivation for the requests
- An explanation accompanied with reasons for complying
- Hints in which circumstances are suggested from which the audience draws the desired conclusions and acts in the desired way

Commercial speech. As defined by the Supreme Court, the concept of commercial speech allows a corporation to state publicly its position on controversial issues. The Court's interpretation of this concept also allows for political activity through lobbying and political action committees. (17)

Compliance strategy. A persuasive strategy designed to gain agreement through coercion. (53)

Consequence. One of the characteristics of newsworthiness of information. Relates to whether the information has any importance to the prospective reading, listening, or viewing public. Is it something that the audience would pay to know? (68)

Controlled information. Information over which you have total control as to editorial content, style, placement, and timing. Examples of controlled information are institutional (image) and advocacy advertising, house publications, brochures, and paid broadcast material (if it is paid placement). **Public service announcements (PSAs)** are controlled as far as message content is concerned but uncontrolled as to placement and timing. (5)

Copyright. Legal protection of intellectual property (for example, writing and artwork) from use by others without permission. (19)

Crosshead. A small, transitional head within an article. (191)

Cutline. The informational description that appears below or next to a photograph or other illustration. Also known as a **caption.** (191)

D

Dateline. A brief notation at the beginning of a press release used to indicate the point of origin. (114)

Defamation. Any communication that holds a person up to contempt, hatred, ridicule, or scorn. (18)

Delayed lead. A type of **news release** lead used to add drama to a story. This type of lead is usually reserved for feature stories and is not appropriate for straight news. (107)

Descriptive data. Information gathered from research that paints a picture of the public being studied by its distinctive demographic characteristics—descriptors such as age, income, sex, education, nationality, and so on. This is information needed for a reader profile. (38)

Design principles. The four basic principles that comprise good design: (234)

- *Balance.* The concept that what is put on one side of the page should "weigh" as much as what is on the other side. All the elements placed on the page have weight, even the white space left by not placing elements. Size, color, and degree of darkness all play a part in balance.

- *Emphasis.* Focusing readers' attention on single elements on a page. Elements are emphasized by assigning them more optical weight than other items on the page. These elements are larger, darker, more colorful, or oddly shaped. They draw the readers' attention first among all other items on the page.

- *Proportion.* A measure of relationship in size. It helps show one object's relationship to other objects in a layout.

- *Sequence.* The order of the elements on a layout. It will literally lead readers through a page.

Display type. Type larger than 14 points, used for headlines and other emphasized elements. (246)

Dissonance theory. A theory formulated in the 1950s stating that people tend to seek only messages that are "consonant" with their attitudes; they do not seek out "dissonant" messages. In other words, people don't go looking for messages that they don't agree with already. This theory also says that about the only way you are going to get anybody to listen to something they don't agree with is to juxtapose their attitude with a "dissonant" attitude—an attitude that is logically inconsistent with the first. (50)

Downward communication. Communication within an organization that imparts management's message to employees. Ideally, even downward communication channels such as newsletters permit **upward communication** through letters to the editor, articles written by employees, surveys, and so forth. (156)

Drop. The amount of white space at the top of a page layout. (241)

E

Elaboration likelihood model. A theory proposed by Richard E. Petty and John T. Cacioppo in 1980 that suggests that persuasive messages are transmitted and received through two different routes: one used by those people who think about messages extensively before becoming persuaded, the other used by those who are unable or unwilling to spend time thinking about a message and so make quick decisions, most of which don't bear directly on the subject matter of the message. (51)

Emotional appeal. Using emotional techniques to persuade an audience. The most common techniques are use of symbols, emotive language, and entertainment. (56)

Entertainment. A communication strategy that encapsulates information within a format that makes it easier to accept or understand. (56)

Event announcement. A form of news release that covers an event: a grand opening of a new site, an open house, or a press conference on an important topic. The primary goal of an event is the generation of publicity. (119)

Exclusive. A press release or other information intended for only one media outlet. The same information may not be released to other outlets in any form. (115)

Extemporaneous speech. A speech given on the spur of the moment, usually with little or no preparation. Basically synonymous with **impromptu speech.** (292)

F

Fact sheet. An information piece that contains just that—facts—and nothing more. It should elaborate on already presented information, such as a news release, and not merely repeat what has already been said. (147)

Feature style. A less objective style of writing that provides less hard information than straight news style. Features generally take a point of view or discuss issues, people, or places. The style is more relaxed, more descriptive, and often more creative than straight news style. (175)

Financial release. This type of **news release** is used primarily in shareholder relations but is also of interest to financial media. (106)

Font. The classification within a given **typeface,** such as bold or italic. (246)

Format (1). The type of music that a radio station plays or the information it provides. For example, some stations play only Top-40 hits. These stations usually cater to a teenage audience. Other stations play only classic rock or jazz, or provide news. Their listeners vary according to their format. (76)

Format (2). The way that you arrange your printed piece—its organizational characteristics. (76)

G

Ghostwriting. Writing something for someone else. Writing that will appear under someone else's name. Examples are corporate letters to the editor and speech writing. (11)

Grid. Another term for the columns used in a layout. (244)

H

Hard news. Information that has immediate impact on the people receiving it. By journalists' definition, it is very often news that people need rather than news that they want. (68)

I

Impromptu speech. A speech given on the spur of the moment, usually with little or no preparation. Basically synonymous with **extemporaneous speech.** (292)

Inferential data. Information gathered from research that allows for generalizing about a larger group or population. This means that the people chosen for the survey must be entirely representative of the larger population comprising the target audience. This allows sampling of a small segment of the target public in order to infer from their reactions the reactions of the larger audience. Inferential research can work only if the sample is chosen completely at random from the larger population. (38)

Interest. One of the characteristics of newsworthiness of information. Relates to whether the information is unusual or entertaining. Does it have any human interest? (68)

Internet (interlocking networks). A large computer network that links several already established computer networks together with a common language. The Internet is a computer network made up of thousands of networks worldwide. (93)

Intranet. An internal network devoted usually to employee or organizational issues and accessed via an internal network or the Internet through a password-protected gateway. (97)

Inverted pyramid style. A straight news story: It begins with a lead, expands on the lead, and proceeds to present information in decreasing order of importance. Also known as straight news style. (107)

Issue statement. A precise definition of the situation, including answers to the following four questions: (28)

1. What is the problem or opportunity to be addressed?
2. Who are the affected parties?
3. What is the timing of this issue?
4. What are your (or your organization's) strengths and weaknesses as regards this issue?

K

Key words. Words used in social media that allow search engines to identify key points in a message. Judicious placement of such words in the text and title also allow those scanning information to focus on the most important ideas. (137)

L

Language fallacy. Typically, an unethical persuasive strategy that involves the actual use of language, including equivocation, amphibole, and emotive language. (11)

Lead. The opening sentences of a straight news story or feature article. In a straight news story, the lead should include the *who, what, when, where, why,* and *how* of the story. Feature leads generally begin by setting the scene of the story to follow. (107)

Logic fallacy. A persuasive technique codified by the Roman orators over a thousand years ago. Commonly referred to as logic fallacies because they are both illogical and deceptive by nature, they include, among others, cause and effect, personal attack, bandwagon, and inference by association strategies. (9)

M

Media advisory. Alerts the news media to upcoming items of interest to their constituents. It's one of the best ways to let them know what's happening and why they should be paying attention. The goal of a media advisory is not to give reporters everything they need to write the story, but rather to get them interested enough to mark their calendars. (132)

Media directory. A publication (electronic or printed) listing various media outlets and their contact information. Publishers of directories offer formats ranging from global checkers that include a variety of sources in every medium to specialized directories dealing with a single medium. (73)

Media list. A personalized list that contains details about local contacts and all the information you need to conduct business in your community. Media lists may include regional and even nationwide contacts, depending on the scope of your operation. A media list, once compiled, should be updated by hand at least once a month. (74)

Memorized speech. A fully scripted speech that the speaker has completely memorized for delivery. (292)

Message strategy. Developing a message, or messages, that will reach and have the desired effect on your target audiences. Message strategies should logically follow your objectives and contribute either directly or indirectly to them. (48)

Micro-blogging. A form of blogging limited by the number of characters allowed (e.g., Twitter). (102)

Newsletter. A brief (usually four pages) printed publication distributed either vertically or horizontally. A newsletter usually contains information of interest to a narrowly defined target audience. The various types of newsletters include the following: (155)

- *Association newsletters* help a scattered membership with a common interest keep in touch.
- *Community group newsletters* are often used by civic organizations to keep in touch with members, announce meetings, and stimulate attendance at events.
- *Institutional newsletters,* perhaps the most common type of newsletter, are usually distributed among employees.
- *Publicity newsletters* often create their own readers. They can be developed for fan clubs, resorts, and politicians.
- *Special-interest newsletters,* developed by special-interest groups, tend to grow with their following.
- *Self-interest or "digest" newsletters* are designed to make a profit. The individuals or groups who develop them typically offer advice or present solutions to problems held in common by their target readers. These often come in the form of a sort of "digest" of topics of interest to a certain profession.

News release. The most widely used of all public relations formats. News releases are used most often to disseminate information for publicity purposes and generally are of three types: **publicity release, product release,** or **financial release.** (106)

O

Objectives. The concrete steps that you need to take to reach your goal. A project's objectives must relate to the purpose of your message and should be realistic and measurable. For public relations writing, there are three types of objectives: informational, attitudinal, and behavioral. (42)

Online newsroom. An online version of a media relations department. Online newsrooms can distribute information to media and others through a broad range of communications methods, including streaming video and audio presentations, interviews, features, webcasts (Web broadcasts), webinars (Web seminars), and blogs (weblogs), along with more traditional printable materials such as press releases, white papers, backgrounders, articles, annual reports, and magazine articles. (84)

P

Peripheral route. One of the two methods by which receivers of messages process information according to the elaboration likelihood model. The peripheral route is used by those who are unable or unwilling to spend time thinking about a message. Instead, recipients using peripheral processing rely on a variety of *cues* to make quick decisions, most of which don't bear directly on the subject matter of the message. (51)

Personnel release. Company announcements of personnel changes, usually promotions or the hiring of new people in important positions. They are a good opportunity to present more detailed biographical information on company personnel and on the company itself. (119)

Persuasion. An information strategy that involves moving someone to believe something or act in a certain way. (49)

Pitch letter. A brief introduction to a subject you intend to cover in more detail in press releases, backgrounders, or other publicity pieces. It is usually intended for a media audience (reporters, editors, news directors, etc.) and not the general public. (129)

Placement agency. An organization that takes information, such as a press release, and sends it out to media outlets using its own regularly updated media lists and computerized mailing services. (75)

Positioning. Placing your piece in context as either part of some larger whole or as a standout from other pieces. Also, roughly synonymous with "branding," or designing your message to stand out from the crowd. (205)

Media kit. One of the most common methods of distributing brochures and other collateral information pieces. Press kits are produced and used for a wide variety of public relations purposes, including product promotion presentations, press conferences, and as promotional packages by regional or local distributors or agencies. (78)

Primary research. Data collected for the first time and specifically for the project at hand. (36)

Privacy. One of the legal terms used to describe infringement. Often referred to as *invasion of privacy*. Its most common forms are as follows: (19)

- *Appropriation.* The commercial use of a person's name or picture without permission
- *Intrusion.* The literal invasion of a person's private space by such means as using telephoto lenses, audiotaping, and trespass

Product release. This type of **news release** deals with specific products or product lines and is usually targeted to trade publications within individual industries. (106)

Profile. A feature story written specifically about a person, product or service, or an organization or some part of it. It profiles the subject by listing facts, highlighting points of interest, and tying the subject to the organization being promoted. (108)

Prominence. One of the characteristics of newsworthiness of information. Relates to whether the information concerns or involves events and people of prominence. (68)

Proximity. One of the characteristics of newsworthiness of information. Relates to whether the information is local. (68)

Publicity. Information dissemination that is not generally paid for but is picked up and passed on by another entity, such as the media. The most common forms of publicity are press conferences and **news releases**. (106)

Publicity release. This type of **news release** covers any information occurring within an organization that might have some news value to local, regional, or even national media. (106)

Public service announcement (PSA). A radio or television spot aimed at providing an important message to its target audience. The PSA is reserved strictly for organizations that qualify as nonprofit under federal tax laws. (267)

Pull quote. A magazine or newsletter device of "pulling" out quotations from the text, enlarging the point size, and setting them off from the text to draw a reader's attention to a point within an article. (192)

R

Reasoned argument. Also known as logical argument, this persuasive strategy uses the techniques of rhetoric as handed down from the ancient Greeks. For persuasive messages, it is important to build the message around a thorough understanding of the psychological state of the audience. (54)

Referral ending. A type of ending for a feature story in which the beginning of the story is referred to in some way to bring closure to the story. (183)

Response ending. A type of ending for a feature story in which a call to action is included. (183)

Rule of ground thirds. A method of working with a page layout that requires that the page be divided into thirds and balanced using a two-thirds to one-third ratio. (237)

RSS. Rich Site Summary, or Really Simple Syndication. RSS allows the placement of news and other brief announcements into a format that can be published to RSS readers and Web pages allowing for a quick scan of the items which are linked to the original, longer version. (93)

S

Sanction strategy. A type of **compliance strategy** that persuades by using rewards and punishments controlled by either the audience themselves or as a result of the situation. (53)

Sans serif typeface. A category of typeface without *serifs*—the lines that cross the end strokes of the letters (*sans*, from the French, meaning "without"). They are usually, but not always, distinguished by uniformity of strokes. They usually impart a more modern look to a publication, especially if used as display type. (248)

Script treatment. An informal narrative account of a television spot. It is not written in a script format but may include ideas for shots and transitions. (270)

Scripted speech. A speech that has been fully scripted and from which the speaker reads, often from a teleprompter. (292)

Search engine optimized (SEO) release. Inserting information and words into social media that will register readily on the major search engines. (136)

Secondary research. Data previously collected, often by third parties, for other purposes and adapted to the current needs. This can include demographic information already gathered by another department in your organization or information gained from research done by other parties entirely outside your company. (36)

Serif typeface. A category of typeface distinguished by a variation in thick and thin strokes and by *serifs*—the lines that cross the end strokes of the letters. Serif type can be further broken down into *Romans* and *slab* or *square serif* faces. Serif faces usually are considered easier to read, especially in body type sizes. (247)

Shooting script. Includes all the information necessary for a complete understanding of a TV spot idea. It fleshes out camera shots, transitions, audio (including music and sound effects), narrative, acting directions, and approximate times. (270)

Signature. Groupings of pages printed on both sides, usually 16 to a signature, but sometimes fewer, and always in multiples of 4. (256)

Slice-of-life spot. A television commercial that sets up a dramatic situation complete with a beginning, middle, and end. In the slice-of-life spot, the focus is on the story, not the characters. The message is imparted through an interesting sequence of events incorporating but not relying on interesting characters. Slice-of-life spots usually use a wide variety of camera movements and postproduction techniques such as dissolves and special effects. (276)

Social media. Works of user-created video, audio, text or multimedia that are published and shared in a social environment, such as a blog, wiki or video hosting site. (96)

Social media release (SMR). Also called a social media press release (SMPR). A form of the traditional news release redesigned for adoption through and by social media. It generally includes key words to optimize search engine recognition, hyperlinks, and audio-video components either embedded or linked. (138)

Social networks. Web-based social networks allow users to interact using e-mail and instant messaging, as well as other forms of exchange and sharing, to build and maintain a community of people with similar interests. (92)

Soft news. News that people want rather than news that they necessarily need. Often entertainment oriented. (69)

Special. A press release or other information written in a style intended for a specific publication but being released elsewhere as well. (115)

Speech. A form of communication, usually interpersonal and somewhat formal, in which a group of people are addressed simultaneously. Types of speeches are typically classified by purpose: (292)

- A speech to *inform* seeks to clarify, instruct, or demonstrate.
- A speech to *persuade* is designed to convince or influence and often carries a call to action.
- A speech to *entertain* covers almost everything else including, celebrations, eulogies, and dinner speeches.

Spot. A broadcast message, either paid-for advertising or a **public service announcement.** (268, 267)

Spot announcement. The simplest type of radio spot that involves no sound effects or music bed and is meant to be read by radio station personnel. (284)

Style sheet. A listing of all of the type specifications that you use in a **newsletter** or other publication. (165)

Subhead. May be (a) a display line enlarging on the main headline, usually in smaller size, or (b) a short heading within the copy used to break up a long block of text. (191)

Summary ending. A type of ending for a feature story in which the main points are summarized. (179)

Summary lead. The most common type of news release **lead**. A good summary lead will answer the key questions—who, what, when, where, why, and how. (107)

Swipe file. A collection of publications and designs done by other people or companies used to help with design, layout ideas, and writing style, as well as to communicate ideas to typesetters and printers. (256)

T

Talking heads spot. A television spot in which the primary image appearing on the television screen is the human head—talking. (273)

Target audience. The end users of your information—the people whom you most want to be affected by your writing. (35)

Timeliness. One of the characteristics of newsworthiness of information. Relates to whether the material is current. If it isn't, is it a whole new angle on an old story? Remember, the word *news* means "new." (68)

Tips/hints release. A release typically using an outline format with plenty of bulleted items. The objective is to position you or your company as an authority on a subject. (124)

Trademark. Legal protection of product names, images, phrases, or slogans from use by others without permission and in a prescribed manner dictated by the trademark holder. (25)

Twitter. A Web 2.0 service that allows users to perform **micro-blogging,** communicating in messages of no more than 140 characters (known as "tweets").

A Twitter subscriber can choose to receive notifications of others' updates via the service's Web interface, cell phone text message, or online instant messaging service. (88)

Two-fold. The most common type of brochure fold resulting in a six-panel brochure. (206)

Type. The generic term for the lettering used in printing. (246)

Typeface. The nearly limitless alphabets and ornaments available as **type.** (246)

U

Uncontrolled information. Information that, once it leaves your hands, is at the mercy of the media. The outlet in which you want it placed has total editorial control over the content, style, placement, and timing. Such items as press releases are totally uncontrolled. Others, such as magazine articles, may receive limited editing but are still controlled as to placement and timing. (4)

Unity. One way of providing readers with a whole by drawing relationships among its various parts. Perhaps the best way to gain unity of design has more to do with an overall look, a unifying design. (241)

Upward communication. Communication within an organization that provides employees a means of communicating their opinions to management. (156)

V

Video news release (VNR). Originally, prepackaged publicity features meant to be aired on local, regional, or national television, VNRs now are news releases designed as feature stories, usually for local television news programs. (265)

W

Webinar. A seminar conducted over the World Wide Web. It is a type of Web conferencing. In contrast to a webcast, which is transmission of information in one direction only, a webinar is designed to be interactive between the presenter and audience. A webinar is "live" in the sense that information is conveyed according to an agenda, with a starting and ending time. In most cases, the presenter may speak over a standard telephone line, pointing out information being presented on screen, and the audience can respond over their own telephones, preferably a speakerphone. (84)

Web 2.0. The second generation of Web development and design. Its key characteristics are the sharing of information rather than the generation of it, and the collaborative nature of the designs that make that sharing possible. (92)

Website. An Internet "publication" composed of any number of Web pages, each hyperlinked to each other and to various other Web sites. (93)

Index